MAKING
THE MOST OF
PROFESSIONAL
SERVICES

MAKING
THE MOST OF
PROFESSIONAL
SERVICES

 Published by Consumers' Association
and Hodder & Stoughton

Which? Books are commissioned and researched by The Association for
Consumer Research and published by Consumers' Association,
2 Marylebone Road, London NW1 4DX and Hodder & Stoughton,
47 Bedford Square, London WC1B 3DP.

British Library Cataloguing in Publication Data
Making the most of professional services.
1. Great Britain. Professional Services
I. Consumers' Association
381'.0941
ISBN 0 340 48876 X

Edited by Edith Rudinger

Research by Halina Sand

Contributions from Allan Blake
                    John Hepworth
                    Robert G Lee
                    Phil Parnham
                    Lynne Thornton

Cover illustration by Julie Tennent

Typeset by Litho Link Limited, Welshpool, Powys, Wales

Printed and bound in Great Britain by Courier International Ltd.,
Tiptree, Essex

Contents

Foreword

Today seems to be the age of the expert – you only need to glance through Yellow Pages to be confronted by a dazzling array of professions, trades and services, all vying for your custom.

Expertise means knowing more about a specialised subject than the man in the street. There is nothing magical about it: it can only be acquired the hard way, the most important part of which is usually practical experience.

If we need expert help, to whom should we go for it? This book is designed to help you understand the nature and special areas of competence of those practising in areas of expertise where professional qualifications are essential.

If you understand what a professional is able to do for you, and what his limitations are, you have a better prospect of resolving your problems. Ideally, you should approach him with the idea of co-operating with him – you need his expertise just as he needs your custom – and a working relationship can be enormously enhanced if there is good will on both sides.

As in all areas of life, prevention is far better than cure. This book offers guidance on both. It warns of likely problem areas, and, in case things should go seriously wrong between you and the professional, it gives an outline of the procedures available to you.

Disputes with professionals will tend to mean that you are somewhat out of your depth, and may have to rely on other professionals to help you. The 'I need a lawyer to protect me from my lawyer' joke can then turn into nightmarish reality; in some circumstances you might also need a lawyer to protect you from your builder, doctor, accountant, tour operator . . . This book should be your guide and ally in facing up to the expert.

How to use this book

The list of contents will tell you where to find each of the various groups of professional services dealt with in this book.

At the end of each section, you will find, under 'Relevant Addresses', the names, addresses and telephone numbers of the most important professional organisations in that field, together with a brief summary (where appropriate) of the information about them.

At the end of the book, under 'Abbreviations', you will find an alphabetical glossary of the acronyms used in the book.

P.S. Throughout the book, for 'he' read 'he or she' (and vice versa).

Introduction

This book is intended to help you in your dealings with the professions. Accountants, lawyers and surveyors are some of the groups you would expect to see included in any book about the professions; but we also include the professions associated with health, and essential services such as the supply of gas, electricity and water and the telephone service, as well as other groups providing services to the general public, such as tour operators and driving instructors. Our definition of a 'profession' is therefore fairly wide, but all the groups we include have one thing in common: they have an expertise and provide a service which you pay for, either directly or through taxation.

There is an important difference between hiring professional services and paying for normal consumer goods. If you buy a washing machine, you shop around for the best bargain and you know how much you will have to pay; it is usually obvious if it does not work properly and you can ask the shop where you bought it to take it back, to replace it or to repair it. You can select the brand name that you think is the best.

When it comes to professional services, the exact amount to be paid is not always established in advance; sometimes you cannot even obtain an estimate of the amount. Clear instructions as to what is actually required often cannot be provided, with reliance being placed on the discretion of the professional. The provision of poor services is sometimes less easy to identify immediately and you cannot take them back once they have been provided (although you could, in some cases, refuse to pay for them).

Finally, the consequences, should things go wrong, can be much more serious – even ruinous, in the case of poor services from solicitors, accountants or doctors.

Introduction

You may be reluctant to challenge the professional provider of the services, because of the mystique cultivated by the 'professional' language and terminology, as well as the letters after the professional's name. All of these are impressive and difficult to understand and can keep you from becoming aware that things are going wrong, or lead you to believe that there is little that you can do about it. The following chapters attempt to overcome some of this professional mystique and enhance the bargaining power that we take for granted in transactions for the purchases of goods, both in the selection of those goods and in taking action if they are not satisfactory. They will provide guidance on:

a) selecting a professional, recognising the professional quali-fications and understanding what they mean; any trade or professional associations that he may belong to and the rules or code of conduct of those associations.

b) if something goes wrong, what to do without going to court: how to use the grievance procedures that may exist for that profession, arbitration procedures that have been agreed under a code of practice, or any other methods that may be suitable for resolving the dispute.

We live in a commercial environment in which we are dominated by the professions and trades, and by their standards of skill, care and integrity on which we must perforce rely. If you buy a house, for example, you may rely on the skills of one or more of these: lawyer, surveyor, building society or bank's financial adviser, builder, architect or planner. Each of these professions has its own rules of good conduct, which may be compulsory or voluntary. If something goes wrong, it is open to you to take legal action if you have suffered loss through the professionals' negligence or breach of contract. Legal action, however, can be costly, lengthy and burdensome, and should, in most cases, constitute a last resort.

Introduction

ENGAGING A PROFESSIONAL

When hiring a professional person, it is important to be aware of the structure of self-regulation that most professions impose upon themselves. These can vary from the ethical codes that apply to the medical profession and the detailed rules of professional conduct that apply to solicitors, to the self-regulatory requirements of financial advisers and the voluntary codes of practice for the telecommunications industry. They usually provide minimum requirements for the protection of the standards of the profession and of the consumers, as well as some form of grievance procedure, which may include concili-ation and arbitration. Some professions have established an 'ombudsman' figure to whom you can take your complaints about certain aspects of the services these professions provide. Others have developed different mechanisms for the aggrieved consumer to pursue any complaint, an example being the establishment of the Solicitors Complaints Bureau by the Law Society to deal with complaints against solicitors.

This book provides information and guidance about these self-regulatory provisions – so that in all your dealings you will be aware of what you can expect from the professional that you have selected – and about the mechanisms of airing any grievances that may arise in your dealings.

It does not follow, however, that there is no remedy for the consumer from firms or individuals who are not members of professional or trade associations: statute and common law see to that. Moreover, in many cases the fact that an individual or firm does not belong to a professional organisation does not necessarily mean that a lower standard of service or less effective complaints procedures are offered.

It is not possible in a book of this size to cover every profession or trade. The ones selected are those offering services which you are most likely to require in everyday dealings. They fall into the broad categories of financial professions, advising professions, property and housing, travel, medical and para-medical matters, essential services of various kinds.

Introduction

General points

Some guidelines relating to specific dealings with professionals providing a service apply generally and can be dealt with in this introductory chapter. The following points need to be considered in nearly all dealings:

o   who are you dealing with?
o   how much will it cost?
o   the nature and terms of the contract for the supply of services between you, the consumer of the services, and the professional who provides them
o   payment.

Who are you dealing with?

It is important for you to know who your contract is with, particularly if things start to go wrong. Not only are the name and address of the person or firm important, but also the form of business through which they are operating.

There are three main types of business: the sole trader, the partnership, the company.

A sole trader means that one person owns a business and runs it, either under his own name or a business name (for instance, Fixit). Sole traders are not companies and you usually deal with the sole trader himself, although he may employ staff to carry out his business. You will often find sole traders referring to themselves as self-employed – this is a common form of doing business in the building trades. In any dealings with this type of business, you are entering into a contract with the sole trader personally.

Two or more people may operate a business together as a partnership. They can trade under their own names or a business name. Partnerships, like sole traders, can employ people to carry out their business.

Both sole traders and partnerships have unlimited liability: if their business gets into financial difficulties, the customers and creditors who are owed money can pursue the repayment of debts against the personal assets of the sole trader or partners until he or they are made bankrupt, as well as against any assets that the business may have.

A company may be trading under a corporate name (such as Fixit Ltd or Fixit plc) or a business name (such as Fixit). Companies have limited liability, as indicated by the name having 'Ltd' (short for Limited) or 'plc' (public limited company) included in it. This is meant as a warning to anyone dealing with the company that if it gets into financial difficulties, customers and creditors are able to look only to the assets of the company – not to any individual's assets – for repayment of any debts; and there may not be any assets left, once the company's bank has recovered any monies that are owing to it. Banks normally get paid first, leaving the ordinary customers with little, if anything, to share out. This is why, when companies go into liquidation, the customer who has paid in advance in cash will be fortunate to get any of his money refunded; and if there is anything to be returned, it will take some time to establish what the assets of the company are and how they should be distributed. (Customers have more protection if they pay by credit card, provided the cash price was more than £100 but under £30,000.) The rule with companies is that generally the personal assets of the shareholders or directors cannot be touched to pay the company's debts.

It is sometimes difficult to discover which type of business you are dealing with – sole trader, partnership or company. This is made more difficult because they could all be using a business name – Fixit, in our example. If, however, businesses do use a business name, they are required to post a notice on the business premises to which customers have access, indicating the name and address (for service of documents) of the individual carrying on the business if he is a sole trader, of each partner if it is a partnership or of the company's registered office. This notice must be displayed 'in a prominent position so that it may easily be read by . . . customers'. This requirement, under the Business Names Act 1985, to publicise the true names and addresses of those carrying on the business, extends also to all business letters, invoices and receipts, and it is a criminal offence not to comply with these requirements.

When dealing with a company, although you will talk to and negotiate with individuals employed by the company, any contract for the provision of services that you enter into is with the company: if you need to talk to a trade association or other body about the services that have been provided, it is the company which you should mention, not any individual in it.

How much will it cost?

When you buy a washing machine, it is usually clear how much you have to pay; the price is agreed in advance and cannot be varied without your consent. With contracts for the provision of services, it is common for no exact price to have been agreed; this often gives rise to disagreements when the customer gets what he perceives to be an excessive bill for the services that have been provided. It takes a lot of courage to refuse to pay.

To make an informed decision as to the amount you should pay and to safeguard yourself from the unexpected large bill, there are mechanisms that you can use. If no price has been agreed between the customer and the professional who is providing the services, the Supply of Goods and Services Act 1982 takes this to mean that the customer has to pay a 'reasonable' charge. However, what may seem reasonable to the professional may not seem reasonable to the customer. Any dispute as to the reasonableness of the charge should be resolved by looking at the normal charges in that profession for similar work. (If the case came to court, it would be for the customer to show that the charge was too high.)

Estimates or quotations (preferably written, dated and signed) provide guidance in advance as to the cost of the services to be provided. Unless there is some express written or oral agreement that the sum quoted is an agreed price, an estimate is only an approximation and is not binding. Quotations, however, are binding.

It is particularly important to ascertain, when seeking estimates or quotations, whether they are inclusive of VAT and other taxes or charges that may be incurred, sometimes referred to as disbursements (for example Land Registry search fees, planning permission, application fees).

An estimate may be exceeded, for instance, if the job turns out to be more difficult than expected, or there is an unexpected increase in the price of materials. However, the increase must be by no more than a reasonable amount. If the increase looks likely to be greater than this, the professional must seek your authorisation before continuing with the work. The problem is that your interpretation of a reasonable increase may differ from the professional's. Therefore it is advisable to instruct the professional to warn you of any significant deviation from estimated costs. One method of keeping a check on the level of fees that you are incurring is to instruct the professional in writing that your permission must be obtained for say, every £500 of extra expenditure; or to restrict the total amount that can be incurred to a maximum of a given amount. The figure should be set at a realistic rate, so that the professional does not have to contact you every day to authorise expenditure, a service for which he may well charge you. Such an arrangement should save you worry about the possibility of large bills being run up without your knowledge. It benefits both sides in that you know exactly where you stand financially and can monitor your expenditure, and the professional is not suddenly confronted with a client who not only cannot understand how such a bill was incurred, but is also unwilling or unable to pay it.

The contract for the supply of services

You enter into contracts every day: whenever you buy a bag of sugar or a newspaper, take a train or a bus journey, buy a meal or send your trousers to the cleaners. Contracts do not need to be in writing. Similarly, when you hire a plumber, solicitor or builder, there is a contract. Contracts for professional services are often not in writing, but instructions as to what is required must none the less be given by the client.

Word-of-mouth contracts may be satisfactory for the provision of some standard professional services where the service that you require is clearly understood, such as bringing about the sale of a house. However, if the service that is to be provided in some way departs from the standard, perhaps because of the type of materials that you want to be used; or the extent of the work is unforeseeable; or you want to specify a period of time within which the service is to be provided or even a specific date for its completion, you need to confirm the agreement in writing to lessen the risk of dispute about the precise terms on which the service is being provided.

Timing

If there is no specific agreement to the contrary, the Supply of Goods and Services Act 1982 takes every contract for the provision of services to include the term that the service will be carried out within a reasonable time. What is reasonable depends upon the facts of each case and on what is generally recognised in the trade as a 'reasonable time'. If there is a specific deadline by which you require the services to be provided, this must be expressly agreed, preferably in writing. There are certain professions that are renowned for the problems they cause in respect of delays: car servicing, building work and legal services fall into this category. The voluntary codes of practice that some professions operate often specifically cover the problems of delays.

Standard-form contracts

Some businesses, such as driving schools and estate agents, operate standard contracts, whereby all their customers are asked to agree to terms and conditions stated on a printed form. The professional will be unwilling to alter this: either you agree to the terms or you go elsewhere. Ideally, you should read the terms before agreeing to enter into the contract, but in many cases this would be a lengthy process; or your attention may be drawn to the terms only by means of a ticket or other document that is given to you, so that you would have to ask specifically to see them in full. An example would be railway tickets and other transportation contracts, and the tickets handed out by pay car parks.

Care and skill
Another term that the law takes to be included in any contract for services is that the supplier will perform his services with the care and skill of a reasonable person in that profession. (Partially exempt from this implied duty are advocates before a court, tribunal, inquiry or arbitrator and the preparatory work carried out by them that directly affects the hearing.)

This implied term means that any professional you hire should at least meet the standards of an ordinary supplier of services of that type; and if special skills are claimed, the standards of someone who ordinarily possesses those skills should be attained.

Builders, contractors and tradesmen doing work on a house have a special statutory duty imposed upon them which they cannot escape. This duty is owed to their customers and subsequent owners in respect of properties that they build, including extensions. It is to see that the work is done in a workmanlike or professional manner, with proper materials and so that, as regards that work, the dwelling will be fit for habitation when completed. Usually building control officers from the local authority inspect the progress at various stages to establish that the builder is complying with the detailed building regulations (and if they do not do this properly, they too could be held in law to be negligent).

Payment for services
In the majority of cases where a service is provided, everything will proceed smoothly and the bill will be paid after the service

has been provided. Should something, however, go wrong, the situation is not the same as if you had bought a faulty appliance: you can send the appliance back, but you cannot send back the unsatisfactory services.

If the services have been substantially performed, the supplier of the services can demand to be paid something, even though the job has not been completed. For example, if the contract was for the rewiring of a house for £1,000 and there are small defects that will cost £100 to correct, the electrician can demand £900, even though the defects were not remedied. Whether or not there has been substantial performance of the contract will depend on the facts of each case.

If there has not been substantial performance of the contract because of the fault of the supplier, he cannot demand any payment. It may be necessary to consult a solicitor to establish whether or not this is the case on the particular facts of your contract.

Some suppliers of services require deposits or advance payments, either as a sign of goodwill, or to cover their costs for necessary expenditure. The contract could provide that payments, for example to a builder, will be made at various stages. You should be wary of any provider of services who wants advance payment in full; he could disappear or become insolvent before the service was provided.

If possible, choose a supplier who does not insist on advance payment in full. If this is not possible (perhaps because this is the usual practice, or because a good discount is offered), at least try to negotiate some retention of the total amount to be paid (for example 10%), so that you will have some bargaining strength if the services provided are faulty in some way. Ultimately, non-payment is the most powerful bargaining factor a customer possesses if the services provided are faulty or inadequate.

It has to be accepted that in the case of some services (holidays, for example), such negotiations are pointless in the face of a standard contract that not only requires you to pay before you receive the service but may also allow the provider of the service to increase the price later through surcharges.

Non-payment can also lead to difficulties if the supplier of the service is in possession of property that belongs to you. This property could be documents (in the case of a solicitor or accountant). In such a case, the supplier of the services has what is called a 'lien' over your goods and can keep your property until the bill is paid, or until you obtain a court order requiring him to return it.

You have more protection if you pay for services costing over £100 with a credit card rather than in cash. This is because the provider of the credit is as liable for any misrepresentation or breach of contract by the supplier as the supplier himself. If a dispute does arise about the provision of the services – or the lack of provision – where the services have been paid for by credit, getting the credit company involved can greatly strengthen your bargaining position with the supplier. The ultimate but rarely used sanction that the credit company has over the supplier is to withdraw the credit facilities. From the point of view of the consumer, involving the credit card company provides an effective way to recoup any losses. Moreover, the credit company can also put pressure on the supplier to settle with you. This joint and several liability that is placed on the credit companies does not apply to agreements of less than £100 or more than £30,000 (not more than £15,000 being paid by credit).

VOLUNTARY CODES OF PRACTICE
Some professions have developed voluntary codes of practice which members of the profession are encouraged to abide by.

The adoption of such codes has been encouraged by the Office of Fair Trading, one of the statutory duties conferred upon the Director General in 1973 being 'to encourage relevant associations to prepare and to disseminate to their members, codes of practice for guidance in safeguarding and promoting the interests of consumers in the United Kingdom'.

There is some evidence that those businesses which have agreed to abide by the codes receive fewer complaints, but the codes have advantages and disadvantages. The advantages are:

○ trading practices which, although lawful, are unfair to consumers can be outlawed by the code

○ consumers normally receive better information about the service they are to be provided with, as well as details – in advance – of any costs, including call-out fees

○ the codes provide for a mechanism for dealing with complaints through arbitration, usually at low cost

○ consumers are assured in advance that the professional they are dealing with has agreed to the minimum standards laid down in the code

○ the codes do not detract from consumers' other legal rights.

The disadvantages are:

○ not all members of the trade or profession may have agreed to abide by the terms of the code; you have to be able to identify those that have not, otherwise your expectations as regards the standard of service may be disappointed

○ even those members who have agreed to follow the provisions of the code may not do so in your case and you may have to pursue them through the complaints machinery

○ the sanctions adopted by trade associations for dealing with members who do not comply with the code vary considerably in their vigour; this obviously affects the implementation of the code by members, as well as your ability to use a breach of the code as a bargaining factor if the services provided are faulty or inadequate.

Consumers should be aware that professional and trade associations exist primarily to serve the interests of their members, and only secondarily to serve those of the consumer. If they formulate codes of conduct or of practice it is in order to preserve the good name of the trade or profession rather than to make sure that justice is done to the consumer (even though they may help him to obtain justice).

Consequently, the sanctions which threaten the breaker of the code are mostly a reprimand or the suspension or termination of membership. In the case of some professions, such as medicine, the law and architecture, such sanctions can cost the culprit his livelihood; but in the case of most other professions and trades he can go on much as before, so the threat is not as serious.

Moreover, only a few professional associations have power to enforce compensation or restitution, or to compel the culprit to make good the damage. To get such a result, you would have to go to law. However, if you do, the fact that your professional has been reprimanded, suspended or expelled by his professional association should add weight to your claim against him.

FORESTALLING PROBLEMS

Complaints against professionals tend to be attributable to either the incompetence of the professional, or to a breakdown in communication between the professional and his client – or, often, to both.

Incompetence is a risk which can be lessened by making an informed choice in finding the right person for the job. Within each profession, some individuals or firms may concentrate on areas requiring special expertise, while others may offer a broad range of services and present themselves as 'jacks of all trades'. Often there are also areas of overlap between professions. For example, all accountants have a basic knowledge of law; similarly, all solicitors have a basic knowledge of accounts. So if you want advice on a company matter, to which profession should you go?

The answer is likely to turn on the precise nature of the problem, and you could in some cases need the services of both the lawyer and the accountant to analyse and advise on different aspects of it. The principle of 'horses for courses' is an important one when choosing a professional.

Introduction

Getting on with the professional

The relationship between a client and a professional is expected to be one of trust. If you begin, at any time, to doubt the advice of the professional you are consulting, you should sort the matter out quickly, because mistrust can jeopardise the outcome of the whole matter.

Failure of communication between professional and client is a constant hazard. The two will inevitably tend to perceive the same matter differently. For a start, the professional has no personal stake (other than the task of earning a living) in the matter about which he is being consulted; and a client who expects a subjective response may be disappointed if this is not forthcoming. In fact, what he really needs is the expert's objectivity and detachment.

The expertise of the professional is his strength, but also a potential source of weakness when it comes to communicating with his client. Many professionals are steeped in their work; their thorough knowledge of their trade makes commonplace to them many expressions and ideas which are obscure to the average client. And so a professional may sometimes express himself in words that are very precise (to him) but which his client either fails to understand at all or (perhaps worse still) interprets wrongly.

For the professional, effective communication is therefore a challenge. If he explains matters in his own terms, he risks being accused of employing jargon or of refusing to give a straight answer to a straight question; conversely, he does not wish to appear to patronise a client. However, it is sometimes extremely difficult to rephrase technical matters in simple terms without trivialising or even introducing ambiguity.

A professional must none the less strive to ensure that he is understood as fully as possible. The trouble is that many clients feel intimidated by professionals and fear that if they admit they do not understand what they have been told, they will be thought ignorant. But the client or customer looking for expertise must make sure that he receives it. So put questions to the expert – many are flattered by an enquiring attitude on the part of their listeners – and go on asking until you know what you need to know.

A concomitant of this is that it pays you, the customer, to get to know your professional. There is a considerable difference between the way you deal with a person known to you only as a voice on the phone or the signature at the end of a letter, and a person you have met face to face. In the same way, it will help him to know you personally.

If you find yourself in a spoken disagreement with the professional, either on the telephone or face to face, try to keep your temper. Even if you find that the other person is being most unreasonable, do not become abusive, storm out or slam the phone down, or you will lose face, even if you are in the right.

Avoiding misunderstandings
In order to have an accurate record of your communications with a professional, be sure to keep a copy of every letter you write to him (and remember to date it clearly). If you are writing in reply to a letter or telephone call, always make reference to it in the letter, mentioning the date. Keep a notebook by the telephone, in order to record the subject of any call to or from the professional and the approximate duration of the call.

IF THINGS GO WRONG
This book concentrates on ways of pursuing grievances which do not involve court action, but recognises the fact that sometimes you may have no other recourse. It is important to be aware that legal remedies may provide an alternative and sometimes simultaneous method of seeking redress (to be used, in most situations, as a last resort).

Invoking the criminal law
Local authorities operate Trading Standards Departments, one of whose functions is to enforce the criminal aspects of consumer protection legislation. They also advise on many areas of

consumer protection. It is a criminal offence to make a false or misleading statement about services, accommodation or facilities. This includes professional services, although it is more frequently used in connection with the provision of holidays and misleading statements in brochures. If a service has been misleadingly described or advertised, contact the local office of the Trading Standards Department with the details. The Trading Standards Officers can initiate criminal proceedings where it seems to them appropriate.

Following a conviction in court, the magistrates or the Crown Court have the power to make a compensation order in favour of any person who has suffered because of the criminal actions. The amounts awarded are not great but can help to compensate for your loss.

There may, however, be occasions when your only recourse is to take legal action in the civil courts.

Civil action

For small claims, currently defined as claims of £1000 or less, there is a special procedure in the county court called small claims arbitration. After the completion of a form called a default summons (Form N1) and the payment of a court fee (which depends on how much you are claiming), the dispute comes before a registrar of the county court.

When completing the form, it is important to know whether you have been dealing with a company or a sole trader or partnership, because if the action is against a company you should insert the company's name as the defendant and the company's registered office as the defendant's address. With sole traders and partnerships, you can use either their real or their business names and the address can be the principal place of business.

The person who is bringing the case is called the plaintiff. The person or company against whom he is bringing it is called the respondent. The action may be for breach of contract or in negligence (that is, a breach of the duty of care owed to the plaintiff, who has suffered loss as a result of it). There are detailed accounts of the small claims procedure in a booklet available from the county court called *Small Claims in the County Court*, specifically drafted with the lay person in mind.

The main advantage of the small claims procedure is that solicitors' costs are not awarded against either side unless the arbitrator certifies that costs were incurred through the unreasonable conduct of the opposite party – for example, if one party fabricated evidence to help his case. Such certifications are, however, extremely rare. The successful plaintiff can claim the costs that are stated on the summons (the fee that you pay when you start the action). Generally, this means that you have a good idea as to how much it will cost to bring the action and need not worry about having to pay the other side's legal costs if you lose. You cannot get legal aid for bringing a small claim.

If the amount you are seeking is just over £1000, you can disclaim the excess and bring yourself within the financial limit, although you must state that you are doing so on the form.

If your claim is outside the small claims limit, any legal action will normally go through the standard county court procedure where legal costs against the loser may be awarded. If you need the services of solicitor, it may be possible for you to get legal aid, depending on your financial circumstances and the nature of the case. You should consult a solicitor before you start a county court action.

CODE ARBITRATION

Small claims arbitration in the county court should not be confused with the arbitration schemes which are offered under the many voluntary codes of conduct that apply to various professions. Most of these codes offer you the option of taking a dispute through an arbitration process; but you cannot be compelled to do so. Any clause in a contract that requires you to go to arbitration cannot usually be enforced.

This 'code arbitration' is not the same as arbitration in the small claims court and the term 'arbitration' to describe the two different mechanisms for resolving disputes is sometimes confusing. Code arbitration usually involves the appointment of an independent arbitrator who decides on the merits of the claim and on the level of any damages that may be awarded, after considering documentation forwarded by both sides in the dispute. It can sometimes involve a hearing, but this makes the procedure much more expensive, which could swallow up all of damages awarded to you, if not more.

While you cannot be compelled to go to arbitration, in many cases the other party cannot be so compelled either, so that arbitration can only happen where both parties agree to it. In most cases, agreement to opt for this voluntary arbitration process binds you not to take the case to court unless there are very exceptional circumstances.

Code or county court arbitration?

If it comes to making a decision as to whether or not to go through the arbitration procedure under a code of practice (code arbitration) or to go through the small claims arbitration in the county court (court arbitration), you may find the following list of their advantages and disadvantages useful.

Jurisdiction – limits on value/subject matter: in court arbitration the financial limit is £1000. Code arbitrations vary as to their financial limits; they sometimes limit the subject matter of an arbitration.

One disadvantage of code arbitration is that it is based on the contract as it stands. You may not challenge the validity of any of its clauses – such as exclusion clauses – as you might be able to do in court.

Cost: both court and code arbitrations involve the payment of an initial fee. It is extremely rare for legal costs to be awarded in court arbitrations: they are not awarded in code arbitrations.

Procedure: the court arbitration scheme provides for an oral hearing. Most code arbitrations do not: the decision is made by the arbitrator based on documents only and there is no opportunity to ask the other side questions face to face. This opportunity does exist in a court arbitration and is a useful procedure if there are questions to which the other side is reluctant to give a direct response (except that the other side may be legally represented).

Awards: it is generally held that court awards are higher than code arbitration awards, although this is only an impression gleaned from some arbitration awards and there is no substantial research to prove or disprove this.

Enforcement: with court arbitration, many of your real problems start after you have won; enforcement of the judgment can be difficult, frustrating, and time-consuming. Reputable firms and companies should pay straight after judgment has been awarded, but the disreputable ones can lead you into a procedural quagmire in your attempts to obtain the damages to which you are entitled. Because code members have to abide by the code, including the arbitration procedure, payment of an award will usually be made without too much difficulty. If not, code arbitrations are technically enforceable in the same way as court judgments; and the association of which they are a member can reprimand, fine and even expel them. (This does not, however, get you your money.)

Ultimately it will depend on the facts in each case as to which method of airing your grievances you select. The following chapters help you to select a professional with whom such problems should not arise, but if you do select one who belongs to an association with a code of practice that includes an arbitration procedure, you have at least a choice as to how to pursue any problems that may arise.

NON-CONTRACTUAL RELATIONSHIPS
A duty of care (under the law of tort) exists in nearly all cases between the provider of a service and the recipient, and is in addition to any contractual duty that may exist; although it is usually the contractual duties that you would seek to rely on if something did go wrong. This is why it is usually important to establish clearly, before you engage a professional, exactly what

you want and when you want it, as well as discussing the price to be paid. If difficulties arise and there are misunderstandings as to what was required, your bargaining strength is considerably weakened if there is no prior written agreement to which you can turn.

In some situations you receive services from a professional but you do not enter into a contractual relationship with him. A good example is your doctor and the supply of medical services under the National Health Service. The absence of a contract does not mean that the doctor does not have to use reasonable care and skill in providing the service. A duty of care does exist between the doctor and the patient, and if that duty is breached through the negligence of the doctor, there are avenues, both legal and non-legal, for pursuing your grievance.

London telephone numbers

On 6 May 1990 the 01 telephone code for London will change to either 071 or 081, depending on the local code that follows it. From that date, people telephoning the 01 code will hear a recorded message telling them to re-dial using either 071 or 081.

USEFUL ADDRESSES

CHARTERED INSTITUTE OF ARBITRATORS
75 Cannon Street
London EC4N 5BH
01-236 8761

**NATIONAL ASSOCIATION FOR CITIZENS ADVICE
BUREAUX (NACAB)**
115 Pentonville Road
London N1 9LZ
01-833 2181

OFFICE OF FAIR TRADING
Field House
15-25 Bream's Buildings
London EC4A 1PR
01-242 2858

Consumer Credit Licensing Branch:
Government Buildings
Bromyard Avenue
London W3 7BB
01-734 5566

Legal Services

In Great Britain at the present time legal advice may be sought from a variety of sources. In the forefront of the legal profession stand solicitors and barristers; but much legal advice that is given does not come from either of these groups.

A solicitor's practice may well encompass legal executives and articled clerks. If you are buying a house, you may decide to employ a licensed conveyancer instead of a solicitor (except in Northern Ireland).

A law centre is obliged to employ at least two qualified lawyers, but most of the other staff will probably not have professional legal qualifications, though they will have received training. The staff of Citizens Advice Bureaux are mostly volunteers who have had some training in particular areas of the law. Such unqualified volunteers are known as 'paralegals'.

This chapter describes the kinds of legal work done by all these people, and the different ways in which they can be of use to members of the public.

The information that follows applies to legal services in England and Wales only: however, the system in Northern Ireland is very similar. Legal services in Scotland will be dealt with separately.

SOLICITORS
When you go to a solicitor's office, how can you make sure that the person who is giving you legal advice is qualified to do so?

It is a criminal offence for a non-solicitor to represent himself as a solicitor. The Law Society will in most cases prosecute anybody who does so. Before being admitted as a solicitor, a person must have passed a number of examinations and served 2 or more years articles of clerkship (an apprenticeship) in a solicitor's office.

Every practising solicitor is required to have a practising certificate, from the Law Society: it must be renewed annually. Thus partners in a firm are required to hold a current practising certificate, and the same is true of solicitor-employees who appear in open court or administer oaths, or whose names appear on legal aid certificates. In fact, all solicitor-employees need practising certificates, unless they are employed only as clerks. It is not necessary for a solicitor to be a member of the Law Society, as the Society exercises statutory authority over all solicitors, whether they are members or not.

Therefore what you need to know is whether your legal adviser has actually been admitted as a solicitor. You should be able to find this out by looking in the *Solicitors' and Barristers' Directory*. As is the case with all such publications, this can never be completely up to date; but the Law Society maintains a computerised register which is available to the public, and this should be up to date. In Northern Ireland, a telephone call to the Law Society in Belfast will confirm whether someone is on the Roll of Solicitors.

But, provided you are satisfied that you are dealing with a firm of solicitors (and you are unlikely to be misled over that), your contract is with the firm, not the individual adviser, whether he is a solicitor or not. So if a dispute arises, this will be between you and the firm, rather than between you and a particular adviser.

But if the firm is not involved in the subject matter of the dispute, your redress will be against the individual, not the firm. An example would be if that person had made an agreement with you to do the work cheaply out of the office, without telling his firm.

Who will your adviser be?

When you arrange to visit a firm of solicitors for legal advice, this does not necessarily mean that the person whom you see will be a solicitor. Firms of solicitors may also employ legal executives who are Fellows of the Institute of Legal Executives; articled clerks who are training to be solicitors; and other executives and clerks.

Even if the person who sees you is a solicitor, he may not necessarily be a partner. Solicitors who are not partners and legal executives may be listed together with partners on, say, stationery and advertisements. However, according to the Solicitors' Publicity Code 1988, the status of non-partners must be indicated – so you should not be misled.

On the other hand, the fact that the name of the person you see is not part of the firm's name, or does not appear on the headed notepaper or the plaque by the office door, does not mean he has no qualifications, as the firm might only have displayed the names of partners. Many firms (particularly the larger ones) employ qualified solicitors who are not partners. Moreover, partnership is not an absolute guarantee of quality.

Under the Solicitors' Practice Rules, a firm must ensure that its office (or offices) is attended each day when it is open to the public or to telephone calls, by a solicitor who has been admitted for at least 3 years. (This rule is often ignored in practice, especially in branch offices.) This solicitor must spend sufficient time at that office to ensure adequate supervision of the staff, and provide the necessary facilities for consultation with clients. He need not be a partner, but the firm must have at least one partner who has been admitted for at least 3 years. Every office of the firm must be managed either by a solicitor holding a practising certificate, or by a person who has been a Fellow of the Institute of Legal Executives for not less than 5 years, 'being of good standing'. This person has to be 'normally in attendance' during all opening hours, but this does not prevent him from being away from the office on clients' business.

According to the solicitors' written Professional Standards, the client should be told the name and status of the person responsible for the day-to-day conduct of his matter, and the partner responsible for its overall supervision; the client should be informed if any change is made, with an explanation. However, this is only a guideline, and does not say at what stage you should be told. Therefore, you might only find out at the end of the interview that the person who has been advising you is not a solicitor; or be told that although he is a solicitor, he will not be dealing with the matter on a day-to-day basis.

The person you actually see may well be, though not a solicitor, perfectly competent to deal with your matter. However, if you wish to insist on seeing a solicitor, ask the person you are seeing if he is one. If too embarrassed to ask directly, consult the *Solicitors' and Barristers' Directory* in the public library.

Even though you may speak to a solicitor whenever you come to the office, this does not mean that a solicitor is personally dealing with your case throughout. Routine matters are often left to non-solicitor employees.

The solicitor's duties and professional conduct

There is a distinction between the solicitor's duties in law and his duties under the rules of professional conduct. A solicitor owes certain duties in law to his client, laid down in various statutes and the rules of common law. If there is a breach of such duties, the client has a right to sue.

The rules of professional conduct are laid down by the Council of the Law Society from time to time, as practice rules, accounts rules, codes, guidance statements and Council directions. You have no legal right to sue for such breaches, but may report the matter to the Solicitors Complaints Bureau, which will take appropriate action. In many cases, a breach of the professional rules will also amount to a breach of legal duties; if so, the client may also be able to sue, if he has suffered loss.

These rules of professional conduct, together with many of the solicitor's legal duties to his client, and the Professional Standards, are consolidated in the *Professional Conduct of*

Solicitors, which is published by the Law Society: this is available to the public, but does not make easy reading for the lay person.

Under the Supply of Goods and Services Act 1982 solicitors are bound to carry out their work with reasonable care and skill; to make a reasonable charge where a fee is not agreed in advance; and, where a time is not stated, to carry out the work within a reasonable time. However, under the Supply of Services (Exclusion of Implied Terms) Order 1982, they are exempt from the duty of care when acting as advocates. This means that you cannot sue your solicitor for the way in which he conducts your case in court or before a tribunal. This is in order to bring solicitors into line with barristers (who also cannot be sued). This may seem an arbitrary exemption. It rests on the notion that otherwise everyone who lost a case would be blaming their advocate, and suing.

The duties of a solicitor under the Solicitors' Practice Rules 1988 include the following:

o   A solicitor must not do anything which is likely to compromise or impair his independence or integrity, his duty to act in the best interests of the client, his proper standard of work, a person's freedom to instruct a solicitor of his choice, or the solicitor's duty to the court.

o   A solicitor may publicise his practice, provided he does not contravene the Solicitors' Publicity Code.

o   A solicitor may accept introductions and referrals of business from another person, and may make introductions and refer business to another person, provided there is no breach of any other rule, and provided that he complies with the Solicitors' Introduction and Referral Code.

o   In connection with investment business, a solicitor must not have any arrangement with another person under which the solicitor could be constrained to recommend some investments or persons but not others.

o   A solicitor must account to his client for any commission received of more than £10, unless he discloses the amount to the client and the client agrees that he should retain it.

o A solicitor should not, as a general rule, act for both the seller and the buyer on a transfer of land (by which is meant realty: house, flat, bungalow). There are, however, a number of exceptions to this rule, provided that there is no conflict of interest: for instance, if the clients are related, or are both established clients. (There is not the same prohibition on acting for both lender and borrower, provided the lender is an institution which provides mortgages in the normal course of its activities.)

o A solicitor must not enter into an arrangement to receive a contingency fee in connection with court proceedings (that is, he must not accept work on a 'no win, no fee' basis).

There are four sets of Solicitors' Accounts Rules (made in 1986 and 1988) which lay down detailed rules for the handling of clients' money, and the keeping of records of such transactions.

The solicitors' Professional Standards cover the areas which are the main source of complaints against solicitors. They are designed to inform clients and reduce potential conflicts. The Standards are guidelines: it will be for the solicitor to judge when a standard can be ignored, but also for him to justify his decision, should the client feel aggrieved. Failure to observe a standard will not of itself give the client a right of action against the solicitor, unless that failure amounts to negligence in the particular case. Similarly, failure to observe a standard will not of itself be grounds for a complaint of misconduct, but unreasonable or persistent failure could well be so.

Choosing a solicitor

It is usually difficult for the Law Society to recommend a particular solicitor: it is therefore best to go by personal recommendations. It is advisable, however, to tell those giving the recommendations what sort of advice you are seeking, as solicitors are increasingly becoming specialists in particular areas. Try to ask more than one person for recommendations, remembering that you will have no claim against any such person if you are not satisfied with that solicitor.

Failing a personal recommendation, you could consult (in a library) the Regional Directory, which indicates the sort of work undertaken by solicitors in your region. However, the information is not sufficiently reliable: it is fairly general and based on the volume of work undertaken; it does not necessarily indicate particular expertise. There will be a number of solicitors undertaking each kind of work, and the directory will not help you decide which of them to choose. Law Centres and Citizens Advice Bureaux will also have copies of the Directory and may in addition advise you on the choice of solicitor. In cases of real difficulty you may be able to get help from the secretary of the local Law Society – contact your library or the Law Society in London for his name and address.

If you are a member of a trade union, professional organisation or trade association, the services of a solicitor (either an employee of the organisation or a solicitor in private practice) may be available to you as one of the benefits of membership – or the organisation may be able to make a recommendation.

Local law centres may also provide referral to appropriate solicitors. They are often well placed to recommend experts in the particular areas of law relevant to the consumer. There is often a mutual referral system in operation between a law centre and firms of solicitors practising in its area.

You may perhaps be introduced to a solicitor by your building society or bank, or some similar organisation, if you are buying a house. The solicitor in England and Wales must comply with the Solicitors' Introduction and Referral Code 1988. He must not reward an introducer; so you can be sure that you have not been referred to that solicitor because he is paying commission. You are not obliged to accept the recommendation.

Eight per cent of solicitors in England and Wales are sole practitioners: that is, they do not have partners, although they may have other people working for them, either assistant

solicitors or clerks. 20% of complaints are about sole practitioners, which means that they attract more complaints, in
proportion to their numbers, than partnerships. This does not
mean that you should not use a sole practitioner: the majority
are good solicitors; and you may find in a sole practitioner
(perhaps a local person you have known for years) the sort of
personal touch that a large partnership may lack.

Advertisements

Solicitors are now allowed to advertise, in accordance with the
Solicitors' Publicity Code 1988. They are allowed to advertise
that they will do particular kinds of work (which suggests one
way of choosing a solicitor).

However, a solicitor is not allowed to advertise that he is a
specialist in a particular field, unless he is a member of a
relevant Law Society panel (there are currently three: Child
Care, Mental Health Tribunal and the Insolvency Practitioners);
or unless he holds the Law Society's Local Government
Diploma.

(The Law Society is considering other panels and qualifications in subjects such as planning, medical negligence and
perhaps matrimonial and criminal law.)

Nowadays most solicitors specialise: either there are
separate departments within the firm, or – as is becoming more
common – the actual firm specialises. A recently published
book, called *The Legal 500*, is a guide to the top 500 firms in the
country (not Northern Ireland), to be updated annually: it is
useful for picking out firms well known for particular work.
However, it has no official standing, and it covers only those 500
firms. These are not necessarily the most expensive firms, but a
number of them will charge more because of their expertise.
There are many thousands of other very good firms, which do
not appear in this book.

Solicitors are not allowed to compare themselves with other
solicitors, or to publish their success rate.

Assessing the cost

Apart from the expertise and competence of a solicitor, an important factor is how much he is going to charge. Although solicitors are not allowed to compare themselves, and therefore their charges, with other solicitors, they are allowed to advertise their charges. But they generally either do not do so, or tend to quote hourly charges – for a good reason. The Code says that they must state clearly what the charges include and in what circumstances they may be increased. It is very difficult to quote a set fee without misleading the public. It is impossible to predict how complicated a particular matter will be, and a long advertisement detailing all the possibilities would be expensive and more likely to put the public off than to make much impact.

Some solicitors, though, have set charges for certain matters, such as conveyancing and wills, although even there the solicitor takes the risk of the occasional complicated case. An hourly rate is not very helpful in telling you how much the matter will cost, as you are not in a position to know how long it will take. On the other hand, it does allow you to compare firms' hourly rates.

You must be a little wary, however, as the hourly rate may depend on the expertise of a particular member of that firm. You might get a less experienced solicitor or legal executive who might take longer, because of inexperience; therefore the final bill could be even higher than a more expensive firm's, if the difference in the comparable charges was not great to start with.

There is considerable variation in solicitors' charges and, subject to the warning just given, you should shop around: always remembering that legal advice is not a commodity, and that the level of charges may just possibly reflect the quality of the service being offered.

Getting in touch with a solicitor
Before consulting a solicitor you may wish to take advantage of the Law Society's Lawline legal information telephone service. It has 115 pre-recorded categories of information, lasting an

average of 5 minutes, which will cost approximately £1-£2, depending on the time of day. The aim of the service is to give you some basic information before you consult a solicitor, but is not intended as a substitute for consulting one. Copies of the Lawline directory can be obtained free by telephoning 0898 600 600. This service is not available in Northern Ireland.

Some but not many firms are willing to give a fixed fee interview: for a fee of not more than £5 (inclusive of VAT), you can have up to a half-hour interview, regardless of your means. You should make sure that the solicitor knows that you are asking for an interview on this basis when you make the appointment, or at the beginning of the interview. This is a voluntary scheme, and a solicitor may decline to give an interview on this basis.

The Law Society's Accident Legal Advice Scheme (ALAS) offers to accident victims or their close relatives a free initial interview with a solicitor, in order to see if it is worth while claiming compensation. Ask a Citizens Advice Bureau or the Law Society for details, or look for the ALAS sticker in a solicitor's office.

Do not be afraid simply to walk into a solicitor's office and ask to see a solicitor. The staff there will be used to this happening: for them it is all in a day's work. But unless you need to have a signature witnessed or an oath administered, it is generally better to make an appointment in advance. When you do so, mention the nature of your business, so that the firm can assess who will be best suited (in terms of legal expertise) to interview you.

Solicitor refusing you

A solicitor is free to decide whether or not to accept a particular client, unless the refusal is on the grounds of race, sex or religion. However, a solicitor must not act where there is significant risk of a conflict of interest between the client and him, his firm or another client. Such a conflict may occur if the client is considering action against another client (a common problem in matrimonial cases); or if two clients are co-defendants in criminal proceedings and the defence of one is to lay the blame on the other.

If there is a conflict of interest between established clients, the solicitor must refuse to act for either, unless he acts for one and the other agrees. Where a client intends to make a gift, such as by will, of a substantial amount to anyone in the firm, or their families, the solicitor must advise the client to seek independent advice about that gift; if the client declines, the solicitor must refuse to act.

A solicitor must refuse to act for a client where another solicitor is already acting in the same matter, unless the client terminates his agreement with the first solicitor, or the first solicitor consents to the second solicitor acting in his place.

This does not prevent another solicitor from giving a second opinion, without the first solicitor's knowledge; but the second solicitor may sometimes be reluctant to do so, on the grounds that he has insufficient information to give such an opinion.

You can terminate your agreement with your solicitor for any reason – that is, you do not need a 'good' reason. However, you may still be liable to pay his bill for work done to date.

If you think your solicitor is providing an inadequate service or has been negligent, it may be advantageous to consult another solicitor before terminating your agreement with the first one. This may either put your mind at rest, or give you the confidence to change solicitors – or even to bring proceedings for negligence against the original solicitor. A solicitor must not terminate his agreement with the client, except for good reason, and on reasonable notice. Examples of good reasons would be where a conflict of interest has become apparent, or there is a serious breakdown in confidence between solicitor and client.

The initial interview
Whatever the nature of your problem, the object of the initial interview with the solicitor is to establish what has to be done and to lay down the ground rules for doing it.

It is in your interest to make the best use of your interview period – to save the solicitor's time and your own money. So make sure to bring with you all the documents and other information relating to your problem. If the business is complicated, write down the essential points beforehand. If you think you may be eligible for legal aid, you should bring your wages/salary slip.

Payment

One of the first things the solicitor will do is to discuss payment with you. Do not be offended by this: it is as much in your interest as the solicitor's that you know where you stand from the outset, rather than suffer a shock when the bill is presented.

According to the Standards, the solicitor should give the client the best information he can about the cost of the matter, and must consider whether the client is eligible for advice and assistance under the 'green form' scheme or for legal aid, which is available to people on low incomes.

Getting legal aid

As not every solicitor is part of the Legal Aid Scheme, you may then be advised to consult another solicitor. Therefore, if you think you are likely to need legal aid, consult the Legal Aid Solicitors' list at the Citizens Advice Bureau, or look for the Legal Aid logo which is usually displayed in solicitors' offices, in the window or in some other prominent position. It should not be necessary for you to go inside to find out.

If all you need is advice, and perhaps some letters written, the solicitor will assess whether you are financially eligible for legal advice and assistance (in both civil and criminal cases) under the 'green form' scheme. He can do do this on the spot, and let you know immediately if you are eligible. You may then not have to pay anything or, if your financial resources are above a certain level, you may have to pay a contribution. The solicitor may ask you for it there and then, though solicitors often waive these contributions. 'Green form' advice entitles you to up to two hours of the solicitor's time (three if the matter is a divorce), but generally no representation in court.

If your case is more complicated, so that you may have to go to court, the solicitor will help you fill in the forms for legal aid; he can work out the figures, but cannot make the decision himself as to whether you are eligible. The DSS will assess your means on the basis of the information you have given on the form, and you may have to go for an interview.

Even if you are financially eligible, legal aid may be refused, because the Legal Aid Office has to decide on the merits of the case you want to bring or defend. Also, legal aid would not be granted for a case which does not need legal representation, for example, a consumer matter such as suing a shop over defective goods, because it is quite easy to bring the case yourself under the small claims procedure in the county court.

It may take 6-8 weeks or even longer before a legal aid certificate is granted, and because your solicitor cannot claim from the Legal Aid Fund for any work he does before the certificate is granted, this will cause some delay in bringing your case. If the matter is urgent, such as getting an injunction against a violent spouse, the solicitor may apply for emergency legal aid, which is much quicker. In certain circumstances, a solicitor may now claim for emergency work done where a certificate could not be obtained because it was out of office hours.

Your own contribution

If you get a legal aid certificate, you may be required to pay a contribution to your legal fees if your income and/or capital are above a certain amount. The Standards provide that if you are legally aided, you should be informed at the outset and at appropriate stages thereafter, about the effect of the 'legal aid charge'. So, before you sign the legal aid forms, the solicitor should warn you about this. Legal aid is really a sort of loan; if you win your case, you have to repay the costs of your case out of your 'winnings'. This does not just mean cash compensation

– it also applies to any property you become entitled to. It also applies to anything you stop the other party claiming, as well as anything you succeed in getting from him, if the legal aid is for defending a case.

However, if you lose your case or do not obtain or successfully defend anything to which a value can be attached, you will not have to repay the money; for instance, when you get legal aid to obtain a custody order. Also, this charge only applies to legal aid and not to 'green form': if you only get 'green form' advice and assistance you do not have to pay anything back. However, if you start with 'green form' and then get legal aid for the same case (perhaps because it becomes clear that you need to go to court) the charge applies to the costs of the 'green form' advice as well as the rest of the costs.

The charge applies to everything which is part of the same matter. So, if you get a divorce because of your spouse's behaviour, and also have to get an injunction to prevent violence, and also a custody order, and financial and property adjustment orders, all these costs will be charged against any property and capital you obtain. Your solicitor should remind you of this at each appropriate stage.

Paying your own fees

If you are not legally aided, and have not previously taken out an insurance policy which will cover the matter, the Standards provide that, whenever possible, the solicitor should give you an estimate of the probable cost; if he is unable to do this, he should at least tell you how the fee will be calculated.

Getting an estimate

He will almost always give you an estimate, not a quotation, that is, a guide to the cost, which should not be exceeded by more than a reasonable amount, but which is not binding. This is because it is extremely difficult to predict how much work will be involved. A matter may look straightforward, but the other side may simply refuse to accept your claim or may come up with a defence which you had not anticipated, and therefore the whole case may take much longer, involve more work and cost more. The solicitor will probably explain that the estimate only covers the basic matter as you have outlined it, and that anything additional, or any complications, will add to the cost. The Standards state that the final amount should not vary substantially from the estimate unless the client has been informed of the changed circumstances in writing; that is, the solicitor must get your authorisation before continuing.

For some matters, such as conveyancing or making a will, you may be able to get a quotation: it is worth asking. Whether you get a quotation or an estimate, the Standards demand that it should be confirmed in writing. However, as the Standards are only guidelines, it is a good idea to make a point of asking for confirmation in writing, especially if the matter is likely to take a long time, because you may have difficulty later remembering what was agreed to.

In Northern Ireland, the Solicitors Practice (Advertising) Regulations 1989 require solicitors to give estimates for work.

The Standards state that the client should be told in appropriate cases that he may set a limit on the costs which may be incurred without further reference to him. Whether or not you have set a limit, you should be told, at least every six months, the approximate amount of the costs to date. In certain cases, your solicitor may deliver an interim bill, which means that you have to pay this, even though the case is not yet over. A solicitor should tell the client at the outset the stages at which this is likely to occur.

No solicitor is allowed to take on a case on a contingency basis, that is, to agree to take a share of your 'winnings', and be paid nothing if you lose.

'Costs'
According to the Standards, the solicitor should warn you that if you lose your case and are not legally aided, you may be ordered to contribute to your opponent's costs; and that even if

you win, your opponent may not be ordered to pay all your costs, and may not actually be able to pay what he has been ordered to pay. Unless you are legally aided, you are responsible for paying your solicitor's costs. Therefore, if your opponent is ordered to pay costs, you cannot tell your solicitor to collect these from him, and that you will pay any balance due. You must pay your solicitor in the first place, and hope that your opponent pays the costs promptly.

The Standards recommend that a solicitor should consider with the client whether the likely outcome will justify the expense or risk involved. Obviously the final decision will rest with you, but the solicitor should give you all the warnings outlined here and then balance these against the chances of a successful outcome. However good your case may be, it is not worth suing someone who will be unable to pay up if you win.

Insurance

It is now possible to take out insurance to cover you for legal bills, although you cannot take it out to cover an existing situation. There is considerable variation in the cover provided and the matters which are excluded. Obviously, the more you pay, the more cover you get. The most common exclusions are divorce, unsatisfactory building work and wills and inheritance. You should read the policy documents very carefully, in order to ascertain the extent of these exclusions, before deciding to take out the insurance. It is also up to the insurance company to decide whether to pursue your case, and if it decides that you should not go ahead, and you insist on proceeding with the case, you will have to pay your own legal bills.

Entering into a contract with a solicitor

Contracts with solicitors are usually oral. This poses a certain problem, in that you may not be able to remember exactly what you said, and it would be as well to have some of the terms (such as estimated cost) documented in correspondence.

In contrast to most other contractual situations, clients tend not to be able to give clear, precise instructions to their solicitors. When you go into a shop, you will probably be able to tell the assistant exactly what you want; but you may spend some considerable time telling your solicitor about your problem without making it clear what exactly you are instructing him to do. (It may be that several legal problems are involved in the one affair, but you want action taken on only one of them.)

If you do know exactly what action you want your solicitor to take, then say so clearly at the beginning. If there are important time limits which the solicitor must comply with, you should make that clear to him; delay is the biggest cause of complaints against solicitors.

Do not worry about talking to him about personal, embarrassing or confidential matters. He has a duty never to reveal not only what you tell him, but also anything else that he finds out while he is acting for you. (Confidentiality may be overridden by a court order in certain circumstances, when the police are investigating a serious crime.)

Giving clear instructions may not be easy if you are in an emotional state, so write to your solicitor afterwards, to confirm them. This is a good idea in any case: it will assist if you later feel that the solicitor exceeded or ignored your instructions.

If you have changed your mind, perhaps because you were in an emotional state at the time, do not hesitate to inform your solicitor of this. Because the contract is oral, this does not need to be in writing; but it may be best to write, in order to avoid confusion. Do not be embarrassed to change your mind: solicitors are used to clients doing this, often at a quite late stage in the proceedings. It is far better to change your mind than to incur further legal costs, and possibly be put through the anxiety of a court case. Not only would the solicitor prefer to have a satisfied client – he would not want a client who might change his mind in court.

Being kept informed

The Standards provide that the client should be told at the outset, or as soon as possible, the issues raised: how they will be dealt with and the immediate steps to be taken. The client should be kept informed of the progress of his matter, and the reason for any serious delay; requests for information should be answered promptly, and the effect of any important document should be explained. The Standards leave it to the solicitor to decide whether he should confirm in writing his advice and any instructions he may receive; you may wish to write to him to request such confirmation.

At the conclusion of the matter, the solicitor should write confirming that it has been completed, and summarising any continuing consequences.

You should be aware, however, that keeping you conscientiously informed will use up some of the solicitor's time, and so will be reflected in the fees.

Complaints about solicitors' charges

If you think your bill is too high, the first thing you should do is take the matter up with your solicitor; he may agree to reduce the bill. If this approach does not succeed, the steps you can take depend on whether or not court proceedings were started in your case.

If court proceedings were started

It does not matter whether your case ever got to court – if proceedings were commenced by either side, you can only challenge the solicitor's charges by applying to the court for 'taxation'. This means that the court will assess how much the bill should be, taking into account factors such as the complexity and importance of the matter, the skills, knowledge and responsibility required, the number and importance of the documents, the value of any property or money involved. Therefore just because the matter did not take very long, you cannot assume that the charges are too high. The court cannot take into account whether the solicitor was acting without your authority, or had agreed to limit his fee. (The steps to take if your complaint falls into this category will be explained later.)

Both you and the solicitor may make representations to the court: for instance, you may want to dispute the number of letters, appointments or telephone calls. If the court decides that you should pay less than half of the charges made, the Law Society will be informed, and may consider whether to take disciplinary proceedings against the solicitor.

It may be advisable to consult another solicitor before applying for taxation. This is because not only will you have to pay a fee to the court to have the bill taxed, but, if the bill is reduced by less than one-fifth, you will have to pay the solicitor's costs of going to court, as well as your own.

Another solicitor will give you an informal opinion on whether the bill as drafted seems too high. You can then decide whether it is worth applying for taxation. Do not be embarrassed to approach another solicitor: the Law Society and the Solicitors Complaints Bureau recommend this course of action.

If no court proceedings are involved

You should ask your solicitor to obtain a remuneration certificate from the Law Society. The Society will then check your solicitor's bill to see that it is fair and reasonable: this will cost you nothing. Under the Solicitors' Remuneration Order 1972, a solicitor cannot bring proceedings to recover his costs unless the costs have been taxed, or he has written to inform the client of his right to ask him to obtain a certificate. Therefore, although it is a good idea to ask the solicitor to obtain a certificate as soon as you receive the bill, if you think the charges too high, do not worry if you did not do so: you will not be taken to court if you have not been informed of your right.

You must apply for the certificate within one month of being told of your right to do so. You cannot apply if you have already paid the bill. However, if the solicitor has deducted his own charges from money he is holding for you, this does not count as your having paid the bill, unless, before the money was deducted, you were given a reasonable opportunity to query the bill, and did not object within a reasonable time.

After you have asked your solicitor to obtain the certificate, he will fill in an application form, and send this, together with your file, to the Law Society, which will send you a copy of the form for your comments; it will then send them to the solicitor for his observations. The Law Society will then consider all the documents, make a decision and issue the certificate.

The Law Society will only consider whether the charge is fair and reasonable for the work done, taking into account (or discounting) similar matters to those considered by the court on taxation. Thus this procedure can only be used if you are either complaining that the charge was too high for the work involved, or that the solicitor did not do all the work he claimed – for instance, you may be disputing the number of appointments, letters and/or telephone calls involved. Note that the remuneration certificate procedure is not available if you agreed the amount of the solicitor's charges in advance of the work being done.

You may apply to the court for taxation of the bill, even though your case did not involve court proceedings. However, because of the risk of having to bear the costs (as explained earlier) it is advisable to apply for a remuneration certificate first. You may then apply for taxation if you are still dissatisfied, although you should think carefully about the low chances that the court will reduce the bill by at least one-fifth, if the Law Society has not done so. If you apply for taxation first, you cannot then apply for a remuneration certificate.

Once you have received a remuneration certificate, you must pay the sum stated, unless you apply for taxation.

COMPLAINTS ABOUT SOLICITORS' CONDUCT

It may be that your grievance is one that can be sorted out between yourself and the solicitor. If this does not succeed, complain to the senior partner in the firm (assuming your solicitor is not himself the senior partner).

Even if the firm compensates you, you may still want to pursue your complaint, for instance, if the solicitor was dishonest. You should then contact the Solicitors Complaints Bureau. There are certain types of complaint which the Bureau cannot handle; but it publishes a leaflet explaining what it can and cannot do, and will advise you on where to take your complaint if the Bureau cannot handle it.

The Solicitors Complaints Bureau

The Bureau was set up in September 1986 by the Law Society; it is separate from the other operations of the Society.

By far the most common complaint has been found to be delay and failure to answer correspondence. Inadequate service or negligence, other than delay or shoddy work, comes next but this is a wide category, general rather than specific. Third comes breach of the professional code (unbefitting conduct). There is then a considerable drop in the number of complaints; only half as many complaints are received about excessive charges, the next category. This is followed by shoddy work; failure to hand over papers; failure to account for profits; breach of undertakings; general dissatisfaction with the legal system and profession; and dishonesty.

What the Solicitors Complaints Bureau can and cannot do

The Bureau cannot deal with a complaint of excessive charges as such. However, if you are complaining that they are excessive because the work was shoddy, or because the solicitor agreed on a fixed fee which he has not kept to, or because he exceeded your instructions, the Bureau can deal with it.

The Bureau cannot deal with negligence. This is not only because of the seriousness of the matter, but because the Bureau has no powers to award compensation. It is therefore necessary to distinguish between negligence and shoddy work (though the distinction is a difficult one to draw in practice). Negligence is a breach of the duty to use reasonable care and skill, and there must be loss in money terms to the client. Shoddy work is usually inadequate work, which falls short of breaching this duty; and it could also be complained of even when the client has suffered no financial loss. The essence of shoddy work, as defined by the Bureau, is that it has caused the client frustration, inconvenience, annoyance and/or dissatisfaction. Delay, however, could also amount to negligence if the client has suffered financial loss because of it.

As well as complaining to the Bureau about your own solicitor, it is also possible to complain about the other party's solicitor. However, if you think that he has acted improperly or illegally, it is advisable to discuss this with your own solicitor. If he agrees with you, and if the misconduct is other than trivial, he must report the matter to the Bureau. If you do not have a solicitor, perhaps because it is a simple consumer or divorce case which you have decided to handle yourself, you can make a written complaint about the other party's solicitor to the Bureau.

Bringing a complaint

Although there is no time limit for bringing a complaint, the longer you wait, the less pressing your grievance is likely to be considered.

Write a brief account of your complaint to the Bureau, giving the name and address of the solicitor you are complaining about. State whether you have approached any other solicitor about the complaint. Do not worry about how much detail to give; just set out your complaint clearly and simply, and the Bureau will ask you if it needs more information. If you do not feel able to write out your complaint yourself, you could go to a Citizens Advice Bureau or other advice centre. Alternatively, the Bureau will put you in touch with a solicitor on its interview panel; you can tell him what your complaint is, and he will help you to set it out. This service is free. The solicitor will, if possible, be one from your area. This solicitor does not become your solicitor, and therefore will not be able to act for you. If you need a solicitor, the Bureau may help you to find one, though it will not recommend any particular firm.

Your complaint will be allocated to an investigation officer (IO) – it takes about a year for the Bureau fully to train an IO. He is instructed to look for reasons to investigate your complaint, rather than reasons not to. If your complaint is not explained adequately in your letter, he may suggest that you see a member of the interview panel to sort out this difficulty.

If you have seen another solicitor about your complaint, the IO will ask that solicitor for comments. If the complaint is about shoddy work, the solicitor complained of will be required to send his file on the matter to the IO. The file will then be investigated by a report writer who is experienced in the area of law you have complained about, and then the file will be vetted by another report writer. If they do not agree, a third report writer will read the file. The solicitor complained of will be given the opportunity to comment on the report.

Whether your complaint is about shoddy work or anything else, if it is decided that there is a case to investigate, the solicitor in question will be asked for his observations or, if the matter looks serious, for an explanation.

In the case of shoddy work, if there is disagreement after the solicitor complained of has made his observations, the whole file and the report on it can be considered by a review panel of practising solicitors.

If the IO or the report writer decides that there is no issue and therefore that your complaint is not to be considered further, or if he is satisfied with the solicitor's reply, you will be told why, including being sent a copy of any reply from the solicitor. A member of the interview panel can be asked to explain this to you. If you are satisfied, the matter will end there.

If you are not satisfied, the IO must refer the file to the Investigation Committee, the majority of the members of which, including the chairman, are not solicitors. (There are 16 members: 10 lay members, 4 non-Council solicitors, 2 Council members.) The Committee can decide either that no further action should be taken and therefore bring the matter to an end or that further enquiries should be made.

If the IO is not satisfied with the solicitor's explanation in the first place, or with the result of further enquiries recommended by the Investigation Committee, he will refer the matter to the Adjudication Committee; he will prepare a report for it, with a recommendation as to the action this Committee should take. The Investigation Committee sees all the cases on the agenda that is prepared for the Adjudication Committee, which may recommend further enquiries before a final decision.

The majority of the members of the Adjudication Committee are solicitors (12 out of 18, nine of these, including the chairman, being members of the Council of the Law Society). This Committee can order your solicitor:

○ to reduce his bill (not because the charges, as such, were too high, but because of the effect on you of, say, his delay or other shoddy work)

○ to pay you interest on your money (when you ask for a 'deposit interest certificate')

○ to correct a mistake, or take other action to your benefit.

The Adjudication Committee can also:

○ order a payment to you out of the Compensation Fund (which is funded out of compulsory annual contributions from solicitors) if you have lost money because of your solicitor's dishonesty, and if there is no other source of recompense, such as insurance

○ rebuke the solicitor

○ refuse to grant, or impose conditions on the solicitor's practising certificate (such as that he should attend a training course)

○ (in extreme cases of dishonesty) find another solicitor to take over the practice and close it down altogether.

The Adjudication Committee has, of course, the option of dismissing your complaint.

The Solicitors' Disciplinary Tribunal

If the above measures are not appropriate and the matter is sufficiently serious, the Adjudication Committee may decide to apply on behalf of the Law Society to the Disciplinary Tribunal. In fact, anyone can apply to the Tribunal without going through the Solicitors Complaints Bureau. However, it is more sensible to contact the Bureau – in any case, the Tribunal cannot order your solicitor to pay you compensation. In the last resort you could still bring proceedings before the Tribunal yourself – but this would be advisable only in exceptional circumstances, and you should consult another solicitor first.

The Disciplinary Tribunal is wholly independent of the Law Society, and of the Complaints Bureau. There are 19 members, 12 solicitors and 7 lay members, all of whom are appointed by the Master of the Rolls. Each case is heard by three of the members: two solicitors, one of whom acts as the chairman, and one lay person. (The Bureau acts as prosecutor in the name of the Law Society for the case: you are not involved – unless, of course, you have decided to bring proceedings yourself.)

The Tribunal can reprimand or fine the solicitor; or suspend him from practice; or order his name to be struck off the Roll of Solicitors. Although being struck off is permanent, as opposed to a suspension which is temporary (usually for up to 5 years), the solicitor may, at a future date, apply to the Tribunal to be restored to the Roll.

The Lay Observer

If you are dissatisfied with the way the Complaints Bureau treated your complaint, you may complain to the Lay Observer, who is appointed by the Lord Chancellor to investigate such complaints. As his name suggests, he is neither a solicitor nor a barrister. You must write to him within three months of being told of the Bureau's decision, giving the Bureau's reference number. His job is to investigate, not your original complaint, but the Bureau: that is, whether the Bureau investigated it fully and fairly. He will ask the Bureau to send him the file on your complaint. Before this is done, the Bureau's Investigation Committee will review the case, and may itself decide to order further investigations.

If the Lay Observer thinks that the complaint was not investigated properly, he can recommend further investigations, but his recommendations are not binding. He will send a copy of his report to you and to the Bureau. The Bureau's Investigation Committee will then review the report, and will notify the Lay Observer of any action it has taken as a consequence. If it appears appropriate to the Lay Observer in the course of examining an allegation, he may make an application to the Disciplinary Tribunal with respect to the solicitor in question.

In 1987 the Lay Observer received 456 complaints (an increase of 15% over 1986, which was itself an increase of 17% over 1985). He was critical of the way 40 cases were handled, although he agreed with the final decision. He recommended further action in 6 cases.

Ironically, a major source of complaint about the Bureau is delay. This is to some extent inevitable, given the increasing number of complaints being handled.

Solicitors in Northern Ireland
The rules for complaining about solicitors in Northern Ireland are much the same as in England and Wales. There is no Complaints Bureau, but the Law Society administers a detailed procedure for handling complaints of alleged professional misconduct by solicitors. There is a Disciplinary Committee and a Lay Observer, operating similarly to the system in England.

Negligence
As mentioned above, the Solicitors Complaints Bureau cannot consider cases of negligence. In theory, if you believe that your solicitor has not carried out his duty with reasonable care and skill, including not carrying out the work within a reasonable time, and you have suffered loss as a result, you should consult

another solicitor. However, it is not always easy for a member of the public to decide whether there was negligence and to take the considerable step of consulting one solicitor about another. There is also an obvious reluctance on the part of some members of a profession to act in proceedings against other members of that same profession, particularly those practising in the same part of the country.

You should therefore start by contacting the Solicitors Complaints Bureau, which will first of all consider whether there is a potential claim for negligence. If there is not, your complaint will proceed through the Bureau's normal complaints procedure; if there is, the Bureau will put you in touch with a solicitor who is a member of its Negligence Panel, and who will give you up to an hour's free advice. This will be enough for him to help you to decide whether to take the matter further, and to give you advice on how to proceed. It may be that there is, in fact, no negligence; and so the Negligence Panel solicitor may advise you to go back again and proceed via the Bureau. If there is negligence, you may then choose whether to ask that solicitor to take on your case on a fee-paying basis (with or without legal aid) or to engage another solicitor.

Although your complaint is about the provision of legal services, it should be treated in the same way as complaints about goods or services. You should already have approached your solicitor and the senior partner of his firm as the first step in the complaints procedure. Now your new solicitor will start by trying to negotiate a settlement.

Under the Solicitors' Indemnity Rules 1975, all principals in a law firm – that is, partners or sole practitioners – are required to be insured for the risk of professional negligence claims against the firm. This means that they are covered whether the negligence was their own, or that of their employees or former employees. However, the disadvantage is that the insurers become involved in the matter, and may be reluctant to accept that there is a case, or to agree to the amount being claimed. Perseverance may sometimes be necessary.

An out-of-court settlement is reached in most cases. However, if yours is not one of these, you can consider arbitration as an alternative to court proceedings.

The Solicitors' arbitration scheme

In 1986 the Law Society set up an arbitration scheme which is run by the Chartered Institute of Arbitrators, and is therefore independent of the Law Society. There is a fixed fee of £46, so arbitration provides a cheap, simple and quicker alternative to court proceedings, without the stress. However, both parties must agree that the the claim should go to arbitration; you cannot insist if the solicitor in question does not agree. The case is dealt with in writing which you may find unsuitable because you would prefer to explain your case orally and have the chance to question the solicitor. There is a procedure for oral hearings in cases where it appears that the matter cannot be dealt with by looking at the papers alone. However, it is not for you to make this decision, and an oral hearing will be much more expensive. If your case goes to arbitration the decision is binding, and you cannot then decide to take the matter to court if you are not satisfied.

Because of the difficulties involved in bringing a claim for professional negligence in court, you should consider arbitration very seriously. Details and application forms are available from the Solicitors Complaints Bureau, the Law Society or the Institute of Arbitrators. A similar scheme operates in Northern Ireland.

Taking a solicitor to court

If arbitration is not acceptable, you will have to start court proceedings. This does not necessarily mean that the case will actually get to court: it may be settled out of court. However, this is definitely not a situation in which you should consider bringing the case yourself, without a solicitor and ultimately a barrister to represent you. It is not at all comparable to a claim for compensation for shoddy goods.

Negligence is a very complicated issue, and you cannot escape the fact that the person you are suing is legally qualified. There is the additional complication that the defendant's insurers are involved. You must therefore get advice on the likely cost of the action, unless you are eligible for legal aid. Unfortunately, many people who are not eligible for legal aid are nevertheless unable to afford legal representation. You are, of course, entitled to bring the case yourself without legal representation, but it may not be wise. You must weigh the time, complexity and stress of handling the case yourself against your chances of success. You may then decide that it is worth reconsidering arbitration.

Should the matter be settled in your favour, in or out of court, the Solicitors Complaints Bureau will then investigate your case, and decide whether any disciplinary action should be taken against the solicitor.

LEGAL EXECUTIVES

The term 'legal executive' tends to be used loosely to describe anyone dealing with legal matters in a solicitor's office who is not a solicitor. However, the code of conduct of the Institute of Legal Executives states that this term should be used only for a person who is a Fellow of the Institute, and the Law Society has agreed that firms shall use it only in this way. In order to become a Fellow, a person must have passed two membership examinations; have been in qualifying employment for five years, at least two of these since passing the membership examinations; and be at least 25. A Fellow is allowed to use the designation F.Inst.L.Ex after his name. A Fellow, although not a solicitor, is a person with considerable experience of legal matters, who has the equivalent of degree-level qualifications.

Do not be misled by anyone describing themselves as a member or associate of the Institute. The former term can indicate that someone has passed all the examinations for Fellowship – but may simply mean that he has enrolled with the Institute. The latter title is used by approximately 2000 members who passed some older examinations which have now been superseded.

'Associate' is not an official designation and they are not entitled to use it after their name.

Members of the Institute (whether Fellows or not) usually specialise in a particular branch of the law. They have some limited rights to appear in court cases before county court judges and registrars, and at tribunals. However, you will not be entering into a contract with a member (unless he is also a licensed conveyancer) because your contract will be with the solicitor who employs him. Any claim against him for breach of contract or negligence will be brought against the solicitor's firm, which will be liable. This does not mean that you are not allowed to sue the employee himself for negligence, but it is more sensible to sue the firm, which has insurance cover.

Complaints against members of the Institute of Legal Executives

Your first step in complaining about any employee should be to complain to his employer, in this case the senior partner in the firm. However, you may feel that the matter is too serious for that, or you may be dissatisfied by the employer's response. If you are seeking compensation, you should pursue the action by taking the steps already described for complaints against solicitors; the same applies if your complaint is really about lack of supervision on the part of the firm, or its poor response to your complaint.

You may also complain to the Institute of Legal Executives about the conduct of any one of its members, whether he is a Fellow or not. All members of the Institute must abide by its code of conduct. The Institute, in fact, receives few complaints from members of the public. Its disciplinary procedure is normally invoked in response to matters raised with the Law Society, or as the result of court proceedings. This is primarily because of a firm's responsibility for its employees with regard to the law of contract and of negligence, which results in complaints being made about the firm rather than the individual.

According to the Guide to Good Practice issued by the Institute, on first taking instructions a member should make clear to the client his own qualification and position in the firm. If you are in doubt, you could ask him or the firm; or, if you prefer, you could ask the Institute. However, your complaint might be not about the person who interviewed you, but about some other person in the firm.

The code of conduct covers a number of matters, such as professional integrity; the interest of the client being paramount; not misusing trust, nor revealing confidential information; not taking advantage of information for personal gain. The code also requires the member to have regard to the Guide to Good Practice which includes: accepting only such work as he is competent to handle; informing the client of the effect of costs; informing the client of the availability of legal aid and of the effect of the statutory charge; avoiding conflicts of interest; keeping the client promptly and effectively informed of progress; and informing the solicitor and the client of undue delay.

If you have a complaint, say, that a member of the Institute is incompetent or caused unnecessary delay or disclosed confidential information, by all means write to the Institute, Institute's disciplinary procedure is purely internal, and there is no power to compensate members of the public.

LICENSED CONVEYANCERS

'Conveyancing' is the legal procedure of transferring the title of property from one owner to another. If you are buying or selling a house, you can use a solicitor to do your conveyancing; you can do it yourself; or you may use a licensed conveyancer. Licensed conveyancing is a new profession, created by the Administration of Justice Act 1985, with a statutory duty to provide an economical and efficient service to the public. It has been in operation since May 1987.

The licensed conveyancer will have passed examinations

which are at the same level as those of the Law Society, but more specialised in the area of the law of conveyancing, including residential and commercial conveyancing.

Like a solicitor but unlike a legal executive, a licensed conveyancer may set up a firm of his own, having first proved his professional competence to the Council for Licensed Conveyancers (the statutory independent governing body of the profession) and held three consecutive annual licences. In such a case, your contract will be with him. However, a licensed conveyancer does not have to set up his own firm: he can work for other licensed conveyancers, or for solicitors. He can also practise in partnerships with other licensed conveyancers, or they can form themselves into companies providing conveyancing services.

A licensed conveyancer must have a current licence on display in any office from which he practises: it must be renewed every year.

You do not need to be worried at the idea of engaging a licensed conveyancer to do your conveyancing. Much of the conveyancing work in a solicitor's office is done by licensed conveyancers and/or legal executives in any case.

It is, however, important that he should hold a licence issued by the Council: one of the less desirable features of the legislation governing the profession is that it does not bestow a monopoly of the word 'conveyancer', and a member of the public could unwittingly engage an unqualified practitioner.

A licensed conveyancer has to have professional indemnity insurance cover of at least £250,000 before starting his practice and must abide by strict rules of practice, professional conduct and accounting as provided by the Council for Licensed Conveyancers. He may employ solicitors, licensed conveyancers, legal executives and other staff and is responsible for the adequate supervision of their work.

Choosing a licensed conveyancer

The deciding factor in choosing whether to use a solicitor or a licensed conveyancer is often the cost. You should shop around, because solicitors are aware of the competition from licensed conveyancers, and you should not assume that a licensed conveyancer's charges will necessarily be cheaper.

Licensed conveyancers are governed by the Council for Licensed Conveyancers. They are subject to the Licensed Conveyancers' Rules of Conduct, Practice and Discipline 1989, which apply whether the licensed conveyancer is in practice on his own account, or in employment. If a licensed conveyancer does not comply with these rules, he can be disciplined by the council for Licensed Conveyancers and may lose his practising licence.

Under these rules, licensed conveyancers are allowed to advertise, and to seek clients in any manner other than unsolicited telephone calls or visits – provided that the client's freedom to instruct a qualified person of his choice is not unduly restricted, and that the licensed conveyancer's reputation for integrity and professional standards is not damaged.

Licensed conveyancers are allowed to enter into arrangements for the introduction of clients to them and by them, provided that the client is informed in writing of the arrangement, and of any commission paid; provided that the client gives written agreement to the payment of the commission; and provided that the licensed conveyancer remains able to advise independently. Therefore you may find that the builder of your house, for instance, will recommend a licensed conveyancer to you; or that the licensed conveyancer will recommend to you someone who can provide a mortgage or insurance. It is up to you to judge whether to accept these recommendations. You should not assume that the person recommended is necessarily the cheapest or the best.

The contract and the licensed conveyancer's duties

Before entering into a contract, the licensed conveyancer must tell you how his fees are calculated, the circumstances in which they might be increased, and about any expenses and VAT: there are certain expenses, such as the Land Registry fee, which have to be paid on top of the licensed conveyancer's (or solicitor's) fee. He must charge only such fees as are fair and reasonable, having regard to the nature of the work and the time taken. If he gives you a written quotation, it cannot be varied without your consent. A licensed conveyancer may charge for the mortgage work which he deals with on behalf of your building society or bank. He must not delay the completion of a transaction because his fees have not been paid.

A licensed conveyancer must not refuse to accept instructions on the grounds of race or sex. But he must refuse to act if there is a conflict of interest. He may act for both sides in a transaction, provided both clients are satisfied that there is no conflict of interest, and have both consented in writing.

A licensed conveyancer must not accept instructions which are beyond his competence; those which he does not have the time or resources to fulfil; or those for which he is not covered by insurance. If a matter arises which is beyond his competence, he must seek other advice, or advise the client to seek it.

He must set out in writing the terms on which he is accepting your instructions, and must not exclude or limit liability for any failure on his (or his employees' or agents') part to use reasonable care and skill. Like all other professionals, he has the duty to use reasonable care and skill.

He must deal with correspondence and other matters with economically reasonable speed; must not cause unnecessary delay; must observe proper standards of professional courtesy and co-operation; and must ensure that the client is kept fully informed. He must treat all information as confidential and must not make unauthorised use of such information.

If a seller instructs a licensed conveyancer to submit

contracts to more than one prospective buyer, the licensed conveyancer must obtain the client's (that is the seller's) authority to disclose this to all prospective purchasers, and if the client does not agree, the licensed conveyancer must cease to act for him. So, if you have lined up more than one purchaser, either for fear of one dropping out, or in order to get a higher price, the licensed conveyancer will not act for you in setting up a 'contract race' unless all the prospective purchasers are told of this. (Solicitors have a similar rule.)

The licensed conveyancer – as any professional – must not take unfair advantage of any disability or lack of knowledge of the client. He must disclose all profits and advantages to him in connection with any transaction of the client's.

Unless required by the client, a licensed conveyancer is not allowed to withdraw from a transaction, except in limited circumstances: for example, if there is a conflict of interest, or if the client does not agree that prospective purchasers in a contract race should be notified of each others' existence. Where he has ceased to act, he must deliver up any documents and money, subject to any right of lien, which means that, like most professionals, he has the right to retain your documents until you pay his fees.

The Council has rules governing the keeping of accounts, the handling of clients' money and the provision of insurance, and spot checks are carried out to make sure the rules are complied with.

Complaints about licensed conveyancers

The first step is to complain directly to the licensed conveyancer and, if he is an employee, to his employer.

Under the Supply of Goods and Services Act 1982, the licensed conveyancer has a duty to use reasonable care and skill, to make a reasonable charge if a fee is not agreed in advance, and not to take more than a reasonable time; his rules of practice contain the same requirements. If what you are complaining about amounts to a breach of the Act, you have the right to sue him. There is no provision for arbitration, and so in theory you must take him to court. There is provision for complaining to the Council for Licensed Conveyancers that its rules have been infringed, but the most the Council can do is refund your fees.

However, you should try to negotiate a settlement with the licensed conveyancer. You can seek the advice of a solicitor in this. The fact that the licensed conveyancer is covered by insurance will help, although the insurance will not cover him for charging too high a fee; any delay complained of must amount to negligence; and the loss you have suffered must be one that can be calculated in money. If the licensed conveyancer is dishonest and has disappeared with your money, you can be repaid out of the Council's compensation fund.

Whether your complaint is of negligence or not, you should complain to the Council for Licensed Conveyancers unless your complaint is about a person who is employed by a solicitor, in which case you can decide to complain instead to the Solicitors Complaints Bureau.

The licensed conveyancer is under a duty to inform you that the Council has a complaints procedure. This applies whether your complaint is about a licensed conveyancer, or about one of his employees or associates.

All you need to do is write a letter to the Council setting out the facts – there is no special form. Notes for the guidance for complainants are being drafted, but are not yet available. The complaint will firstly be considered by the Investigating Committee, which must decide whether the case ought to be referred to the Discipline and Appeals Committee. The licensed conveyancer will be approached for his response to the complaint. If the Investigating Committee decides that the case should be referred to the Discipline and Appeals Committee, it may also direct that the conveyancer's licence should be suspended until a decision has been reached about the complaint, if this appears necessary for the protection of the public.

The hearing

As soon as possible after the referral, the licensed conveyancer will be sent a notice of hearing, giving details of the allegations, together with a date for the hearing. The complainant (you) will be sent a copy of the notice, and of the Discipline and Appeals Commitee (Procedure) Rules.

The hearing will be not less than 28 days after the posting of the notice. You are entitled to attend, and may conduct the case if you wish, but are not obliged to do so and it is highly unlikely, in fact, that you would want to: this provision is designed for cases where the complainant is a member of the legal profession. The case against the licensed conveyancers will be pursued on your behalf by a solicitor, with a legal assessor present, at no cost to you.

If the Committee upholds the complaint, it may revoke or suspend the licence, or direct that it should be subject to conditions; impose a fine; or reprimand the licensed convey-ancer. If it appears to the Committee that the quality of the service provided by the licensed conveyancer to the client was not such as could reasonably be expected of him, the Committee may order him to refund or remit the whole or part of the fees paid to him, and there is also some provision for the payment of interest. However, the Committee has no power to award damages if your loss exceeds the amount of the fee.

To obtain compensation, you will have to go to court – if you can afford to, and if the size of your loss justifies it. But you should consider complaining to the Council in any event, not only because a breach of professional conduct should be reported, but because if your complaint is upheld, this might encourage the licensed conveyancer to reach a settlement out of court.

Barristers

A barrister's training is similar to a solicitor's. He obtains a law degree (or a degree in some other subject followed by a one-year diploma course in law) and then a one-year vocational course leading to the Bar Final examinations. (In Northern Ireland, a two-year certificate course replaces the diploma course.) Having passed these (and fulfilled some other conditions) and having been 'called to the Bar', he is allowed to call himself a barrister, even before starting pupillage. This is the equivalent of solicitors' articles – a way of learning on the job – and lasts one year during which the new barrister is guided by a senior one, the pupil-master. After the first six months of pupillage, a barrister is allowed to accept work on his own account.

There are two types of barristers: 'junior' barristers and Queen's Counsel (sometimes referred to as 'silks'). Although to become a QC a barrister has to have been in practice for a number of years and to be of a certain standing, this does not mean that the so-called juniors are necessarily less experienced or have less ability. QCs are paid higher fees, and in most cases are required to have a junior barrister in attendance (there are now a few types of case, such as guilty pleas and some appeals, where a QC can appear alone).

People tend to think of barristers as required only for court appearances. However, you may also use a barrister for specialist advice, or for drafting documents. Similarly, some people think that solicitors cannot appear in court, and that you must therefore have a barrister. In fact, solicitors can appear in magistrates' courts and the county court, and have some other limited rights to appear in court. Although barristers have training in advocacy, this does not mean that they are necessarily better than solicitors in court; thus, a newly qualified barrister may not be as good as an experienced solicitor who has been appearing in court for years. You should also take into account the fact that, if you have been consulting him for some time, your solicitor is more likely to be familiar with your case.

You need to understand some rather strange conventions regarding barristers. First, you cannot instruct a barrister directly as you would a solicitor: you must go through a solicitor or, in some cases, through some other professional. It does not matter that you may think that you do not need the services of a solicitor: for instance, if you have received a court summons, are quite clear as to the situation, and simply want someone to stand up in court and represent you. It is the solicitor who briefs, that is, instructs the barrister: you do not have a contract with the barrister because he is employed by the solicitor, but you will be responsible for his fee.

Naturally, if you know of a barrister because he has been recommended to you, or because you have used him before, you can ask your solicitor to brief that particular barrister. Unlike a solicitor, a barrister is not allowed to refuse to take on any client who comes along (the 'cab rank' rule), unless he is already booked for a case which is likely to come to court at the same time, or is representing the other side in the case. This is because everyone is entitled to representation; and if barristers were allowed to refuse cases, it might happen that a particularly controversial person would not be able to get anyone to represent him. However, even though you do not have a contract with the barrister, you are allowed to refuse to have a particular barrister represent you, either from the outset or at any stage, if you do not have confidence in him, or for some other reason.

As a general rule, the barrister is not allowed to see you except in the presence of someone representing your solicitor's firm (it need not actually be your solicitor). Similarly, there has been in the past a strict rule that there must be someone to represent the firm throughout any court proceedings. You may find that because the qualified staff is needed elsewhere, the solicitor will send a secretary to the court, or even someone specially engaged, who knows nothing about the law or about your case. There is little you can do about this, but it should happen less often now, because the rules have been relaxed in a large number of cases. You may find yourself being accompanied only by your barrister when it is unnecessary to have a representative of your solicitor present.

Proposals for other changes in the way the legal profession works have been embodied in the Lord Chancellor's 'green papers' which are now actively under discussion in many quarters.

A barrister's costs can be paid out of the Legal Aid Fund in the same way as a solicitor's, provided the Legal Aid Office agrees that a barrister is necessary for the case. However, legal aid is not as a general rule, available for those cases which go not to the court but before tribunals, such as industrial tribunals for employment cases, and social security appeal tribunals.

PROBLEMS WITH BARRISTERS

The most common complaint is that on the day of your case, a completely different barrister turned up. This is particularly frustrating if the original barrister had been involved in your case for months, and the new barrister was given the file only the evening before, and had little time to familiarise himself with it. This problem is usually caused by the first barrister being double-booked. Although each case is set down to be heard on a certain day, no one can be absolutely sure how long it, or the cases before it, will take. Therefore, if a barrister has another case the day before, or has a very short simple case, and this takes longer than expected, or is delayed because the case before overran, another barrister will have to take over. There is nothing you can do about it. It is the fault of neither barrister, and it would be unreasonable to ask barristers to leave long gaps between cases as a precaution. They themselves tend to blame the court lists (in which cases are set down for hearing) for the occurrence of double-booking; cases may be adjourned or rescheduled without prior notice.

You cannot sue a barrister over the way in which he conducted your case in court, even if you think he was negligent. This may seem unfair – but if suing one's barrister were allowed, every person who lost a case would (in theory) do so.

You can sue a barrister if he has been negligent elsewhere than in court: for instance, if he gave you negligent advice, or prepared the case negligently. You would have to prove that he failed to take reasonable care or use reasonable skill. In addition to this, you would have to show that you had suffered loss which can be calculated in monetary terms. Very few such cases are brought against barristers.

If the barrister has not been negligent, but you feel he has not conducted himself in a manner befitting a barrister, by disclosing something you told him in confidence, or if you object to the way in which he conducted his interviews with you, you will not be able to sue him (unless the offence complained of comes within the Sex Discrimination or Race Relations Acts), but you may complain to the General Council of the Bar.

How to complain about a barrister

If your complaint is of a fairly minor nature, you should first complain to your solicitor: it was he who instructed that barrister, and therefore may be able to take the matter up with him. If this fails, you could write to the head of the barrister's chambers; but this may not do much good because chambers of barristers are not partners, which means that they are not legally responsible for each other. Each barrister is a sole practitioner.

For more major complaints you should address yourself directly to the General Council of the Bar. Although you cannot sue a barrister for negligent advocacy, you can complain about this to the Bar Council. You can also complain of any other breach of professional standards or conduct. You will be sent a complaint form to fill in, accompanied by notes for guidance. You should fill in the form in detail, and if you have any witnesses, you should ask them to write out a statement or put their names on the form. (The Bar Council is in the process of changing its procedures.

The complaint form goes to the Professional Conduct Committee, which has both barristers and lay representatives, appointed by the Lord Chancellor. The barrister is notified of the complaint and asked to answer it in writing. The Committee is entitled to seek additional evidence from anyone. It will dismiss a complaint only if the lay representatives agree to this.

The Committee may decide to deal with the matter by writing to the barrister, or by directing him to attend on the Chairman (for a severe reprimand). You will be notified of such a decision. It may decide, however, that proceedings should be brought against the barrister before the Disciplinary Tribunal, which consists of a judge as chairman, a lay representative and three barristers. Another barrister prepares the charges and prosecutes the case. It will not cost you anything. If the barrister you are complaining about denies or disputes the charges, you will probably be called as a witness.

If the complaint is upheld, the Tribunal may reprimand or discipline the barrister. The ultimate sanction is to disbar him so that he would not be allowed to practise.

You will be notified of the Tribunal's decision; but even if this is in your favour, the Tribunal has no power to award you compensation.

Complaining about Northern Ireland barristers

If complaining to your solicitor fails to resolve the matter, write to the Professional Conduct Committee of the General Council of the Bar in Northern Ireland. This may either deal with the complaint itself, or refer it to a specifically appointed disciplinary committee of the Executive Council of the Inn of Court of Northern Ireland. At least one member of this committee must be a judge. The proceedings will be similar to those in England.

Other sources of legal advice

If you do not fall within the financial limits for legal advice and assistance, you can turn to other sources of help.

Legal advice centres

These advice centres are set up by Citizens Advice Bureaux, local authorities and various charitable organisations. They are informal, non-profit making legal offices, staffed by volunteer lawyers, who give their services free on a part-time or rota basis. They offer free legal advice, but do not handle any casework. They are there to deal with straightforward cases where a little advice is all that is needed, such as consumer complaints against shops; or to give some preliminary landlord and tenant or matrimonial advice, and to help you to decide where to go next. They will not act for you, but you could decide to ask the solicitor who gives you advice at the centre to take on your case (for a fee, or with legal aid) at his firm's office. That solicitor must make sure that you know that you are free to instruct any other solicitor.

It is becoming quite common for individual firms of solicitors to offer free legal advice at certain times, usually one evening a week. Although these are not legal advice centres, properly speaking, the situation is similar, in that there is no contract between the solicitor or firm and the person being advised. Such firms are hoping that the advice-seeker will then return to consult the solicitor on a fee-paying basis. Nevertheless, this is a valuable service. You can usually find out about such free advice from advertisements in the local newspaper, or from the Citizens Advice Bureau.

Because the advice is free, you do not have a contract with anyone. However, the solicitor will still have a duty, under the law of negligence, to use reasonable care and skill. If you believe the advice was given negligently and you have suffered loss which could be given a money value, you would have the right to sue the adviser. Such claims are bound to be rare, given that if the original case was serious, you would have been advised to seek professional advice elsewhere.

If you want to complain about some other aspect of the adviser's conduct, or the way in which the centre is run, you could first complain to the person in charge and, if not satisfied, to the organisation which set up the centre. You could take the matter further by complaining to the adviser's professional body; for instance, the Law Society if he is a solicitor.

Law centres

A law centre gives free legal advice, like a legal advice centre, sometimes on a 'green form' basis, but in addition takes on the whole case: that is, it will actually represent you in legal proceedings. Law centres do not take on every kind of work; the Solicitors' Practice Rules prevent them from competing for some types of cases, such as those involving conveyancing and matrimonial work. Personal injury and adult criminal work are also excluded, except in special circumstances. They are therefore likely to concentrate on welfare rights, housing, employment, immigration, juvenile crime and debt. Different law centres may specialise in different types of cases, depending on what is important to people in that area. They will have particular regard to work for which legal aid is not available, such as tribunal work.

As law centres are not required to make a profit, they may also take on group work, such as campaigns to do with local planning, or may undertake monitoring or research. If the law centre cannot take on your case, it will refer you to a solicitor who can help you – for instance, one who specialises in adult criminal work – or to the Citizens Advice Bureau for consumer advice.

Some of the caseworkers in law centres are paid employees, and the rest are volunteers. In many cases, up to half the staff are legally qualified as either solicitors or barristers. Law centres are required to employ at least two lawyers, one of whom should be a solicitor with three years' practising experience. The rest of the staff need not be legally qualified, but will generally be specialists or experts in other fields, such as community work, and will have received some practical training. Both the type and the extent of the training given vary from centre to centre: the Law Centres Federation organises basic and specialist courses, but otherwise training is done within the individual centres. Many law centres pay all employees at the same rate, regardless of their qualifications. An important facility provided by law centres is that staff come from a range of backgrounds, and between them may speak a number of different languages.

There are several situations in which a law centre is of particular value:

○ where people do not qualify for legal aid, either because it is not available for their case, or because they are not eligible, yet cannot afford to pay for legal representation

○ where it is important to have someone who comes from the same background and/or speaks the same language and can relate to the client

○ where the matter is a general local issue rather than one individual's case.

Law centres tend not to specialise in ordinary consumer matters such as sale of goods or supply of services, where it is not difficult to deal with the case without legal representation.

Solicitors employed at law centres must comply with the Solicitors' Practice Rules, including the rules about the management and supervision of the office, holding a current practising certificate, complying with the accounts rules, and being insured against claims for professional negligence.

Complaints about law centres
Although there is a Law Centres Federation, each law centre is independent, and is responsible to its local management committee. This has members from the community: both individuals and representatives of local organisations, and also ex-officio members such as local councillors, and a member of

the local Law Society. Their membership is renewable annually.

If you have a complaint, you should write to the chairman of the management committee. If you are dissatisfied with the response, you can complain to the Law Centres Federation, and the matter will be considered by its executive committee. There is no formal procedure for complaint, but this is currently under discussion. The only real sanction which the Federation possesses is to expel a centre from membership. As each centre is independent, this will not affect the centre directly. However, it will affect the centre's reputation, and may have an impact on its funding. Also, under the Law Society's rules, a solicitor must not say that he is working for a law centre unless this centre is a member of the Federation.

As the advice is free, you have no contract with the law centre or the individual worker. Therefore any claim would have to be under the law of negligence.

If you have a complaint about a solicitor or barrister who is employed at a law centre, and are not satisfied with the response from the centre or from the Federation, you can complain to the Law Society or the Bar Council, as explained earlier.

The Free Representation Unit (FRU)

If your case is to go before a tribunal and you cannot afford to pay for representation (legal aid not being available), you can turn to the Free Representation Unit. FRU is a charitable organisation, which receives funding from the Bar Council and individual members of the Bar. FRU has a few full-time staff but relies heavily on Bar students and those in pupillage. This does not mean that their representatives are wholly inexperienced: they all have degrees, and receive training from FRU. After this training they must attend two cases with a senior representative, and must produce a written opinion on each. FRU was successful in 78% of its cases in 1987/8. You must be referred to FRU by Citizens Advice Bureaux, advice centres or solicitors: FRU cannot accept referrals direct from clients.

Consumer Advice Centres

These are centres set up by some local authorities which give advice only on consumer matters, that is, disputes involving goods or services. The advice is free. Unlike in most legal advice centres and law centres, all the staff are employees rather than volunteers. The staff members receive training but are usually not legally qualified. However, unlike most lawyers, they have a detailed knowledge of the comprehensive law relating to consumer rights. They will negotiate with traders, and help with writing letters and preparing a case for court. Some centres will actually send someone to accompany you to court – but not represent you – if staffing permits. This is particularly useful when you consider that many solicitors will not take on small consumer complaints.

A trader is more likely to pay attention to representatives of the local authority, particularly as they are more likely to visit or telephone than to write. Advice centres are expensive for a local authority to run, so they tend to be situated only in large cities.

You have no contract with an advice centre, any more than with any other of the 'free' centres mentioned. Any complaints should be made to the person in charge, and thereafter to the local authority.

Citizens Advice Bureaux (CABX)

In 1939, Citizens Advice Bureaux were set up by local authorities at the request of the government. They are now separate independent local organisations which come together as an Association in England and Wales, and an Association in Scotland. They are rather different from the other advisers dealt with here because they do not confine themselves to legal advice. However, approximately 90% of the advice (varying from bureau to bureau) is concerned with the law. As with law centres and legal advice centres, the advice is free.

There are other similarities to legal advice centres (which may in fact be set up by CABx), in that apart from the manager and administrative staff, most of the advisers are volunteers who give their services free, and do not represent individuals in legal proceedings. They take on casework, in the sense that they will negotiate, say, if a person is in debt, or help with writing letters, and in certain cases, may help an individual to prepare a case for court.

Although most of the staff members are not legally qualified, they all undergo basic training, the emphasis in which is on acquiring the necessary skills. With the expertise the CABx have acquired over the years and their extensive information base (which is brought up to date monthly), a bureau may be able to resolve a case on its own. Alternatively, after preliminary advice, the bureau staff will be able to refer clients either to a solicitor giving advice at the bureau, or to a law centre, or to other advisers. The CABx will refer individuals to solicitors who take part in the £5 fixed-fee interview scheme, or who give initial advice free of charge; or to a law centre if they need representation and legal aid is not available, and they cannot afford to pay a solicitor. CABx can also arrange for free advice from an accountant, or a free survey to be done on a property; or can help to find an expert to examine goods about which there is a dispute.

CABx are often a first recourse, because many people have never heard of law centres, and cannot afford a solicitor (or think that they cannot afford one, because they do not know about legal aid). Some people think that their problems are too trivial to be of interest to a solicitor (which may be true, as in consumer matters) or are simply afraid of consulting a solicitor. CABx are particularly valuable because of the range of advice available. A significant and growing problem is debt, especially multiple debts. Often the debtor does not know that anything can be done and does nothing but worry while the debts mount up. CABx can help a person work out what he can afford to pay and help him to reach an agreement with the creditors.

A person may have money worries without actually being in debt, in not having enough money to live on, and CABx may be able to help him to apply to government or charitable agencies. There may be housing problems or social welfare problems. It may be that a person is more in need of counselling than advice. In all these cases, the CABx can either help the individual directly or refer him to those who can help.

CABx also get a significant number of referrals from solicitors and law centres; usually consumer cases and people in need of debt counselling. Sadly, CABx also get a number of people coming to them after consulting solicitors, not because they have been referred by the solicitor, but to ask for an explanation of what the solicitor said, which they found incomprehensible. The problem may lie partly in the fact that the person was upset, and did not take in what was said; or did not dare say he did not understand, either through pride, or because he was overawed by the solicitor and the atmosphere of a solicitor's office. However, the fault often lies with solicitors, who may use too much legal jargon, do not take the time to repeat explanations and often (usually unintentionally) have an intimidating manner.

Complaints about the CABx
As is the case with both legal advice centres and law centres, you have no contract with the CABx. Although each bureau has a duty to take reasonable care, the nature of the advice is such that you would be unlikely to find cause to allege negligence on the part of the bureau. Morever, the duty of care would not be that of a lawyer (unless the advice was actually given by a lawyer at the bureau) but merely that of an adviser; in other words, you cannot expect someone who is not legally qualified to have the same knowledge of the law and skill in applying it as someone who is. Therefore any complaint would probably be about the service provided by the bureau, or the conduct or inefficiency of an adviser, rather than about negligence.

CABx are controlled by the National Association of Citizens Advice Bureaux (NACAB) and the Scottish Association of Citizens Advice Bureaux (SACAB). All CABx are required to display a poster about making complaints about the CABx, and forms for this should also be on display. Although complainants are encouraged to use the forms, it is acceptable if you just write a letter or a note with your complaint. If your complaint is made to the CAB you are complaining about, that bureau is obliged to inform NACAB or SACAB. If you write directly to NACAB or SACAB, a copy of your complaint will be sent to the bureau for a response. If that is not satisfactory, the matter will be dealt with by the area office. NACAB or SACAB possesses the ultimate sanction to close down a bureau.

'Which?' Personal Service

The 'Which?' Personal Service was set up by Consumers' Association. In order to obtain help and advice from the Service, you must be a member of the Service (not merely a member of CA), for which there is an annual subscription. The Personal Service gives help and advice on consumer matters, such as sale of goods, hire purchase, holidays, insurance, and poor workmanship and services in general. It cannot help with disputes between landlord and tenant, welfare benefits, wills and foreign law, High Court actions or where you have already instructed a solicitor.

The 'Which?' Personal Service will not only advise you as to your rights, but also draft letters for you to send. It will take up the complaint on your behalf with the retailer or manufacturer, and help you take your case to court. If your case raises an important matter of principle affecting all consumers, the Personal Service may be prepared to pay legal costs; and if the law is inadequate, may, through Consumers' Association, bring pressure to bear for changes in the law.

Trading Standards Departments

Trading Standards Departments, which are part of the local authority, exist to enforce the criminal law, such as the Trade Descriptions Act (TDA). Therefore they are not really advisers; however, most of them will give simple quick consumer advice over the telephone (this is far more limited than the advice you can get from any of the other advisers referred to earlier). Thus, for example, they are able to advise consumers as to whether the shop can really insist that defective goods must be returned within seven days. There are some Departments which will take matters further than this, and will actually speak to the trader, although this will be unofficially. If your complaint also reveals a criminal offence, they will then be able to take the matter up officially, and you may benefit indirectly, for instance, by being awarded damages if there is a conviction under the TDA.

However, as it is not the job of Trading Standards Departments to give advice (though in Scotland many of them offer money advice casework), you should seek it only if it is along the lines of the example. Otherwise you should consult one of the other advisers mentioned. If you are trying to find an expert to look at workmanship or goods which you think are defective, the Department should be able to put you in contact with such a person, or a professional or trade association which can do so.

Legal services in Scotland

Scotland has its own legal system, which in many respects differs from that of England and Wales. The following discussion of Scottish legal practice dwells chiefly on the differences, and in areas where none are indicated, it can be reasonably assumed that the Scottish practice is very similar or identical to the English practice described earlier.

SOLICITORS IN SCOTLAND

Scottish solicitors and advocates are often wrongly regarded as being the exact equivalent of English solicitors and barristers; there are, however, significant differences.

Practising solicitors in Scotland must have passed a number of examinations, obtained a law school Diploma (a one-year course) and completed a two-year traineeship. They must then be enrolled as solicitors and hold a current Practising Certificate issued by the Law Society of Scotland. All solicitors are members of this Law Society, which is their regulatory body.

It is an offence for a non-solicitor to represent himself as a solicitor and any such person will be prosecuted by the Crown Office. If you are in any doubt as to whether someone is entitled to act as a solicitor, you can check the position with the Law Society of Scotland.

Your contract is with the firm rather than the individual adviser. In Scotland the contract is usually based on the law of agency: in instructing a solicitor, you are authorising the firm to act as your agent.

The partners of a firm are jointly and severally liable. This means that in an action of negligence, for example, you are entitled to sue any one or all of the partners or the firm itself, except where the person complained of was not acting in the course of his employment.

Who will your adviser be?
Solicitors in Scotland traditionally give advice on all aspects of a client's affairs, not necessarily the purely legal ones. In most cases you will be dealing with a practising solicitor; occasionally with a trainee. Some firms employ non-solicitor staff with training and experience in specific areas of legal administration, who may be able to assist you in a particular matter.

As in England, only practising solicitors may be partners, but there may be fully qualified solicitors in the practice who are not partners. The Solicitors' Practice Rules at present prohibit the naming of non-solicitors on firms' notepaper.

In Scotland, unlike England, solicitors appear in the majority of Court actions; only practising solicitors and advocates are authorised by the courts to appear on behalf of clients.

The solicitor's duties and professional conduct
The Rules of Professional Conduct governing Scottish solicitors are laid down partly by statute, partly by Professional Practice

Rules authorised by the Lord President of the Court of Session and partly in terms of unwritten or common law provisions. The Law Society of Scotland hopes to set up a Code of Conduct in the near future and then to authorise a publication detailing the professional practice obligations of a solicitor.

The following are some of the rules governing the conduct of a Scottish solicitor at present time:

○ A solicitor must not do anything which is likely to compromise or impair his independence or integrity, his duty to act in the best interests of the client, his duties as an officer of court, his proper standard of work, or the client's freedom to instruct a solicitor of his choice.

○ A solicitor may publicise his practice, including his charges, provided he does not contravene the Solicitors (Scotland) (Advertising) Practice Rules 1987.

○ A solicitor may accept introductions and referrals of business from another person, and may make introductions and refer business to another person, provided the solicitor does not share his fees with an unqualified person.

○ A solicitor must not conceal any commission which he may receive as a result of placing clients' business.

○ A solicitor must not act for more than one party, where the interests of those parties might conflict: this includes sellers and buyers on a transfer of property. There are some exceptions to this rule, provided there is no conflict of interest: for instance, where the clients are related, or are both established clients. A solicitor may act for both a borrrower and a lender, provided he is merely giving effect to the terms of a loan agreement already agreed between the parties.

○ Although a solicitor in Scotland may accept work on a 'no win, no fee' basis, he must not enter into an arrangement to receive a contingency fee in the sense that he would receive, as his fee, a proportion of any award made by a court to the client.

There are a number of specific solicitors' accounts rules, principally the Solicitors (Scotland) Accounts Rules 1981 and 1986 and the Solicitors (Scotland) (Accountant's Certificate) Rules 1981 which lay down detailed rules for the handling of clients' money and the keeping of records of such transactions.

In addition, solicitors are obliged to contribute to the Scottish Solicitors' Guarantee Fund, which will refund to any client money which has been stolen by a solicitor in the course of his acting as a solicitor. They are also obliged to be members of the Law Society of Scotland's Insurance Indemnity Scheme which provides minimum standards of professional negligence insurance to all practising solicitors in Scotland.

Choosing a solicitor

The Law Society of Scotland cannot recommend a particular solicitor. Failing a personal recommendation, you could consult, in a library, the Regional Directory which indicates the sort of work undertaken by solicitors in your region. You can also write to the Law Society, indicating the type of advice or service you require; you will be provided with the names of two or three firms of solicitors in your area who may be suitable. The Citizens Advice Bureau may also be able to advise you. As in England, solicitors' advertisements are permitted to indicate that they will do particular kinds of work, but not that they are experts in a particular field.

Many firms are willing to give a free first interview. Not all firms advertise this fact, however, and you are advised to enquire. In addition, two schemes are administered by the Law Society of Scotland, namely: ALAS, which provides a free initial interview in respect of a potential claim for damages following an accident; and HOME FREE, a Home Advisory Service for home owners and prospective home owners, where the first interview is also free. If you are not sure whether a solicitor offers these schemes, you can check with the Law Society of Scotland.

Payment of fees and outlays

In the case of many of the services provided by solicitors, you will not only have to pay the solicitor's fees for the work done on your behalf, but also refund the outlays and expenses he has incurred on your behalf, such as the payment of stamp duty in buying a house, or the dues charged by the court, when there is a court action.

The solicitor should try to give you the best information he can about the likely costs, and he must consider whether you are eligible for advice and assistance under the legal aid 'pink form' scheme which is available to people who are on a low income and do not have much in the way of savings. It is similar to the English 'green form' scheme. You may not have to pay anything; or if your financial resources are above a certain level, you may have to pay a contribution. The solicitor will collect it there and then, if possible. The Legal Advice and Assistance Scheme in Scotland is not particularly generous, but your solicitor will guide you as to how much work he will be able to undertake on your behalf under the Scheme.

If you have to go to court, the procedure for finding a solicitor who undertakes legal aid work is on much the same lines as in England and Wales. The application is submitted to the Scottish Legal Aid Board; the delay in granting the certificate may be eight weeks, or more. If the matter is urgent, such as getting an interim interdict (injunction in England) against a violent spouse, the solicitor may apply for emergency legal aid which is much quicker.

You may be required to pay a contribution to your legal fees and outlays if your income or capital is above a certain amount. The 'Solicitors' Standards' referred to in the English scheme do not apply in Scotland, but the situation is similar and you should be advised of the position by your solicitor.

Legal aid in Scotland is granted on the same conditions as in England: if you win your case, you must repay the costs out of your 'winnings', in money and in kind; if you lose, you do not have to repay anything.

Paying your own fees

The situation as regards obtaining an estimate for legal fees and outlays, insurance for legal expenses and responsibility for payment is very similar to that in England. The solicitor has a duty to the Court not to bring before it an action which the solicitor is convinced will be unsuccessful: and accordingly the solicitor may, despite your willingness to pay, refuse to act for you.

Contract with a solicitor in Scotland

Contracts with solicitors are almost always oral, and are usually based on the law of agency. What was said earlier with respect to England and Wales about giving instructions to a solicitor applies equally in Scotland.

Most solicitors will write to you confirming what advice has been given and the completion of the various stages and of the whole transaction or case. Where you are receiving legal aid, however, the Scottish Legal Aid Board will not pay for letters confirming advice. Where you are meeting the costs yourself, you may wish to ask the solicitor to provide written confirmation at appropriate stages.

Complaints about solicitors' charges

Again, the procedure is similar to that in England. There is, however, no system of remuneration certificates; so regardless of whether there have been court proceedings, if you wish to dispute the solicitor's bill, you must require him to have it taxed. Taxation is carried out by the Auditor of Court.

Complaints against solicitors

The Law Society of Scotland has a duty to consider complaints made against solicitors, to ensure that all solicitors maintain high standards of professional conduct.

If you have a complaint, there are steps you should take:

○   Tell your solicitor about your problem, as it may be possible to sort things out. If you remain dissatisfied, ask to see the senior partner.

o   If you are still not satisfied, write to the Society, setting out the facts as clearly as possible and giving the name and address of the solicitor. The Society normally sends a copy of your complaint to the solicitor concerned, so that he has an opportunity to answer it. Usually a copy of his reply will be sent to you for your comments.

The Society employs its own staff, trained to deal with complaints. Often a complaint can be dealt with through an exchange of letters. If appropriate, the complaint will be passed to one of the Society's Complaints Committees made up of solicitors and non-solicitors. This will investigate the details of the complaint. If it thinks the complaint is justified, the Society will take appropriate action, and will notify you of its decision.

When can the Society take action?

The Society can take disciplinary action when it is satisfied that a solicitor has either provided an inadequate professional service or has acted in an unprofessional manner, or both.

A finding of inadequate professional services (IPS) will be appropriate in cases of poor, shoddy or negligent work, where the solicitor has not provided the service reasonably expected from a competent solicitor. For example, he may have failed to advance work at a reasonable pace, carried out work badly, or made a mistake in the course of work which had otherwise been well done.

A finding of professional misconduct or unprofessional behaviour ('misconduct') may be appropriate where the solicitor's ethical standards, as distinct from the services provided, have seriously departed from the high standards of conduct expected of a reputable solicitor. Misconduct has occurred when a solicitor has acted where there was a conflict of interest; behaved dishonestly; failed to communicate with a client; or the like. Sometimes the same conduct – such as serious delay – will result in a finding of both IPS and misconduct.

You do not need to decide whether you think your complaint involves IPS or misconduct: the Society will form its own view on the basis of the information which it receives from you.

What the Society can do
In all cases of alleged IPS and/or alleged misconduct, the Society can call for explanations and, if necessary, examine the solicitor's files. Having completed such investigations as it considers necessary, the Society can decide:

o   to take no action
o   in cases of IPS, to order the solicitor to reduce, refund or waive fees and/or expenses; to rectify mistakes or pay for another solicitor to do so; or direct the solicitor to take such other action as the Society thinks appropriate
o   in cases of misconduct, to issue a formal reprimand to the solicitor (which is noted on his official record) or in less serious cases, write deploring or regretting the solicitor's conduct
o   in serious cases, to prosecute the solicitor before the Scottish Solicitors' Discipline Tribunal, which is an independent body appointed by the Lord President of the Court of Session. If the solicitor is found guilty, the Tribunal may censure, fine or suspend him from practice, or strike him off the roll of solicitors. The Tribunal may also order the solicitor to pay the costs of the prosecution.

What the Society cannot do
The Society cannot give legal advice. It cannot order your solicitor to release documents if you have not paid his proper fees and outlays.

If you are satisfied with your solicitor's services, but consider his fee to be unreasonable, the Society cannot help: you must ask for taxation. Nor can it order your solicitor to compensate you for any substantial loss resulting from his negligence.

If you are complaining about a solicitor who acted for another party in any business, the Society will not investigate your complaint unless it is supported by the solicitor who acted for you.

Generally, the Society will not consider a complaint of IPS if:

o you have not lodged your complaint within six months of becoming aware of the cause of complaint

o your complaint is considered to be relatively trivial

o the alleged IPS relates solely to your solicitor's conduct in court

o your solicitor has provided a competent service, and you are complaining only about the way in which he has used his professional judgement

o the complaint is purely one of professional negligence, and the Society considers that if there is merit in it, you may have grounds for a claim for damages against your solicitor.

The Client Relations and Complaints Office
The Society handles complaints through this Office, which is staffed by experienced solicitors; it not only investigates complaints, but also gives general advice about making complaints. If you need further information, telephone the Complaints Secretariat.

The Scottish Solicitors' Discipline Tribunal
If the matter is sufficiently serious, the Council of the Law Society of Scotland may refer it to the Scottish Solicitors Discipline Tribunal, which closely resembles in its workings the Solicitors Disciplinary Tribunal in England, and is able to impose similar penalties; likewise, it cannot grant compensation.

Taking a solicitor to court
The information on this topic with regard to English solicitors applies also in Scotland, except that the option of arbitration is not available.

The Lay Observer for Scotland

He is appointed by the Secretary of State for Scotland, and works in the same way, in almost every respect, as the English Lay Observer; the period allowed for bringing complaints about the Law Society's handling of cases is, however, longer.

Negligence

If you decide to bring a claim for negligence against a solicitor, and are unable to find a solicitor who is prepared to act for you, you should write to the Law Society of Scotland giving full details. The Society will appoint a solicitor (referred to as a 'troubleshooter') to advise you.

Scottish solicitors, like English ones, are required to be insured for professional negligence claims (in terms of the Master Policy of the Law Society of Scotland). The Solicitors' Arbitration Scheme does not operate in Scotland.

ADVOCATES

In Scotland the equivalent of a barrister is known as an advocate. All advocates have to be members of the Faculty of Advocates, which is based in Parliament House, Edinburgh. In most respects the work of a Scottish advocate is similar to that done by his English counterpart although, unless your case is being heard in either the High Court or the Court of Session, you are more likely in Scotland to be represented by a solicitor. However, there are important differences in the organisation of the Scottish Bar. For instance, the Scottish Bar does not have a chambers system. There are only about 250 Scottish advocates currently in practice. The leader of the Scottish Bar is known as the Dean of Faculty. He is primarily responsible for discipline of members of the Bar in professional matters. As practice at the Bar involves the provision of service to the public, a strict code of professional conduct has to be complied with by all practising members. A breach of professional conduct will result in disciplinary action. The Faculty of Advocates operates a disciplinary procedure. Any complaint should be investigated impartially; and proceedings may be instituted before a Disciplinary Tribunal comprising both lawyers and lay persons. Any complaint should be made in writing to the Dean of Faculty.

OTHER SOURCES OF LEGAL ADVICE
There are no licensed conveyancers or legal executives in Scotland. Legal advice centres and law centres operate as in England. Scottish Citizens Advice Bureaux were discussed together with their English counterparts.

USEFUL ADDRESSES

COUNCIL FOR LICENSED CONVEYANCERS
Golden Cross House
8 Duncannon Street
London WC2N 4JF
01-210 4559

Code of conduct: yes
Complaints procedure: yes
Complaint-handling charge: no
Disciplinary sanctions: reprimand, fine, suspension, disqualification; also, loss/refund of fees, payment of costs

FACULTY OF ADVOCATES
1 Parliament Square
Edinburgh EH1 1RF
031-226 5071

Code of conduct: adherence to professional standards
Complaints procedure: conducted by the Dean of Faculty
Complaint-handling charge: no
Disciplinary sanctions: reprimand; disbarment

FREE REPRESENTATION UNIT (FRU)
13 Gray's Inn Square
London WC1R 5JP
01-831 0692

Membership: law students and pupil barristers
Membership list: not available
Code of conduct: yes
Complaints procedure: yes
Complaint-handling charge: no

GENERAL COUNCIL OF THE BAR (BAR COUNCIL)
11 South Square
Gray's Inn
London WC1R 5EL
01-242 0082

Code of conduct: adherence to professional standards
Complaints procedure: investigation by Professional Conduct
    Committee (PCC)
Complaint-handling charge: no
Disciplinary sanctions: reprimand; disbarment

GENERAL COUNCIL OF THE BAR OF NORTHERN IRELAND
Bar Library
Royal Courts of Justice
Belfast BT1 3JX
0232-232721

Code of conduct: adherence to professional standards
Complaints procedure: investigation by Professional Conduct
    Committee (PCC)
Complaint-handling charge: no
Disciplinary sanctions: reprimand; disbarment

INSTITUTE OF LEGAL EXECUTIVES
Kempston Manor
Kempston
Bedford MK42 7AB
0234-841000

Membership: by examination; annual subscription
Style of qualification: F.InstL.Ex (Fellows only)
Membership List: not available; list of Fellows published in the
   Solicitors' and Barristers' Directory
Code of conduct: yes
Complaints procedure: yes
Complaint-handling charge: no
Disciplinary sanctions: yes

LAW CENTRES FEDERATION (LCF)
18-19 Warren Street
London W1P 5DB
01-387 8570

LAW SOCIETY
113 Chancery Lane
London WC2A 1PL
01-242 1222

Membership: solicitors only; voluntary; annual subscription
Style of qualification: none
Membership List: computerised register available to the public
Fee guidelines: for legal-aid work information is available from
   the Legal Aid Board
Code of conduct: yes
Complaints procedure: the Solicitors Complaints Bureau
Complaint-handling charge: no
Disciplinary sanctions: see Solicitors Complaints Bureau and
   Solicitors' Disciplinary Tribunal

LAW SOCIETY OF NORTHERN IRELAND
90-106 Victoria Street
Belfast BT1 3JZ
0232-231614
Membership: all solicitors in Northern Ireland
Style of qualification: solicitor
Membership list: firms undertaking legal aid work only; free on
    request
Fee guidelines: no, except for legal aid
Code of conduct: yes
Complaints procedure: yes
Complaint-handling charge: no
Disciplinary sanctions: referral to disciplinary committee, which
    can impose fine, suspension, disqualification

LAW SOCIETY OF SCOTLAND
26 Drumsheugh Gardens
Edinburgh EH3 7YR
031-226 7411

Membership: all solicitors in Scotland
Style of qualification: solicitor
Membership list: available from Publications Department
Fee guidelines: no
Code of conduct: yes
Complaints procedure: yes: to Complaints Secretariat
Complaint-handling charge: no
Disciplinary sanctions: referral to Scottish Solicitors' Discipline
    Tribunal, which can impose fine, suspension, disquali-
    fication

LAY OBSERVER
Royal Courts of Justice
Strand
London WC2A 2LL
01-936 6695

Code of conduct: yes
Complaints procedure: yes, regarding Solicitors Complaints
    Bureau's treatment of complaints about solicitors
Complaint-handling charge: no
Disciplinary sanctions: recommendations only

LAY OBSERVER FOR NORTHERN IRELAND
Room 407
Clarendon House
Adelaide Street
Belfast BT2 8ND
0232-244300

LAY OBSERVER FOR SCOTLAND
30 Castle Street
Edinburgh EH2 3HT
031-226 2503

LEGAL AID BOARD
Newspaper House
8-16 Great New Street
London EC4 3BN
01-353 7411

**NATIONAL ASSOCIATION FOR CITIZENS ADVICE
BUREAUX (NACAB)**
115 Pentonville Road
London N1 9LZ
01-833 2181

Complaints procedure: yes
Complaint-handling charge: no
Disciplinary sanctions: bureau could be closed

SCOTTISH ASSOCIATION OF CITIZENS ADVICE BUREAUX (SACAB)
26 George Square
Edinburgh EH8 9ND
031-667 0156

Complaints procedure: yes
Complaint-handling charge: no
Disciplinary sanctions: bureau could be closed

SCOTTISH SOLICITORS' DISCIPLINE TRIBUNAL
22 Rutland Square
Edinburgh EH1 2BB
031-229 5860

SOLICITORS COMPLAINTS BUREAU
Portland House
Stag Place
London SW1 5BL
01-834 2288

Code of conduct: yes
Complaints procedure: yes
Complaint-handling charge: no
Disciplinary sanctions: rebuke; intervention in a solicitors' practice, referral to Solicitors' Disciplinary Tribunal

SOLICITORS' DISCIPLINARY TRIBUNAL
60 Carey Street
London WC2A 2JB
01-242 0219

Disciplinary sanctions: reprimand; fine; suspension; removal from roll of solicitors

WHICH? PERSONAL SERVICE
Consumers' Association
2 Marylebone Road
London NW1 4DX
01-486 5544

Membership: open to all
Code of conduct: no
Complaint-handling charge: annual subscription

London telephone numbers

On 6 May 1990 the 01 telephone
code for London will change to
either 071 or 081, depending on the
local code that follows it. From that
date, people telephoning the 01
code will hear a recorded message
telling them to re-dial using either
071 or 081.

Financial Services

The world of personal finance and investment has undergone a far-reaching revolution in recent years, and the financial and investment professions have altered accordingly.

New Acts of Parliament, culminating in the Financial Services Act, have made enormous changes in borrowing money, in buying on credit and in insurance and investment. A brief look at the most important legislation is necessary to understand the role of the professionals involved and their new responsibilities and liabilities.

THE CONSUMER CREDIT ACT 1974

In 1971 the Crowther Committee Report on Consumer Credit took note of the enormous growth in the use of credit for buying goods and houses. It found the two major problems to be that unscrupulous lenders might try to induce borrowers to agree to one-sided and onerous agreements, and also that the borrowers themselves might be tempted to borrow too much for their own financial benefit.

The subsequent Consumer Credit Act passed through Parliament in 1974, but the majority of its provisions came into force through statutory instruments (regulations) over a period of at least ten years following that date.

The Act protects individual borrowers in a number of different ways which are summarised below. In order to be covered by the Act, an agreement must be for credit not exceeding £15,000, and made with an individual. Certain agreements which fall into this category are, however, exempt:

these include loans for the purchase of land (which, in law, includes houses and other real property) and certain charge card agreements, such as American Express and Diners Club.

Licensing
The Act brought into force a licensing system supervised by the Director General of Fair Trading. It requires lenders to obtain a consumer credit licence. Licences may be refused or revoked, and if an unlicensed trader engages in an activity for which a licence is required, there is provision for fines (up to £2,000) or imprisonment (up to two years). An agreement made in such circumstances is unenforceable unless the Director General makes a 'validating order' confirming it.

Advertising
There are regulations for the form and content of credit advertisements, and offences are committed if false and misleading advertisements are published.

Canvassing personal loans
A canvasser commits an offence if he canvasses a loan off trade premises, unless he does this at the prospective borrower's request.

Withdrawal and cancellation
A prospective debtor (borrower) or hirer (hire-purchaser) can withdraw from a transaction at any time before the offer has been accepted, either orally or in writing.

Agreements can be cancelled if they were made orally but away from the creditor's trade premises. Having received the statutory second copy of the agreement, the debtor can cancel during a period of 5 days, in writing. He is entitled to the return of his deposit and must make the goods available for collection by the creditor. These provisions are intended to cover the situation in which a doorstep salesman makes a credit transaction appear very attractive, but with thought and consideration it becomes much less so.

Hire-purchase and conditional-sale agreements can be terminated at any time before the final instalment, but in this case the debtor is normally required to make his payment up to one half of the total price, and the goods must be returned.

A right to pay off early and obtain a rebate
The debtor can do this if he gives notice to the creditor and pays all sums due (such as interest charges). Under the Consumer Credit Act there are Early Settlement Rebate Regulations which lay down the formulae to be used in calculating rebates.

Rights to prevent 'snatch-back' of goods
In hire-purchase and conditional-sale cases the Act prevents a creditor from going into the debtor's premises to repossess goods. In the case of 'protected goods' (where the debtor is in breach of his agreement and has paid one-third or more of the total price) the goods cannot be recovered by the creditor without a court order.

In this case the court can make a time order, enabling it to re-schedule payments at a level that, in its view, the debtor can afford.

No extortionate credit bargains
Credit arrangements (for credit of any amount) can be set aside or rewritten by the court, on application by the borrower, if it thinks they are grossly exorbitant or otherwise grossly contravene the principles of fair dealing.

Liability for defects
If goods bought through credit agreements prove defective, the Act gives certain extra rights to the debtor. In the normal three-party credit agreement between credit company, retailer and debtor, the creditor and retailer are both singly and together liable for the defects. This applies only where the price of the goods is not less than £100 and not more than £30,000. A

particularly useful consequence of this is the purchaser's right to take action against a credit-card company if goods bought with the card prove defective, and the seller of the goods cannot (or will not) meet the liability.

These rights do not apply to hire purchase and conditional sale agreements, where the goods still belong to the creditor, until the option to purchase is taken up.

The right to see a credit file

Anybody who enters into a credit agreement is likely to appear in the files of one of the credit reference agencies, which keep records of people's credit transactions. Traders consult these agencies before granting credit to customers, in order to assure themselves that it is safe to do so. The files record both those transactions in which the customer met his obligations, and those in which he defaulted.

Anyone applying for credit of up to £15,000 has the right to be given by the trader the name and address of any agency that has been consulted about him. There are, at present, four national credit reference agencies, and some local agencies. The Act gives a consumer the right to ask a credit reference agency, at any time, for details of his file, by written request plus a small fee (currently £1). If the consumer believes that the file contains incorrect information, he can give notice for it to be removed or amended. If nothing is done to his satisfaction, he can apply to the Director General of Fair Trading, who can make any order he thinks fit in the circumstances.

The agency must notify each person to whom, within the preceding six months, it has given information relevant to the financial standing of the consumer, that the incorrect information should be amended or removed.

THE BUILDING SOCIETIES ACT 1986

Over recent years, building societies have changed greatly. This statute came into force because of the building societies' huge assets and increasing financial power; because of increasing demand amongst members for additional services; and in general, because of the greater sophistication of the financial world in which the building societies are involved.

The Act provided for the setting up of a Building Societies Commission with the remit of protecting members, promoting financial stability and ensuring that, in spite of changes, the societies' main purpose will continue to be raising money and advancing it to members by security of mortgage.

Nevertheless, it allows societies to diversify their activities; for example, into making unsecured loans and making loans for the purchase of mobile homes, and also into new services, for example, foreign exchange, the provision of insurance and estate agency. It also provides for the protection of investors in the (extremely unlikely) event of a building society becoming insolvent.

An interesting element is the scheme for the investigation of complaints made by individuals about action taken by a building society. Each society is required to be a member of an investigation scheme headed by an ombudsman.

THE BANKING ACT 1987

The scope of this Act is narrower than it appears: it is primarily concerned with the interests of depositors alone. The Act details the duties and powers of the Bank of England, which is given supervisory functions and certain specific regulatory functions. A new Board of Banking Supervision is established. Only authorised institutions may accept a deposit. The Act continues the Deposit Protection Board set up by the Banking Act 1979 for the protection of depositors. A Deposit Protection Fund is created by contributions from authorised institutions.

A person who has a deposit with such an authorised institution may receive, should it become insolvent, a compensation payment amounting to up to three quarters of his deposit (up to a maximum limit of £20,000).

The Act contains detailed provisions controlling the use of banking names – and the Bank of England can object to misleading or undesirable names. The Act also confirms the obligation of secrecy on supervisors and those who acquire supervisory information.

THE FINANCIAL SERVICES ACT 1986
This Act provides a complete review of the regulation of investment business and came about following the Gower reports into investor protection.

In recent years, the financial services industry has undergone a transformation. The Stock Exchange's system of fixed minimum commissions and its single-capacity dealing system (the separation of market makers – jobbers – trading only as principals, and not directly with the public, from brokers, trading only as agents on behalf of the public) were abandoned.

The Stock Exchange's rule book was removed from the scope of the legislation about restrictive trade practices. At the same time, financial services conglomerates emerged because of the removal of restrictions on the outside ownership of Stock Exchange member firms. This upheaval gave scope for an increase in what could politely be called conflict of interest – impolitely, abuse of duty and fraud.

Some kind of regulation was vital. The 1986 Act provided for regulation by 'Self-Regulating Organisations' (SROs), which would be under the general oversight of an independent commission. This commission became the Securities and Investments Board (SIB).

The carrying on of investment business is prohibited without authorisation by SIB or by the appropriate SRO. It is a criminal offence to contravene this rule, and firms which enter into agreements in contravention cannot normally enforce them. An investment business can be authorised directly by SIB, or indirectly through membership of a recognised SRO.

The Act makes somewhat similar provision for people certified by 'Recognised Professional Bodies' (RPBs) such as the Law Society, who do investment business which is incidental to their main activities. If RPB members whose activities are covered by the Act do not apply for certification, then they must join an appropriate SRO or seek authorisation directly from SIB itself.

One of the most profound changes brought about by SIB under the Financial Services Act comes from the polarisation of those selling life assurance into either independent advisers, able to recommend any product, or tied agents selling the products of one company. This rule has been greatly criticised, and has been particularly inconvenient for the High Street banks which, before the Act came into force, assumed the role of impartial advisers, but were able at the same time to sell their own range of unit trusts and insurance-related investments. Of the 'big four' banks, only the National Westminster Bank has now decided to be an independent adviser.

Investment advertising by unauthorised persons and the making of misleading statements are criminal offences under the Act. SIB has a rule book which is constantly updated: it has the duty of introducing regulations for the conduct of investment business. It provides a 'cooling-off' period for purchases of certain investments and provides for the safekeeping of clients' money. Those carrying out investment business must be fit and proper to do so (the previous records of firms and their officers are taken into account). Investment businesses are required to have proper regard to a client's best interests in any advice they give, and all their published recommendations must be researched and capable of substantiation.

Unsolicited visits and telephone calls to sell investments are for the most part banned (an exception is life assurance and unit trust selling where, if the sale is the result of a 'cold call', a 14-day cooling-off period is provided). Clear warnings must be given in advertisements about matters such as the volatility or the marketability of a product.

At the present time, there are the following self-regulating organisations:–

○ The Association of Futures Brokers and Dealers (AFBD) embraces the London commodity markets.

○ The Securities Association (TSA) is concerned with dealers in quoted securities and international dealings, such as Eurobonds and Euroequities.

○ The Financial Intermediaries, Managers and Brokers Regulatory Association (FIMBRA) is concerned with independent intermediaries. FIMBRA members offer advice (which must be independent) on investments.

○ The Investment Management Regulatory Organisation (IMRO) is concerned with firms specialising in discretionary investment management.

○ The Life Assurance and Unit Trust Regulatory Organisation (LAUTRO) is concerned with the sale and marketing of life assurance and unit trust products by company representatives of its members.

In short, the intention of the Act was to prevent individuals or firms from taking on investment business unless they were honest and capable; to provide their clients with adequate complaints procedures; to provide a compensation fund if firms should go out of business; and to provide protection to clients while firms are in business. Whether this measure will be successful, only time will tell.

THE INSURANCE BROKERS (REGISTRATION) ACT 1977
This Act was passed for the registration of insurance brokers and for the regulation of their professional standards.

The Act established the Insurance Brokers Registration Council (IBRC) which registers insurance brokers (only those so registered may use the word 'broker' in their trading title) and maintains a register of practising insurance brokers. The IBRC has made rules about the annual auditing of accounts of insurance brokers, the segregation of clients' monies, and the necessity of maintaining certain solvency ratios. There is a statutory code of conduct to which all insurance brokers must adhere. An investigating committee and a disciplinary committee have also been established to look into any alleged breaches by insurance brokers of the code and other requirements under the Act. All insurance brokers must have professional indemnity insurance to a mandatory quality and quantity. IBRC also operates a grants fund to mitigate losses by personal clients arising from an insurance broker's failure to account for monies, or the fraud or dishonesty of an insurance broker.

THE INSURANCE COMPANIES ACT 1982

This Act provides that only authorised or exempted businesses can carry on insurance business in the UK. Accounts must be filed with the Secretary of State; life insurance and general insurance must be separately accounted for. A 'requirement of solvency' is laid down and important powers of intervention are given to the Secretary of State.

Intermediaries who are connected with insurers are required to disclose this fact. Proposers (that is, people applying) for life insurance are given a statutory cooling-off period before committing themselves. It is an offence to make false or misleading statements to induce someone to enter into an insurance contract.

Following this outline of the most important recent legislation affecting the world of finance, it is now possible to look at the financial professions individually.

Providers of investment advice

As mentioned earlier, since the Financial Services Act came into force, the provision of investment advice and the professional conduct of the advisers have come under the supervision of a number of self-regulating organisations. There is a certain amount of overlap between their activities, reflecting the multiple functions of some of the firms they supervise, so that some firms concerned with life insurance and investment may come under the supervision of more than one SRO.

SECURITIES AND INVESTMENT BOARD (SIB)

SIB itself is a private limited company – not a government department – whose aim is to achieve a consistent level of both investor protection and overall efficiency in financial markets. The rules of SIB are in the process of being crystallised into guiding principles of conduct, the first of which states that investees must act with fairness and diligence in relation to investors 'to the greatest extent practicable in the circumstances, the investor's interest being paramount'.

SIB has a complaints procedure for both directly authorised and self-regulating organisations. The aggrieved client should complain to the firm itself in the first place: if not satisfied, he should write to SIB, giving full details. SIB will try to conciliate, but if this fails, the case will go before the Independent Investigating Panel (if appropriate). Further conciliation will be attempted, and, if necessary, arbitration.

Firms can be reprimanded (publicly or privately), or their authorisation to carry on investment business may be withdrawn. Injunctions may be taken against firms that break the rules – SIB is even empowered to petition for the winding-up of a defaulting company or partnership.

SIB has a compensation fund, but it is available only in cases of insolvency: otherwise, the only way the client can secure compensation is by action in the civil courts.

SROs have rules as strict as those of SIB. Many of the rules are much the same for both, though adapted to their members' particular circumstances.

One rule requires members to be members of the Investment Compensation Scheme, established under the auspices of SIB. (At present, this does not apply to life assurance companies and building societies; nor to members of RPBs, such as accountants and lawyers.) The maximum compensation (to be awarded if a firm responsible for loss caused by negligence or fraud is wound up or goes into liquidation) is 100% of losses up to £30,000, together with 90% of any further loss up to £20,000, making a total of £48,000.

THE ASSOCIATION OF FUTURES BROKERS AND DEALERS (AFBD)

This is another SRO within the Financial Services Act. Investment in futures means trading in options, currencies and commodities in the future, in the hope that their value will rise. It is a highly speculative business.

AFBD includes members of the London International Financial Futures Exchange (LIFFE), trading in futures in currencies and options; the Futures and Options Exchange (London-Fox) trading in futures in such things as sugar, cocoa and coffee; the International Petroleum Exchange, trading in futures and options contracts in oil and oil products; the London Metal Exchange, dealing in copper, zinc, aluminium, nickel, silver and lead futures; and the Baltic Future.

Members include futures brokers, dealers and advisers, banks, stockbrokers, money brokers and bullion dealers. To qualify for membership, they must:

o   enjoy a suitable financial and business standing
o   carry on business efficiently, honestly and fairly
o   comply with the conduct rules of AFBD
o   have means of ensuring that their employees are them-
    selves fit and proper persons
o   have adequate means and financial resources to comply
    with AFBD rules, and to carry on investment business.

The rules include the following requirements: entering into a written contract with customers, setting out the investment services to be provided and the remuneration to be charged; making unsolicited calls on clients only in accordance with the rules; holding customers' money on trust in a separate client account; maintaining a minimum amount of financial resources to support investment business; and submitting regular financial reports to AFBD. All members must give AFBD access to their premises and books, and must submit to regular unannounced inspections by AFBD inspectors.

AFBD's leaflets emphasise that potential customers should

not allow themselves to be 'talked over', or persuaded to enter transactions, and that a hasty decision can, and often does, result in loss.

Anyone complaining about a member firm is asked first to draw the matter to the attention of the firm itself. If he is still dissatisfied, the matter should be referred in writing to AFBD. It will be investigated fairly and impartially, and may be referred to the business conduct committee. If the decision is to take no action, the customer may be entitled to initiate arbitration procedures. An attempt to conciliate may be made, and if this fails, the customer may either initiate arbitration procedures, or himself refer the matter to the business conduct committee.

Where the case is referred to the business conduct committee, there will be an investigation and adjudication. As a result, the member complained of may be censured, fined, expelled or suspended; or an order may be made for compensation to be paid to a customer. Any decision of the committee may be appealed against, by either the member complained of or by the complainant.

In the case of arbitration, claims for sums not exceeding £35,000 are usually decided on the basis of written representations. If more than one arbitrator is appointed, at least one will be an independent lay member of the Council of AFBD.

Since these regulatory powers and sanctions can be very useful, a potential investor should make sure that the firm with which he is dealing is a member of AFBD, by looking for its logo on advertising and letterheads, or checking with AFBD or SIB. Nevertheless, there is no substitute for an investor making sure for himself that a proposed investment is suitable for him, and that he is in a position to bear any resulting loss.

THE SECURITIES ASSOCIATION (TSA)

This is the SRO responsible for all types of investment business (with certain exceptions). Most stockbroking firms belong to TSA. It has set up a complaints and conciliation bureau: a brochure giving details of its powers is available to the public and, by the TSA rules, member firms must inform the public about its existence.

TSA members are required to deal promptly and correctly with customers' complaints; if a customer is not satisfied, he should contact the compliance officer of the firm, who will arrange for the complaint to be dealt with by a senior official who was not directly involved in the case. At this stage, the firm is obliged to inform the customer of his right to refer the matter to the complaints bureau.

The bureau can only handle complaints which are not already the subject of litigation or arbitration, and which are about something that happened after 29 April 1988. From May 1990 onwards, complaints must be about something which happened less than two years before the complaint was made. The aggrieved customer should write to the complaints bureau, giving full details.

The complaint will be investigated free of charge. TSA rules require members to co-operate fully and promptly. The complaints bureau may refer the case back to the firm concerned, or try to conciliate in order to reach a settlement; it may also decide that no action is warranted. If agreement follows conciliation, this removes the right to go to court or to arbitration. If the bureau takes no action, then the customer may take the complaint further.

TSA has a consumer arbitration scheme for cases that are not settled by conciliation. 'Private customers' (which includes individuals, partnerships or small companies) and 'expert investors' having a claim against a member firm for £25,000 or less, may use the scheme.

The claimant must pay a registration fee of £10, and also pay all his directly incurred costs; TSA pays the costs and expenses of the arbitrator and any hearing. The arbitrator will award costs against either party only if he considers its case to be frivolous and totally without merit: even then, there is a maximum of £500.

Each party is required to sign a submission agreement. An

independent arbitrator is appointed, and usually decides the case on the basis of documents submitted. He may make an award, giving reasons. His decision is final.

For larger claims (usually more appropriate to some of the institutional disputes), there is a further arbitration scheme, which is not free, and involves legal representation.

An independent complaints commissioner oversees the work of the complaints bureau. He will not reopen any case, but will consider whether the Bureau has been correct, fair and prompt. His address is: The Complaints Commissioner, c/o TSA Tribunal Secretariat, The Stock Exchange Building, Old Broad Street, London EC2N 1EQ.

If any complaints prima facie involve a breach of TSA rules, they are passed to the TSA investigations team; this may result in members being fined, suspended and ultimately expelled from the Association.

THE FINANCIAL INTERMEDIARIES, MANAGERS AND BROKERS REGULATORY ASSOCIATION (FIMBRA)

This Association regulates firms which provide independent financial services to the general public, including investment advisers and private portfolio managers. It has members who offer advice on a wide range of investments, from life insurance and unit trusts to shares, debentures and gilts (government securities which provide a fixed interest payment twice yearly and return a guaranteed sum after a specified number of years).

The rules of FIMBRA require its members to demonstrate that they are members of FIMBRA, chiefly by incorporating its logo in their letterheads and advertising.

Members of FIMBRA are 'strongly advised' to take out professional indemnity insurance. This is not however, at present, a condition of membership, because SIB does not insist on it: but there are plans to make such insurance cover compulsory. Before being allowed to join FIMBRA, prospective members must pass a solvency test, which varies according to the kind of work they do.

A FIMBRA member is expected to be independent, to recommend suitable investments, and to suggest particular products which have performed well in the past, and which can reasonably be expected to out-perform the rest of the market in future. He should know a great deal about his client, which may involve asking him detailed questions about his income, tax position and other investments.

FIMBRA members must at all times ensure that their clients understand the risks that they are running in making a particular investment. (In normal circumstances, life assurance is expected to be risk-free, unit trusts slightly riskier, and individual investments in shares, riskier still.)

Members are required to keep detailed records of transactions entered into on behalf of clients, and to keep copies of each written complaint about their conduct of investment business. These must be dealt with by a competent and experienced officer of the company, and complainants must be informed of their rights of complaint to FIMBRA, which also has the power to monitor members' behaviour by a system of random checks by officers of FIMBRA.

There are detailed requirements to do with financial accounting, including various duties imposed by the Financial Services Act as to keeping of clients' money (in particular, holding it on trust in a separate bank account). Provisions also exist as to standards of advertising to be observed; these are intended to keep clients as well informed as possible.

Complaints about a FIMBRA member

Complaints about FIMBRA members are investigated free of charge. If there is to be a formal investigation, they must allege a contravention of FIMBRA rules, and must be presented in writing.

On receiving the complaint, the chief executive may appoint an investigation team before which the individuals concerned will be asked to state their case. It may request documents to be provided, and also reasonable access to premises, in appropriate cases.

If the chief executive finds prima facie evidence of a member's misconduct, the proceedings will be referred to a disciplinary panel or to a 'summary process', if the member agrees to submit to it. At the conclusion of the summary process, the chief executive may reprimand a member, in private or in public; require him to take such action as is necessary to remedy the situation; or refer the case against the member to a person authorised by the FIMBRA Council to resolve disputes between members and clients.

A disciplinary panel can order the following sanctions: termination of membership; imposing special conditions on membership; a reprimand, either in private or in public; referral of the case to a person authorised by the FIMBRA Council to resolve disputes between members and clients.

FIMBRA insists that the prospect of a fee must never influence the advice that independent intermediaries give to a client. The FIMBRA rules on 'best advice' require independent advisers to recommend the most suitable product for a client. Intermediaries who deal in all types of investment must take investment trusts, which do not pay commission, into account when considering investment opportunities. However, the FIMBRA guidelines state that where a non-commission-paying product appears to be the best for the client, the intermediary can ask for a fee to make up for loss of commission.

Complaints about FIMBRA, or any other SRO, should be addressed to the Securities and Investments Board.

INVESTMENT MANAGEMENT REGULATORY ORGANISATION LTD (IMRO)

IMRO is specially responsible for the regulation of corporate investment managers and advisers: that is, professionals who manage investments and who give advice about investing money and switching it from one company to another. IMRO members include unit trust managers and pension fund managers.

Complaints about IMRO members

IMRO members, like all businesses coming under the Financial Services Act, must show their membership on their letterheads, and members must give details to the public of the organisation and its address. Any complaint received by IMRO may be either investigated, or passed to SIB or other regulating organisation, or even to the police or the Department of Trade. No fee is charged. In many cases, a complainant need only express his dissatisfaction to the firm in question, as the IMRO rules require members to notify it about all complaints which have not been resolved to the customer's satisfaction within four weeks. Complaints to IMRO should be in writing, but need not follow any particular form.

A complaint could be about a breach of the IMRO rules; a breach of customer agreement; a breach of statute; malpractice or impropriety; or the repetition of an action that had been the subject of an earlier complaint.

Every member is obliged to submit to IMRO a quarterly summary of all complaints received. If he does not hear further from a customer within four weeks of responding to a complaint, he is entitled to treat the complaint as settled. But if a customer remains dissatisfied four weeks after the complaint was received, IMRO must be notified.

If a customer claims to have suffered financial loss because of an IMRO member's action (or lack of it), the member's first response must contain a notice that the customer may direct his complaint to a referee. The member must co-operate fully with any attempt at conciliation by the referee, and if the customer accepts adjudication by a referee, the member must agree.

You may be entitled to use the referee system without being yourself the customer of an IMRO member. You may do so, for instance, if you have invested in unit trusts managed by an IMRO member, and you want to complain that you have lost money through the actions of the management. If the member is also a member of the Insurance Ombudsman Bureau, the complaint will be referred there.

There are also other conditions:

o The IMRO member must have been given four weeks in which to settle the matter.
o The matter must be referred to the referee within 18 months of the problem arising.
o The complaint must not normally involve a sum exceeding £100,000.
o The complaint must be about something that happened after 29 April 1988.
o The firm about which the complaint is made must be an IMRO member at the time of complaint.

Since April 1989, the referee has been the Investment Referee, handling complaints on behalf of both IMRO and FIMBRA, but remaining independent of both organisations. No fee is charged unless the referee decides that the customer had acted unreasonably in the circumstances.

The referee will attempt conciliation, and if this does not succeed, will offer adjudication. This will be as informal as possible, and may be based wholly on documents, though in some cases there may be an informal hearing. The IMRO member and his customer must co-operate with the referee. At conciliation, no rights to further action are given up; but if the customer agrees to adjudication, he must agree to give up all other legal remedies. The referee's award will be final and binding on both parties: the Investment Referee Scheme can award compensation up to £50,000 for loss due to negligence. In answer to a complaint, a member may request the referee to adjudicate on a complaint he has against the customer, on the same subject. If the referee finds the complaint genuine, he may invite the customer to pay an amount to the member: this is not binding.

The Investment Referee can be contacted directly by writing to the Investment Referee Scheme, 6 Frederick Place, London EC2R 8BT. Any complaint sent in this way should be as detailed as possible, setting out dates and reference numbers, and enclosing copies of relevant letters or documents.

Although the referee's award is final and binding on both parties, either party, with the leave of the court, may appeal on a point of law to the High Court as provided by the Arbitration Act 1979. The referee must notify the complainant of this right of appeal.

The referee scheme is a useful alternative to other methods of claiming compensation. The conciliation procedure would be sufficient in most cases; and adjudication is usually preferable to court procedure, because of its informality, speed and cheapness. But, as in other arbitration schemes, the eventual award may be lower than would have been awarded by a court; it only applies to cases where the claim is for less than £100,000 (if the referee decides to award more, he can only invite the member to pay it); and the right of appeal is limited.

THE LIFE ASSURANCE AND UNIT TRUST REGULATORY ORGANISATION (LAUTRO)

LAUTRO is a self-regulating organisation, set up in 1986 by the life assurance and unit trust industries with the object of seeking recognition under the Financial Services Act 1986. It regulates the marketing of life assurance by life assurance companies and of unit trusts by management companies of authorised unit trust schemes.

Any company coming under its jurisdiction can be recognised by either a statement of membership or a logo (on its advertising or on its premises). Consumers can contact LAUTRO direct or through its members, who are required to provide the address if requested; or through advisory bodies such as Trading Standards Departments and Citizens Advice Bureaux.

LAUTRO maintains, jointly with FIMBRA, a register of salesmen and intermediaries. Furthermore, an indemnity scheme has been provided to cover losses of client money held by life assurance companies or their agents before the setting up of a contract of insurance, should the company become insolvent during that period. This supplements the scheme of the Policyholders Protection Act 1975.

Under the Financial Services Act 1986, the Chief Registrar of Friendly Societies is required to establish a scheme for compensating investors, and these societies must be covered by this scheme, as a condition of LAUTRO membership.

LAUTRO is responsible only for the marketing of unit trusts; the Investment Management Regulatory Organisation (IMRO) is responsible for investment management. Unit trust management companies share in compensation arrangements administered by IMRO.

The rules of LAUTRO contain a code of conduct for members, containing these significant features:

○ Members must exercise due skill, care and diligence in business dealings, and should deal fairly with investors.

○ Company representatives may make unsolicited calls on investors, but must recognise and respect the right of the investor to terminate the call at any time. If coming by appointment, the representative should state the purpose of the call, identify himself as representing a particular company, and show the investor his business card.

○ The business stationery of members should give full details of their company and indicate that they are members of LAUTRO.

○ Members' representatives should at all times ensure that investors receive the best advice. This means that they must take an investor's financial circumstances into consideration; must not make unfair criticisms of other investment contracts, and must not sell an investment unless they are authorised and competent to advise on the matter.

○ Members representatives must keep detailed records of all transactions, and must treat all information received as confidential.

○ A person who at any time acts as a company representative must not at the same time also be an independent intermediary.

An important part of the rules contains detailed provisions limiting the power of members to offer or give commission to any person who is not an authorised person, as well as further details about the amount of commission permitted to independent intermediaries.

Complaints about LAUTRO members

The primary responsibility for investigating alleged misconduct amongst members lies with the LAUTRO enforcement staff, under the direction of the Monitoring Committee and the Chief Executive.

If the Monitoring Committee finds a complaint justified, it may require the member concerned to take certain action. In the case of serious breaches of rules, in particular where there is concern regarding the protection of investors, the Committee may institute proceedings before the Disciplinary Committee. Sanctions for misconduct range from private reprimand to termination of membership.

LAUTRO's complaints procedures are coupled with those of the insurance ombudsman, for those members who are also covered by the Insurance Ombudsman Scheme, but with the ombudsman taking due account of LAUTRO rules.

Complaints received are sifted jointly by the ombudsman and LAUTRO. Those cases which show no evidence of serious breach of rules or of a consistent pattern of ignoring or neglecting rules are referred directly to the ombudsman. Serious breaches are dealt with by the LAUTRO enforcement staff.

Complaints alleging that a business is being carried on without authorisation are, like all allegations of unauthorised trading, referred to the Securities and Investments Board. Complaints about LAUTRO itself are investigated under the direction of the organisation's chief enforcement officer and a report is made to SIB.

THE UNIT TRUST ASSOCIATION (UTA)

This is not an SRO under the Financial Services Act 1986, but is represented on the board of IMRO and of LAUTRO. UTA's general role is to provide information on the unit trust industry. It also has a brief to promote unit trusts generally. Its Unit Trust Customer Standards Committee is formulating a code of practice for the unit trust industry.

A unit trust is essentially a trust, and so must have a trustee. This is usually a clearing bank or large insurance company, which acts as custodian of the fund's assets and is responsible for ensuring that the management company complies with the Financial Services Act. Although unit trusts can go down in value because of a general decrease in the value of shares, no holder of unit trusts should lose money through fraud.

Unit trusts can be bought directly from a management group, or from independent financial advisers, such as stockbrokers, insurance brokers and specialist unit trust brokers. Independent advisers earn a commission from selling the unit trusts; from 1990 they will have to reveal the amount. The rate agreed by the industry is 3%. Unit trusts may be sold by cold-calling (uninvited) salesmen, but in such cases, the buyer may cancel within 14 days of receiving a notice telling him of his right to cancel.

Complaints about dealings in unit trusts should be addressed, first of all, to the unit trust management company itself (the trustee); and if this is not fruitful, to the SRO concerned. This will be IMRO in connection with investment business, or LAUTRO in connection with the marketing of life assurance or unit trust products.

The Unit Trust Association may be of help because of its knowledge and experience of the industry, in giving advice to potential complainants.

Members can be identified by the words 'Member of the Unit Trust Association' printed on promotional literature and sometimes letterheads. No fees are charged for advice.

The unit trust ombudsman

His duties are to advise, conciliate and adjudicate on complaints from personal unit holders about unit trust management companies which are members of the scheme. This appointment is the result of powers given to LAUTRO by the Financial Services Act 1986, to regulate the marketing of unit trusts and life insurance. The unit trust ombudsman reports to an independent Council. He works alongside the insurance ombudsman and has the power to make awards of up to £100,000 against member companies; his decisions are based primarily on legal principles, but also on good investment and marketing practice.

Complaints can only be made to the unit trust ombudsman if the unit trust company and the complainant have failed to reach agreement, and the matter is referred within six months of the company's final reply.

Stockbrokers and market makers

Stockbrokers are agents for the selling of shares in companies, and may also give general investment advice.

How should you go about choosing a stockbroker? The best way may well be to follow a recommendation by a bank, a solicitor or a friend. The amount of money available for investment is an important factor, as some large firms may not be interested in small investors. A broker may offer 'execution only' services, that is, buying and selling without giving advice. In such a case, the minimum sum which the firm may require to be invested may be as low as £500.

Another consideration is the organisation of the firm, and its experience in dealing with private clients. Some stockbrokers deal mostly with companies, and are not geared up to deal with individuals. Moreover, a provincial broker may offer a more personal (and faster) service than would be available in the City of London. The recent spate of privatisations of public enterprises has created a large number of small purchasers; and institutions such as banks and building societies have introduced stockbroking services which may be more suitable for someone making small transactions.

Stockbrokers are unlikely to turn down a potential client (unless he has a record of not settling accounts), but some may decide that a particular client's needs are not right for them. You, the client, should be equally discriminating: it is, after all, your money which is being invested.

Costs are an important factor. You may be charged an annual fee, plus a percentage commission on every deal. There are now no standard rates of charge, so you may be able to negotiate. But be careful: a small annual fee may be offset by a large commission charge, and vice versa.

Potential investors should bear in mind the following points:

○ Check that your investment adviser has authorisation under the Financial Services Act 1986. If this is not clear from logos and letterheads, then you should ask the Securities and Investments Board.
○ Find out whether your adviser is independent or tied to one company (independent advice is nearly always best).
○ Get second (or even third) opinions before committing yourself to any investment suggested.
○ Do not respond to a 'cold call', that is, someone coming uninvited to your house to try and sell you investments; at the very least, get some independent advice before clinching the deal.
○ Ask your advisers what commission they will get for selling you different types of investment.
○ Use only those advisers who are covered by a professional indemnity insurance.

○ Do not be afraid to complain if things go wrong. All the SROs have complaint-handling procedures, and their members are required to mention these to clients. If you do not get a satisfactory response when you first make your complaint, do not be discouraged – persist. The SROs are there to help and advise investors – make sure that they do this in your case.

Banks

Bankers provide many different services, so that the right bank for an individual's current or deposit account may well not be the best choice for investment advice.

How do we know that a bank really is a bank? This should not be a problem to the majority of bank customers who deal with the 'big four' national banks, but it could be one for anybody involved with 'fringe' banks. The Banking and Companies Acts provide restrictions on the use of the word 'bank' and help to avoid confusion and, at times, fraud.

Many banks have different managers dealing with different areas of business. Some provide their customers with their own 'personal banker', who is often a relatively junior staff member and serves the purpose of taking pressure off senior staff.

Banking is not a registered profession; anyone employed by a bank on banking business might reasonably call himself a banker. However, many members of a bank's staff will have passed examinations to achieve particular banking qualifications, the most widely held being those awarded by the Chartered Institute of Bankers (CIB). The Institute keeps a list of its members, and may be contacted to establish whether someone is a member: but the absence of CIB qualifications should not be taken to mean a lack of experience or competence. Many bank staff who have not qualified through the Institute are highly experienced and may have specialist qualifications in accountancy or law, or those offered by the Building Societies Association (which will be dealt with later).

The Chartered Institute of Bankers has a disciplinary committee which can act only in case of personal misconduct by its members. It does not operate a code of conduct for members.

The costs of banking

Most people use banks for straightforward current and/or deposit accounts, and for them the question of costs can be very important. The best advice is to shop around to find the best bank for their purposes: one offering the lowest bank charges and the highest interest rates on deposits. The large banks publish their interest rates in the financial newspapers and in their branches. Financial services are very competitive so, as a rule, interest rates do not vary too much between different banks.

When it comes to bank charges, competition between the banks is also very fierce. Most of them offer free banking when the account is kept in credit. A warning here: if the account becomes overdrawn at any time and for any amount during the bank's charging period, the bank will apply charges for the whole of that period. This is a rule which is strictly applied, and the fact that banks require five working days to clear a deposited cheque can cause problems.

For clients whose finances are such that they are apt to let their accounts go into the red at fairly regular intervals, many banks provide special accounts: for example, ones where bank charges are payable, but at the same time interest is paid when the current account is in credit. This sort of account can be very useful, to offset the cost of bank charges. All the 'big four' banks have recently introduced systems of current accounts which pay interest.

COMPLAINTS ABOUT A BANK

As in the case of most other consumer complaints, a letter to the bank's manager or area manager (depending on the circumstances) may be effective and is preferable to a long-drawn-out procedure. However, if this proves unsatisfactory, then more formal procedures should be undertaken.

The banking ombudsman

He is independent of the banks and his function is to resolve complaints and disputes and to act as an impartial adjudicator. You do not lose any legal rights by complaining to the ombudsman, but you should first give the bank a chance to sort out the problem, either locally or at its head office. Only when the bank's own complaints procedure has been exhausted can the ombudsman formally consider a complaint. Complaints can be made about all types of personal banking service, including credit cards, cash, dispensing machines and mortgages, overdrafts and bank charges.

The great majority of banks providing personal banking services are members of the Banking Ombudsman scheme, and so are certain other designated associates, such as the Joint Credit Card Company (Access), TSB Trustcard, Barclays Bank and Midland Bank Trust Companies, and National Westminster Home Loans.

The banking ombudsman can investigate a complaint only if all of the following conditions apply:

o the bank or company is a member of the scheme
o the complaint is about something which happened on or after 1 January 1986
o the complaint is sent to the ombudsman within six months of the complainant's reaching deadlock with the bank and being informed of the existence of the ombudsman
o the claim is for under £100,000
o the complaint relates to services provided in England, Wales, Scotland or Northern Ireland.

The ombudsman will not hear complaints already dealt with by him or by a court; nor a complaint concerning a guarantee given by a company or by an individual to support a company.

Forms of complaint are sent on request by the ombudsman's office and should be returned together with a letter explaining what the bank has done wrong, what loss has been suffered, and what remedy is required. For the complaint to be investigated, all those concerned in making the complaint must usually have given their consent.

The complaint will be dealt with in confidence. If the ombudsman thinks it justified, he will try to get the bank to settle it informally; and if this cannot be done, he will make a formal recommendation for a settlement. If he thinks the complaint unjustified, he will write and inform the complainant.

There may be a problem for the consumer in the fact that there exist, in addition, an insurance ombudsman and a building societies ombudsman. The present banking ombudsman claims that in practice there is no problem about deciding to whom one should take one's complaint, because of the good working relationship that exists between the three ombudsmen, and their consequent ability to redirect cases, where appropriate.

Investment advice from banks

If investment or other financial advice is required from a bank, then the choice of bank should depend a great deal on the quality of senior staff. The only sensible advice to a potential customer is to rely on any local recommendation that may be available – particularly from other professional people, such as local solicitors or accountants, who will know which bank has the best reputation.

As was explained earlier, under the Financial Services Act 1986, institutions offering investment advice must be regulated. As well as supervision from the Bank of England, banks need separate authorisation for their activities in such areas as life assurance and unit trust management, securities dealing, trusteeship and general investment management. They are, consequently, accountable to most of the regulatory bodies: to FIMBRA, IMRO, LAUTRO, TSA or directly to SIB.

A particular problem for banks is the SIB rule of polarisation, which is that a person selling or advising on life assurance must act either as an independent intermediary, or as a company representative. If a bank decides to sell its own life assurance and unit trust products, then its branch managers may not give advice about the market as a whole. This means that a manager is debarred from recommending the products of other institutions, even if he thinks these more suitable to the customer's needs. Instead, if the product of his own bank is not appropriate, he must refer the client to another part of the group, which is authorised as an independent intermediary. As stated before, of the 'big four' High Street banks, only the National Westminster Bank has chosen to become an independent intermediary.

Banks and finance companies require a credit licence from the Office of Fair Trading to carry out their business of giving consumer credit, even if some of the agreements they make are exempted from the provisions of the Act. If agreements are entered into when the creditor has no licence, they are unenforceable, unless the Director General of OFT makes a validation order.

FINANCE COMPANIES

Finance companies are alternatives to banks when it comes to borrowing money. Many of them are, in fact, authorised banks under the Banking Act 1987. There is a trade association called the Finance Houses Association (FHA) whose members are financial institutions providing instalment credit services. A list of FHA members is available to the public.

They are required to comply with a code of practice: to behave with integrity and responsibility, to provide adequate training for members of staff, to follow any guidance from the Bank of England or FHA, and to notify FHA of anything adversely affecting the reputation of the industry.

In consumer transactions it is a member's duty to:

o   ensure that all relevant statutes are complied with
o   ensure that where a consumer believes he has been unreasonably refused credit, the application is reviewed
o   advertise prudently
o   put no pressure on a consumer to enter into a loan

o   monitor the activities of credit brokers
o   continuously examine debt-collecting procedure
o   ensure that if any credit agreement is made on the security of a debtor's home, the debtor is aware of this
o   provide correct information to credit reference agencies
o   encourage suppliers of goods financed by his firm to maintain high standards of quality and service.

Complaints about finance houses

If a complaint is made to the Finance Houses Association, it will refer this to the chief executive of the member-firm concerned, and if this does not solve the problem, FHA will conciliate.

If this is unsatisfactory, the consumer may agree to arbitration, operated by the Chartered Institute of Arbitrators. The cost of this is low, the consumer's liability being limited to twice the registration fee (between £17 and £46, depending on the amount in dispute). The arbitrator's decision is based on written submissions, and is final.

Unless the consumer has agreed to arbitration, there is nothing to prevent him from seeking redress through the courts. Clearly, a finance company which is a member of FHA should be chosen in preference to one not subject to regulatory procedures such as these.

FLEXIBLE FRIENDS?

In this modern financial world, credit cards are increasingly important. These can be very useful for providing 'easy' credit facilities, but it must be remembered that most credit card companies charge interest rates which are higher, usually, than those charged by banks for overdrafts or personal loans.

In finding out the cost of credit, the vital figure is the annual percentage rate (APR), which is reached by a complicated calculation and shows the cost over a year. When stated in monthly terms, it can appear to be far more reasonable. The APR is calculated by adding up all the charges involved in borrowing, not only interest but also fees, and any compulsory expenses, such as taking out insurance. It also takes into account the repayment period. For example, with £1000 borrowed and repayable monthly over a year, the average debt during the year is £500, because half-way through the year half of the debt has been repaid, even though interest is charged throughout the year on the whole £1000.

Building Societies

At present there are ll4 building societies competing for customers who require loans, wish to invest money, or have need of any of their other ever-expanding services.

The choice of building society depends greatly on personal preference, and also on the kind of offer made by the society for the service required. In the case of loans, for example, the majority of societies charge very similar interest rates, but some 'special offers', such as fixed-interest loans, can be significantly different. However, anyone intending to use a building society should be certain that it is a member of the Building Societies Association (BSA). To be members, societies must be authorised by the Building Societies Commission to accept shares and deposits.

If, in the opinion of the BSA's council, it is detrimental to the reputation or interest of the Association, or to its members, or to the public, that a particular building society should continue as a member, it can be expelled – this has not, in fact, happened for many years. Building societies in general are regulated by the Building Societies Commission, under the Building Societies Act 1986.

The Commission is required by statute to protect members, while at the same time promoting their financial stability. It is required to ensure that the main business of a building society remains the lending of money to its members under security of mortgage. This does not mean, however, that the societies are totally restricted to this role; they are allowed to diversify into the making of unsecured loans, and into new services, such as foreign exchange, provision of insurance and estate agency.

Like banks, building societies require authorisation from various SROs for their retail investment services. When building societies undertake to provide consumer credit, they must, like banks, be licensed under the Consumer Credit Act.

Most building society loans – that is, loans financing the purchase of land or dwelling(s) on any land – are secured by mortgage of that land, and are thus exempt from the provisions of the Act. Nevertheless, with building societies moving into the business of unsecured loans, and therefore making regulated agreements, credit licences will, in some cases, be required.

When it comes to the deals offered by the building societies to their investors and borrowers (that is, interest rates offered on deposits or interest charged on loans), there is little to choose between them. Interest rates can be very volatile, and can change very quickly; the changes are generally the same for all building societies. In the case of loans, a fixed-interest version is preferable when interest rates are likely to rise, but not when rates begin to fall.

The various deals that are on offer can be compared with each other by consulting consumer advice journals and the financial pages of the national newspapers.

COMPLAINTS ABOUT BUILDING SOCIETIES

In a similar way to banks, the first avenue of complaint is to the building society concerned, initially to the local branch, and eventually to the head office. This resort to the society's internal complaints procedure is normally a requirement before any complaint can be made to the building societies ombudsman.

The ombudsman scheme was set up under Part IX of the Building Societies' Act 1986. Complaint forms may be requested from the ombudsman's office. They require the complainant to state the complaint, the loss caused, and the amount of compensation claimed; they contain a waiver of the duty of confidence owed by the building society to its members and shareholders. Details of the scheme are available from the societies and from Citizens Advice Bureaux. The conditions for a complaint to the building societies ombudsman are:

o   It must relate to matters such as share accounts, borrowers, money transmission, foreign exchange.
o   It must be about a breach of obligations under the 1986 Act or any contract, or unfair treatment, or maladministration.
o   It must have caused financial loss, expense or inconvenience.

The ombudsman will not investigate if:

o   The complaint is frivolous.
o   The complaint is the subject of court proceedings in the UK.
o   The complaint is related to a decision on creditworthiness taken by proper procedures.
o   The complaint has to do with matters which occurred before the completion of a mortgage or an investment (in particular, faulty valuations).

The ombudsman may order a building society to pay compensation of up to £100,000.

If the society decides not to comply with the ombudsman's decision, it must, within 28 days, undertake to give notice of its reasons in its next directors' report, and also to give notice to the public in any way the ombudsman may require. A further option for the society is to request the ombudsman to state a case for the opinion of the High Court on any question of law. The obligation of the society to comply will then be suspended until the decision or any decision on appeal.

At the beginning of 1988, 9% of complaints to the ombudsman had been about automated teller (hole in the wall) machines; 9% had been about insurance; 4% about interest on early redemption of loans; 3.9% about penalty interest on withdrawing an investment; 6% about discrepancies on investment accounts caused by societies thinking that entries in passbooks were unauthorised. Complaints about MIRAS, further advances and miscellaneous types of fraud amounted to another 6%. (The remaining complaints fell into many small categories.)

Hard times

Recently, some building societies have been offering 'rescue loan packages' to people with serious debt problems. These are usually a form of re-mortgage, not second mortgages, with the loan large enough to settle current debts. The interest rate charged is higher than for unencumbered borrowers but a great deal lower than that charged by many finance companies. The National Association of Citizens Advice Bureaux advises people to see one of its counsellors before taking out another loan in this way.

Accountants

Any business registered for VAT is required by HM Customs and Excise to keep detailed records, and company law requires every company to keep proper accounting records, to file annual accounts, and to have its books audited annually.

Moreover, prospective businesses need advice about their viability and pricing and financing; businesses in operation need advice on controlling costs, managing cash, raising finance, managing growth, buying, selling or merging, and minimising tax liability.

Many individuals may well ask at this point: 'Why do I need an accountant, anyway?' The answer is that individuals can benefit greatly from accountants' advice on subjects ranging from filling in tax forms to tax planning and investments.

Many accountants practise in the form of partnerships. The best way to find a suitable firm is through personal recommendation. Which practice is best suited to one's needs depends on many different factors, such as the personalities of accountant and client, the size of the job, the specialist skills required, the location of the firm's offices and the fees charged. (Accountants claim that their fees pay themselves through the increased efficiency, tax advantages or higher profits enjoyed by their clients.)

Qualifications

Whoever the accountant chosen, he should be a qualified member of a recognised professional association.

The members of the Chartered Association of Certified Accountants (ACCA) may call themselves certified accountants. Associates become Fellows after five years of membership. Members in practice require a practising certificate, obtained after undergoing the necessary training.

The members of the Institute of Chartered Accountants in England and Wales (ICAEW) may call themselves chartered accountants. Members in practice require a practising certificate, which can be obtained by passing professional examinations, serving a training contract with a practising firm and completing post-qualification requirements. The members of the Institute of Chartered Accountants of Scotland (ICAS) may also call themselves chartered accountants.

Other professional associations involving accountancy include the Institute of Chartered Accountants in Ireland, the Chartered Institute of Cost and Management Accountants, and the Chartered Institute of Public Finance and Accountancy.

All these bodies together form the Consultative Committee of Accountancy Bodies, set up in 1974 to co-ordinate the views of the profession as a whole, with the intention of keeping accounting and auditing standards in line with current requirements.

In the United Kingdom, the accountancy profession is not regulated by the government, except in relation to statutory audit, insolvency work and investment advice. It is independent and self-regulating. As a result, anyone can set up as an accountant, and offer services (except for the three just mentioned) to the public. Therefore it is most important to make sure that the accountant you employ is a member of one of the associations mentioned here.

None of the associations provides any guidelines as to a scale of fees. The amount of fees charged will depend on the nature of the work, the extent of the expertise required, on who actually does the work (that is, partner or trainee accountant), and the time spent. It is very important that anyone about to employ an accountant should make sure to find out what his hourly rates are and to obtain an estimate beforehand of the amount that is likely to be charged. If extra work is done which was not anticipated at the beginning, the accountant may increase the fees; but under the Supply of Goods and Services Act 1982 there is an overall requirement that if no agreement has been made as to fees, the fees charged will be reasonable.

Where investment advice is concerned, the provisions of the Financial Services Act 1986 apply also to accountants. Here, too, statutory regulation is administered by self-regulating organisations. The accountants' professional associations are the 'recognised professional organisations' which authorise them to carry on the business of giving investment advice.

COMPLAINTS ABOUT ACCOUNTANTS

If an accountant should give cause for complaint, all of the professional associations provide remedies. The Institute of Chartered Accountants in England and Wales has a guide to professional ethics, providing detailed rules for members' activities.

Generally speaking, these prescribe integrity and objectivity; a regard for technical and professional standards; conduct exhibiting courtesy and consideration, and such as is consistent with the good reputation of the profession and the Institute. Members must ensure that their clients are not misled as to fees. In conducting their clients' business, members should make no improper use of information entrusted to them; and there are detailed rules as to financial involvement with clients' affairs.

Since January 1989, all member firms of the Institute must have professional indemnity insurance, in a form laid down by the Institute, if they conduct investment business. All other member firms will be required to have such insurance from the beginning of 1990.

The minimum level of cover is £50,000 for a sole practitioner. For a firm the level of cover is £50,000 or 2.5 times the estimated gross fee income for the ensuing year, whichever is the higher, but not more than £500,000.

Anyone may make a complaint to the Institute by writing to the Director of the Professional Conduct Department, with details of the grievance, and copies of relevant documents. These will first be examined by the secretariat of the Institute – which will not, however, consider complaints about fees; these may have to be settled in a court of law.

If the complaint remains unresolved, it will go to the Institute's investigation committee, which, if it thinks that a prima facie case has been made out, may bring proceedings against the member complained of before the Institute's disciplinary committee. (In exceptional circumstances, if the committee decides that the matter is one of great public concern, a different procedure, under what is known as the Joint Disciplinary Scheme, may be followed.)

If the complaint is found to have been justified, the member may be fined, or have his practising certificate removed or even be excluded from the Institute. He may be ordered to pay costs.

However, the Institute has no power to order a member to pay compensation to a client – if that is what is wanted, it can be pursued only through the courts. The disciplinary committee is advised by an independent lawyer, and the appeal committee is chaired by an independent lawyer.

The Institute of Chartered Accountants of Scotland has a very similar system to its English counterpart, including an ethical guide, an investigation committee and a discipline committee. Complaints should be addressed to the Secretary of the Institute. ICAS considers questions of fees: it has auditors to whom disputes may be remitted for adjudication. Both parties must agree to this, and must also consent to be bound by the

135

outcome, and to make arrangements for the payment of any fee settled on.

The Chartered Association of Certified Accountants also has a similar procedure for complaints. The complaint (with documents in support of the allegations) should be set out in writing, and sent to the Association's legal department. The majority of complaints are resolved by correspondence.

If this fails, there is an investigations committee, which may decide that a prima facie case has been made against the member and refer the matter to a disciplinary committee for a decision. Penalties including fines, costs and exclusion from membership can be imposed on the member. There is provision for an appeal committee, if necessary.

Like the Institutes, the Association has rules of professional conduct and will appoint an arbitrator, to settle complaints if both parties consent to this. The Association will likewise appoint an arbitrator to determine a fee dispute. Since 1989, all its members must be covered by professional indemnity insurance.

The insurance profession

The type of insurance which has grown particularly rapidly in recent years is life insurance, both in itself and in connection with pension schemes and/or mortgages. A multiplicity of life insurance schemes has become available from diverse sources: not only insurance brokers, but banks and building societies, with advice also being offered by other professionals.

The people in the business of selling insurance with whom members of the public are most likely to come into contact are intermediaries who sell the products of insurance companies. Before the 1970s there was no legislation to prevent anyone at all from setting up in business as an insurance salesman. This gave great scope for negligence and fraud. At present, the authorisation and registration provisions in the Insurance Companies

Act 1982 and the Insurance Brokers (Registration) Act 1977 (as explained earlier) provide a great deal of protection to the public. Insurance intermediaries may be accountants, solicitors, building societies, estate agents, mortgage brokers or many other related professionals: the term 'insurance brokers' is sometimes loosely – but incorrectly – used for these as well as for the registered insurance brokers.

SIB rules insist that anyone selling life insurance must identify himself as belonging to one of two distinct groups: either wholly independent intermediaries, or representatives selling the products of one company only, so that the market is polarised.

The right advice about choosing an insurance policy or scheme should be based on the circumstances of each individual case; so independent professional advice is essential. When looking for an adviser, personal recommendation is the first thing to go by. However, there are many professional associations in the insurance field, and it would be unwise to rely on someone who was not a member of such an association.

The Chartered Insurance Institute (CII)

Anyone who is employed or engaged in the insurance industry can be a member. Most members either are employees of insurance companies or sell insurance on a commission basis.

Diplomas of Associateship and Fellowship are awarded to those who complete the Institution's examinations and Fellows may use the titles 'Chartered Insurer' or 'Chartered Insurance Practitioner', according to their occupation within the insurance industry.

The Institute has a code of conduct requiring members to give to the public full information about the suitability, scope and limitations of any insurance contract being negotiated. Members must also comply with the law in general, and must ensure that any advertisements and public announcements will not bring the Institute into disrepute. Furthermore, members who do not comply with the current standards of professional conduct may be subject to the procedures of the disciplinary committee.

Complaints about CII members

Complaints should be addressed to the Secretary-General, and will be investigated. The Institute says that in the whole period of existence it has never yet been necessary to resort to arbitration.

The British Insurance and Investment Brokers' Association (BIIBA)

Members of the Association are insurance or investment brokers. They are subject to the Financial Services Act and must be registered as insurance brokers with the Insurance Brokers Registration Council which was established under the Insurance Brokers Registration Council Act 1977.

The Association has approximately 4000 member firms, a list of which is available in libraries and Citizens Advice Bureaux. Another way of ascertaining that a firm is a member is to ask to see its annual membership certificate.

The Association does not attempt to control fees, chiefly because its member firms usually deal on a commission basis. But it has a code of conduct, which is the same as that of the Insurance Brokers Registration Council. This specifies the kind of behaviour which will be treated as unprofessional conduct, for example:

○ breach of the duty of utmost good faith and integrity
○ not doing everything possible to satisfy the insurance requirements of clients, and not placing the interests of those clients before other considerations
○ making misleading or extravagant statements when advertising.

Brokers are also required to explain to clients, if asked, the relative cost of different types of insurance. Again, if asked, they must disclose what commission they are getting, as well as any additional charges, before closing the deal. When the proposal form is being filled out, a broker is required to make it clear to the client that all answers or statements on the form are solely the client's responsibility.

Complaints about BIIBA members

Complaints about members of BIIBA should be sent (giving details) to the consumer relations officer at BIIBA House. A member who is in breach of statutory duties can be expelled from the Association, but the main disciplinary sanctions are governed by the Insurance Brokers Registration Council.

The Institute of Insurance Consultants (IIC)

Members of the Institute are insurance or financial consultants; they do not necessarily have to pass examinations (although rules of the Institute allow it to make the passing of an examination a condition of membership, or of a higher grade of membership).

To qualify for membership, an intending member must have a minimum of two years' experience as an insurance intermediary; must hold professional insurance cover; must provide references; and must give an undertaking that he will either not handle clients' money or will keep all clients' money in clients' trust accounts. Before his membership is renewed, a member is required to give proof that his professional insurance cover is still in force, and to provide a solvency certificate.

The Institute does not provide a scale of fees, because its member firm generally deal on a commission basis.

However, in the case of life insurance and investment business, members can choose whether to declare the rate of commission they receive, or tell clients that they charge fees only according to the scale laid down by their regulatory body (which, in such a case, is likely to be the LAUTRO or SIB).

The Institute of Insurance Consultants has a code of conduct which requires the utmost integrity from all members in dealing with fellow members and others. Information given to a client must be to that client's best advantage, and advertising must not be misleading or extravagant. Each member must comply with any legislation applicable to the particular client's business, and ensure that his employees understand and apply the code of conduct.

Complaints against IIC members

There is a complaints and disciplinary committee to investigate complaints and infringements of the code. These may include discrimination, fraud, contravention of legislation or engaging in deceitful or otherwise unfair or improper business practices. If a member is found guilty of any of these, his membership may be suspended or cancelled.

Anyone with a complaint against a member should send it in writing to the Institute's head office. An investigation and regulation officer will conduct initial enquiries before submitting the case to the disciplinary committee, if he thinks this necessary.

The Institute of Insurance Brokers (IIB)

Membership of this Institute is strictly confined to insurance brokers registered with the Insurance Brokers Registration Council, having satisfied the Council that they have adequate qualifications and experience.

There are no rules as to fees (because members are paid by commission), but there is a code of conduct which regulates good practice. Brokers must display in their offices a notice stating that a copy of the code is available on request.

The code defines good practice as conducting business with the utmost good faith and integrity; doing everything possible to satisfy the insurance requirements of clients; and not making misleading statements when advertising. Specific examples of unprofessional conduct are: not explaining, when asked, the different terms and costs of the different types of insurance available; not declaring the rate of commission, when asked; withholding from clients any written information without adequate and justifiable reasons; and not having proper regard for the wishes of a client who wants to terminate an agreement.

A member must obtain the consent of a client before disclosing or using information he has acquired about him.

Any advertising must conform to the code of the Advertising Standards Authority, and must clearly distinguish between those benefits which the insurance policy is bound to provide, and the ones which will accrue if the insurer's own forecast of future events is correct.

Complaints about IIB members

Any complaints about members should be sent to the Institute, whose disciplinary committee will investigate them thoroughly. All members of the Institute are required to have at least £250,000 insurance cover in respect of errors or omissions causing loss to consumers.

The Corporation of Insurance and Financial Advisors (CIFA)

The Corporation is the trade body for independent financial advisers. Membership is open to any independent financial adviser who is able to meet the strict criteria and code of conduct set by the Corporation. Members applying to the Corporation are required to have at least two years' appropriate experience. For Associateship, a minimum requirement of four years' senior experience is necessary; Associateship may also be awarded to those who sit and pass the Associateship examination. Fellowship of the Corporation requires, in addition to many years of proven expertise and experience at senior level, the submission of a thesis on a given subject and/or the sitting and passing of the Fellowship examination. Companies may be incorporated into membership; such incorporation carries the designation of 'Incorporated Insurance & Financial Advisors'.

It is mandatory for all applicants who join the Corporation to have professional indemnity cover of at least £250,000; but where the applicants are also authorised by FIMBRA, this cover may be reduced to £100,000. On applying to join the Corporation, applicants must provide copies of their current consumer credit licence and professional indemnity cover. For companies being incorporated, a certificate of solvency must be produced. Incorporated companies are also required to produce a current certificate of solvency on renewal. When an applicant is being considered for membership, the Corporation makes numerous searches to ensure that the applicant is a fit and proper person to become a member of CIFA.

No guidelines are provided by the Corporation as to scale of fees which members should charge where fees are appropriate.

The Corporation has a strict code of conduct which all members of the Corporation must follow. All members must act in their clients' best interest and must, at all times, give 'best advice'.

Complaints about CIFA members

Any complaints concerning business handled by a member of the Corporation should be reported to CIFA Headquarters for investigation and consideration by the disciplinary committee, which has powers to suspend or expel any member from the Corporation if the complaint is found to be justified.

The Life Insurance Association (LIA)

Members are collective investment advisers (principally on life insurance, pensions and unit trusts) or financial planners. Generally speaking, the aim of LIA is to promote professionalism, ethics and good practice. Applicants for membership may become provisional members after six months in insurance and can become full members after two years.

The Association has a code of conduct which embodies fundamentally the same principles as those of the other insurance associations. Its ethics committee deals with complaints about members, with an ultimate sanction of expulsion. Complaints must be in writing and addressed to the ethics committee, and must be in connection with the business carried on by LIA members.

Society of Pension Consultants (SPC)

The membership of the society is corporate (not open to individuals), and brings together a wide range of professionals such as actuaries, solicitors, accountants, bankers and investment analysts whose work has to do with the establishment and operation of pension schemes.

The Society has a code of conduct which aims to ensure that members act with the utmost good faith, integrity, honesty and concern for those who seek advice. Members must act impartially and independently, keeping the interest of their clients paramount at all times; a member company must offer advice only in areas in which it is proficient.

The rules of the Society include disciplinary procedures which may culminate in loss of membership. This may be of some help to a complainant, but the Society emphasises that invoking the statutory protection for investors may often be a more attractive alternative. The Society decided at the outset of investor-protection legislation that it could not properly combine its role as an advocate of members' views with the power to put them out of business.

The more general aim of the Society is to draw on the knowledge and experience of its members to influence legislation and other developments relating to pensions, and to raise professional standards in all aspects of pension services.

The Occupational Pensions Advisory Service (OPAS)

This service is a charity whose object is to give advice and assistance to members of the public on matters relating to occupational pension schemes. However, complainants are asked to put their query first to the administrators (usually trustees) of the scheme in which they are involved.

OPAS can be approached directly, or through local advisory services such as Citizens Advice Bureaux. It has a network of 150 advisers throughout the UK, backed by a panel of experts, who take over if the problem is a complex one. It provides guidelines as to the types of cases where it may be able to help, based on the fact that the service relates to occupational, not personal pension arrangements, and that it can do no more than clarify the general terms and options available. OPAS cannot give financial advice or help with negotiations about joining or changing to an occupational scheme, nor can it advise on funding arrangements, personal pensions or free-standing AVCs (additional voluntary contributions).

Although it does not undertake formal arbitration or initiate legal action, it will explain how someone can take such action. It is not a pressure group for improvements, nor an advocate of one type of pension scheme over another.

The service can be of great help to holders of occupational pensions, but only in the way of advice.

Lloyd's

Any insurance policy issued by Lloyd's underwriters will have been effected through a broker, and any complaints about policy effected by a UK resident in his private capacity should be made in writing to Lloyd's Consumer Enquiries Department.

This department deals with complaints and disputes in connection with UK personal insurance policies effected with underwriters at Lloyd's. It also investigates third-party complaints, and complaints relating to brokers: the service is free. The nature of the investigation differs from case to case, but can involve full access to underwriters' files, interviews with the interested parties, and the seeking of legal opinion.

The chairman or deputy chairman of Lloyds can be asked to intervene in a dispute. Lloyd's are also members of the Insurance Ombudsman Bureau.

Lloyd's subscribe to the Statement of General Insurance Practice which contains recommendations for best practice in insurance matters such as proposal forms, claims and renewals.

Lloyd's Motor Underwriters Association (LMUA)

Membership of this Association is restricted to Lloyd's Motor Underwriting Syndicates whose principles of conduct are

144

expressed in the Statement of General Insurance Practice. Complaints regarding the business of individual Members are always referred to the Lloyd's Consumer Enquiries Department. LMUA has now joined the Insurance Ombudsman scheme.

The Association of British Insurers (ABI)

This Association emphasises that it is a trade association and not a professional association, so that it exists primarily to further the aims of its members, rather than to help the public.

However, in 1988 the ABI produced a code of conduct for non-broker intermediaries who sell motor, home, travel or other general insurance. The essence of the code is that such intermediaries must tell future policy holders whether they represent one company or several, and are required to take out professional indemnity cover in the same way as registered brokers.

This code has been criticised because it is voluntary, and because it does not provide for a compensation fund. The ABI's reply is that since it is a trade association, any control can only be voluntary; and that a compensation fund is not necessary, because of the indemnity regulations.

LOSS ADJUSTERS AND LOSS ASSESSORS

Loss adjusters are professional people who are qualified to decide how much insurers should pay towards the cost of claims. For example, they may be called upon to assess how much of the damage to a roof was done by a storm, and how much was due to poor condition in the first place. Loss adjusters are independent, but their fees are paid by insurance companies.

A loss assessor is an independent professional who may be called in by an insured person to help with the settlement of his claim. It is the insured person who pays the assessor (usually on a percentage basis); the fee must be paid whether the assessor argues the case successfully or not.

The professional associations for these professions are as follows:

The Chartered Institute of Loss Adjusters (CILA)

Members of the Institute are required to pass a series of professional examinations to become Associates. The Institute has a code of conduct, the fundamental principle of which is the preservation of impartiality – so that, for example, the Institute will not sanction a member and an insurer sharing profits.

All complaints about members should be sent to the Charter and Etiquette committee and will be fully investigated.

The Insurance Adjusters Association (IAA)

Members (who may include surveyors, solicitors and other professionals) must pass examinations similar to those set by the Chartered Institute of Loss Adjusters.

Complaints of unprofessional conduct are investigated by the Council and may result in suspension or expulsion. In some cases, complaints may be sent for arbitration by the insurance ombudsman.

The rules of conduct include a general requirement of impartiality and a duty to act exclusively on behalf of insurers.

The Institute of Public Loss Assessors (IPLA)

Members of the Institute are public loss assessors but may also belong to other professions, such as surveyors or architects.

To obtain membership, candidates must have experience in loss assessing, and must submit a thesis.

The Institute has no rules as to the amount of fees. Its code of conduct requires the preservation of complete impartiality, complete independence and complete integrity. Complaints about members, giving full details, should be addressed to the Secretary. A full investigation by the Institute's national council will follow.

Why all these associations?

The existence of such a number of professional associations connected with insurance has important implications for members of the public who intend to make contracts of insurance.

As explained earlier, there are statutes which provide that insurance brokers must be registered, and that only authorised companies may carry on insurance business in the UK. What extra advantages are given to the public by the professional insurance associations?

In the first place, a number of these associations were involved in drawing up the statutes. Although such associations are formed for the benefit of their members, it is in their interest to carry out a thorough screening of potential members and to discipline current members who transgress their rules.

Secondly, the very fact that an insurance company, a broker or an intermediary is a member of a professional association is an assurance to the wary consumer that he is dealing with a responsible organisation.

Thirdly, the existence of different kinds of insurance association may help in choosing the right person to ask advice from. For example, if you want detailed and independent advice on choosing the correct pension for your circumstances, you may consider employing a pensions consultant (preferably a member of the Society of Pension Consultants), paying a fee direct to the consultant. This advice will, however, cost you something in the region of £50-80 an hour. Members of the Society are also willing to act for clients on the basis of commission from an insurance company, with no direct charge to the client. Insurance brokers would argue that they could give you equally independent advice, free and with no obligation. The final choice must rest with you.

COMPLAINING ABOUT INSURANCE

There are numerous bodies to which complaints to do with insurance can be taken. Though most of the insurance associations have codes of conduct and complaint-handling procedures, the independent agencies may, in general, prove more effective.

The Insurance Ombudsman Bureau

The insurance ombudsman can attempt to settle a dispute in which an insurance company is involved, provided that it is a member of the Voluntary Insurance Ombudsman Scheme (most companies are). It must be emphasised that the ombudsman can only handle complaints against companies – not against brokers or intermediaries. The complainants must be private policy-holders, and the dispute must be with their own insurer, not someone else's. Typical complaints have been that the amount offered by a company to settle a claim was too low; that a company turned down a claim unreasonably; that there was delay in settling a claim. Generally speaking, policyholders have complained when they felt they had not been treated fairly in some way.

The ombudsman's work is supervised by an independent council, and together the two are called the Insurance Ombudsman Bureau. The scheme is an alternative to legal proceedings.

The complainant should approach the insurance ombudsman only if he and the head office of the insurance company have failed to reach agreement; he may contact him through the local office of the insurance company or through the chief executive at its head office, but many complaints are made directly to the ombudsman. A complaint must be made, preferably in writing, within six months of the company's final decision on the dispute. It should include details such as the name of the company and the policy number, together with a brief outline of the reasons for complaining, and should be sent to the Insurance Ombudsman Bureau.

The ombudsman will investigate; he usually makes a decision based on documents and may use expert advice. On rare occasions he may call a hearing, which the complainant will be asked to attend. If the complaint is accepted, the ombudsman may order the insurance company to make an award of up to £100,000; or he may prefer to make a recommendation without any financial award. If the complainant rejects the ombudsman's decision, this does not affect his right to take legal proceedings.

Arrangements have been made with LAUTRO for the unit trust ombudsman to work alongside the insurance ombudsman in the same bureau, and using the same administrative facilities. This has extended the scope of referrable complaints to cover unit trusts and has added good investment or marketing practice to good insurance practice as part of the rationale for awards.

The Insurance Brokers Registration Council (IBRC)
This was set up by the Insurance Brokers (Registration) Act 1977. To make a complaint about a broker, write to the Registrar at the Council's office.

The Council will investigate alleged breaches of the IBRC rules. However, complaints about the alleged negligence of brokers would have to be dealt with by the courts.

The Policyholders Protection Board
This Board was set up under the terms of the Policyholders Protection Act 1975. It is concerned only with insurance companies which are in financial difficulties; usually, with those already in liquidation. Either the Board or the liquidator will get in touch with the policyholders.

The Personal Insurance Arbitration Service (PIAS)
The Arbitration Service aims to help policyholders with claims arising from personal insurance. Policyholders may be referred to the service by the insurance company concerned, if it is a subscriber to the service, or through the Association of British Insurers.

There is no charge to policyholders for the service, which is based at the Chartered Institute of Arbitrators. Application for arbitration must be made through and with the agreement of the insurance company, from which an application form can be obtained. This names the parties involved, and contains a brief outline of the dispute and a signed declaration by both parties that they agree to arbitration, and to be bound by the arbitrator's decision. Awards under the Arbitration Service are legally enforceable in the courts. As with other arbitration, you cannot go back to taking legal action against the company concerned if you are dissatisfied with the arbitrator's decision.

Chartered Institute of Arbitrators

Arbitration is a process which requires that the parties to a dispute should consent to refer their dispute either to an arbitrator of their choice, or to one appointed by an independent body, such as the Chartered Institute of Arbitrators.

An arbitrator who is a member of the Institute is normally an expert in the field of dispute, as well as having qualified in the law, practice and procedure of arbitration. In general, therefore, arbitration is a secondary profession.

The Chartered Institute of Arbitrators is the professional body for arbitrators, drawing its membership from across the professional spectrum, as well as from commerce and industry.

The Institute has at present two grades of member: Associates and Fellows. Entry into the Associate grade is by examination or by arbitration experience. Associates become Fellows by examination, and by being able to show that they possess judicial capacity. Listing on the Panels of Arbitrators is restricted to Fellows who have successfully completed pupillage under a practising arbitrator.

Membership of the Panels is reviewed every three years and the members have to show to a Panel Sub-Committee that they have kept themselves up to date in the law, practice and procedure of arbitration.

The Institute provides no guidelines for fees. It does not have a code of conduct, but members are expected to behave in a professional manner, offering only the highest standard of service. If a member of the public wishes to complain about an arbitrator who is a member of the Institute, an investigation will be undertaken by the Institute's Professional Conduct Committee. Details of the complaint should be sent to the Secretary. If parties feel that the arbitrator has not acted judicially, or has made a fundamental mistake in law in the course of an arbitration, then their recourse is through the courts.

In 1988, the Consumer Arbitration Agreements Act was passed. It affects the validity of agreements to submit to arbitration made by consumers. If a claim amounts to £500 or less, then the consumer cannot be forced to submit his claim to arbitration, even by express agreement, such as having signed a contract form. If a claim amounts to between £500 and £5000, any agreement to submit to arbitration can only be enforced if it can be shown that it would not be detrimental to the interests of the consumer.

The Act is applicable when the dispute is one that can be taken to the small claims court, as an alternative to arbitration. It is a statute of some value to a consumer, who now does not have to have arbitration forced upon him (if the conditions of the Act apply) in cases where arbitration would be the more expensive alternative.

USEFUL ADDRESSES

ASSOCIATION OF BRITISH INSURERS (ABI)
Aldermary House
Queen Street
London EC4N 1TT
01-248 4477

Membership: voluntary
Membership list: free on request
Fee guidelines: no
Code of conduct: yes, for intermediaries in general insurance
Complaints procedure: yes
Complaint-handling charge: no
Disciplinary sanctions: no

ASSOCIATION OF FUTURES BROKERS AND DEALERS (AFBD)
5th floor, Section B
Plantation House
5-8 Mincing Lane
London EC3M 3DX
01-626 9763

Membership: voluntary; members must be in good business standing
Membership list: free on request from AFBD
Fee guidelines: no
Code of conduct: yes
Complaints procedure: yes
Complaint-handling charge: no
Disciplinary sanctions: rebuke; fine; suspension; expulsion; payment of compensation

BANKING OMBUDSMAN
Citadel House
5-11 Fetter Lane
London EC4A 1BR
01-583 1395

Complaints procedure: yes
Complaint-handling charge: no
Powers: monetary award to complainant

BRITISH INSURANCE AND INVESTMENT BROKERS' ASSOCIATION (BIIBA)
BIIBA House
14 Bevis Marks
London EC3A 7NT
01-623 9043

Membership: voluntary; members must be registered under the Financial Services Act 1986 and/or be registered insurance brokers
Membership list: available in libraries, CABx, etc; local lists free from BIIBA
Fee guidelines: no; payment is usually by commission
Code of conduct: yes
Complaints procedure: yes
Complaint-handling charge: no
Disciplinary sanctions: expulsion

BUILDING SOCIETIES ASSOCIATION (BSA)
3 Savile Row
London W1X 1AF
01-437 0655

Membership: voluntary: society must be authorised by the Building Societies Commission
Membership list: free on request
Code of conduct: no; members must conform to Building Societies Act 1986
Complaints procedure: each member has own procedure, after which recourse is to the Building Societies Ombudsman
Disciplinary sanctions: expulsion

BUILDING SOCIETIES OMBUDSMAN
Grosvenor Gardens House
35-37 Grosvenor Gardens
London SW1X 7AW
01-931 0044

Complaints procedure: yes
Complaints-handling charge: no
Powers: monetary award to complainant

153

CHARTERED ASSOCIATION OF CERTIFIED ACCOUNTANTS (ACCA)
29 Lincoln's Inn Fields
London WC2A 3EE
01-242 6855

Membership: conditional on passing professional examinations; also open to chartered accountants
Style of qualification: ACCA (Associate); FCCA (Fellow)
Membership list: from the Membership Department
Fee guidelines: no
Code of conduct: yes
Complaints procedure: yes
Complaint-handling charge: no
Disciplinary sanctions: rebuke; fine; suspension; withdrawal of practising certificate or insolvency licence; exclusion; fine

CHARTERED INSTITUTE OF ARBITRATORS
75 Cannon Street
London EC4N 5BH
01-236 8761

Membership: voluntary; conditional on passing professional examinations
Style of qualification: ACIArb (Associate); FCIArb (Fellow)
Membership list: available from the Institute
Fee guidelines: no
Code of conduct: no
Complaints procedure: yes
Complaint-handling charge: no
Disciplinary sanctions: reprimand; supension; expulsion

CHARTERED INSTITUTE OF BANKERS
10 Lombard Street
London EC3V 9AS
01-623 3531

Membership: voluntary; professional examination qualifications
    required
Style of qualification: ACIB (Associate); FCIB (Fellow) DipFS
    (Financial Studies Diploma)
Membership list: enquiries as to membership answered
Code of conduct: no
Complaints procedure: yes, in cases of individual misconduct
Complaint-handling charge: no
Disciplinary sanctions: termination of membership

CHARTERED INSTITUTE OF LOSS ADJUSTERS (CILA)

Manfield House
276 Strand
London WC2R 0LR
01-240 1496

Membership: professional examination qualifications and prac-
    tical experience required
Style of qualification: ACILA (Associate); FCILA (Fellow)
Membership list: free of charge from CILA office
Fee guidelines: no
Code of conduct: yes
Complaints procedure: yes
Complaint-handling charge: no
Disciplinary sanctions: reprimand; suspension; expulsion

CHARTERED INSTITUTE OF PUBLIC FINANCE AND
ACCOUNTANCY (CIPFA)

3 Robert Street
London WC2N 6BH
01-930 3456

CHARTERED INSURANCE INSTITUTE (CII)

20 Aldermanbury
London EC2V 7HY
01-606 3835

Membership: voluntary; professional examination qualifications required
Style of qualification: ACII (Associate); FCII (Fellow)
Membership list: available from the Institute
Code of conduct: yes
Complaints procedure: yes
Complaint-handling charge: no
Disciplinary sanctions: reprimand; suspension; expulsion

CORPORATION OF INSURANCE AND FINANCIAL ADVISORS (CIFA)
6-7 Leapale Road
Guildford Surrey GU1 4JX
0483-39121

Membership: voluntary; experience required; professional examination qualifications required for Fellowship
Style of qualification: MCIFA (Member); ACIFA (Associate); FCIFA (Fellow) *Membership list:* local list free on request from CIFA head office
Fee guidelines: no
Code of conduct: yes
Complaints procedure: yes
Complaint-handling charge: no
Disciplinary sanctions: expulsion

FINANCE HOUSES ASSOCIATION (FHA)
18 Upper Grosvenor Street
London W1X 9PB
01-491 2783

Membership: voluntary
Membership list: free on request from FHA office
Code of conduct: yes
Complaints procedure: yes
Complaint-handling charge: no
Disciplinary sanctions: warning; expulsion

FINANCIAL INTERMEDIARIES, MANAGERS AND BROKERS REGULATORY ASSOCIATION (FIMBRA)
22 Great Tower Street
London EC3R 5AQ
01-929 2711

Code of conduct: yes
Complaint-handling charge: no
Disciplinary sanctions: reprimand: restrictions on firm's business; expulsion

HOME SERVICE INSURERS GROUP
Aldermary House
Queen Street
London EC4N 1TT
01-248 4477

Code of conduct: Financial Services Act 1986
Complaints procedure: yes, for 'industrial life' insurance
Complaint-handling charge: no
Disciplinary sanctions: no

INSTITUTE OF BANKERS IN IRELAND
Nassau House
Nassau Street
Dublin 2
Republic of Ireland
0001-793 311

Membership: voluntary; professional examination qualifications required
Style of qualification: MIB (Member); MIB Grad (Graduate); FIB (Fellow)
Membership list: membership enquiries answered
Code of conduct: voluntary code of ethics
Complaints procedure: yes
Complaint-handling charge: no
Disciplinary sanctions: loss of membership

INSTITUTE OF BANKERS IN SCOTLAND
20 Rutland Square
Edinburgh EH1 2DE
031-229 9869

Membership: voluntary; professional examination qualification required
Style of qualification: DIP IB (Scot) (Diploma); AIB (Scot) (Associate); FIB (Scot) (Fellow)
Membership list: not available
Code of conduct: in preparation
Complaints procedure: no
Disciplinary sanctions: termination of membership

INSTITUTE OF CHARTERED ACCOUNTANTS IN ENGLAND AND WALES (ICAEW)
PO Box 433
Chartered Accountants' Hall
Moorgate Place
London EC2P 2BJ
01-628 7060

Membership: all chartered accountants must belong
Style of qualification: ACA (Associate); FCA (Fellow)
Membership list: available from head office
Fee guidelines: no
Code of conduct: yes
Complaints procedure: yes
Complaint-handling charge: no
Disciplinary sanctions: ranging from fine to exclusion from membership

INSTITUTE OF CHARTERED ACCOUNTANTS IN IRELAND
Chartered Accountants' House
87-89 Pembroke Road
Dublin 4
0001-680 400

INSTITUTE OF CHARTERED ACCOUNTANTS OF SCOTLAND (ICAS)

27 Queen Street
Edinburgh EH2 lLA
031-225 5673

Membership: all chartered accountants must belong
Style of qualification: CA
Membership list: may be consulted in libraries
Fee guidelines: no
Code of conduct: yes
Complaints procedure: yes
Complaint-handling charge: no
Disciplinary sanctions: rebuke; suspension; withdrawal of prac-
    tising certificate/permit; fine; expulsion

INSTITUTE OF INSURANCE BROKERS (IIB)

Barclays Bank Chambers
College Street
Rushden
Northamptonshire NN10 0NW
0933-4l0003

Membership: restricted to registered insurance brokers
Membership list: available on request
Code of conduct: yes
Complaints procedure: yes
Complaint-handling charge: no
Disciplinary sanctions: reprimand; expulsion

INSTITUTE OF INSURANCE CONSULTANTS (IIC)

PO Box 38l
121a Queensway
Bletchley
Milton Keynes MK1 1XZ
0908-643364

Membership: voluntary; higher grades of membership may require examination qualifications
Style of qualification: M InstIC (member); A InstIC (Associate); F InstIC (Fellow)
Membership list: may be consulted at IIC office or in libraries
Fee guidelines: no
Code of conduct: yes
Complaints procedure: yes
Complaint-handling charge: no
Disciplinary sanctions: suspension; termination of membership

INSTITUTE OF PUBLIC LOSS ASSESSORS (IPLA)
14 Red Lion Street
Chesham
Buckinghamshire HP5 1HB
0494-782342

Membership: voluntary; experience and presentation of thesis required
Style of qualification: MIPLA (Member); FIPLA (Fellow)
Membership list: available from IPLA office
Fee guidelines: no
Complaints procedure: yes
Code of conduct: yes
Complaint-handling charge: no
Disciplinary sanctions: termination of membership

INSURANCE ADJUSTERS ASSOCIATION (IAA)
152 Commercial Street
London E1 6NU
01-377 0282

Membership: voluntary; professional examination qualifications required, plus experience in an adjusting firm
Style of qualification: AIAA (Associate); FIAA (Fellow)

Membership list: available from Secretary of IAA
Code of conduct: yes
Complaints procedure: yes
Complaint-handling charge: no
Disciplinary sanctions: suspension; expulsion

INSURANCE BROKERS REGISTRATION COUNCIL
15 St Helen's Place
London EC3A 6DS
01-588 4387

Code of conduct: yes
Complaints procedure: yes, against insurance/life assurance brokers (not complaints alleging negligence)
Complaint-handling charge: no
Disciplinary sanctions: deregistration

INSURANCE OMBUDSMAN BUREAU
31 Southampton Row
London WC1B 5HJ
01-242 8613

Complaints procedure: yes
Complaint-handling charge: no
Powers: monetary award to complainant

INVESTMENT MANAGEMENT REGULATORY ORGANISATION LIMITED (IMRO)
Centre Point
103 New Oxford Street
London WC1A 1PT
01-379 0601

Complaints procedure: yes; referee procedure available
Complaint-handling charge: no, unless complaint unreasonable
Disciplinary sanctions: monetary award

LIFE ASSURANCE AND UNIT TRUST REGULATORY ORGANISATION (LAUTRO)

Centre Point
103 New Oxford Street
London WC1A 1QH
01-379 0444

Code of conduct: yes
Complaints procedure: yes; direct to LAUTRO, except where LAUTRO members complained of subscribe to the Insurance Ombudsman Bureau or IMRO Referee Scheme, when complaint should be made to these
Complaint-handling charge: no
Disciplinary sanctions: reprimand, order for compensation, restrictions on business, suspension, expulsion

LIFE INSURANCE ASSOCIATION (LIA)

Citadel House
Station Approach
Chorleywood
Rickmansworth
Hertfordshire WD3 5PF
09278-533

Membership: voluntary; restricted to life, pensions and unit trust advisers
Style of qualification: MLIA (Member by Diploma); ALIA (Associate); FLIA (Fellow); all require professional examination pass
Membership list: not available
Fee guidelines: no
Code of conduct: yes
Complaints procedure: yes
Complaint-handling charge: no
Disciplinary sanctions: suspension; expulsion

LLOYD'S
One Lime Street
London EC3M 7HA
01-623 7100

Code of conduct: yes
Complaints procedure: yes, for complaints about Lloyd's syndicates or brokers only
Complaint-handling charge: no
Disciplinary sanctions: ranging from reprimand to deregistration

LLOYD'S MOTOR UNDERWRITERS' ASSOCIATION (LMUA)
Irongate House
Dukes Place
London EC3A 7LP
01-626 7006/7235

Membership: voluntary; only Lloyd's Motor Underwriters/ Syndicates may belong; all are members
Membership list: free on request from LMUA office
Fee guidelines: no
Code of conduct: yes
Complaints procedure: consumer complaints are referred to Lloyd's Consumer Enquiries Department
Disciplinary sanctions: no

OCCUPATIONAL PENSIONS ADVISORY SERVICE (OPAS)
8A Bloomsbury Square
London WC1A 2LP
01-831 5511

Code of conduct: no
Complaints procedure: yes
Complaint-handling charge: no
Disciplinary sanctions: no

PERSONAL INSURANCE ARBITRATION SERVICE (PIAS)
c/o Chartered Institute of Arbitrators
75 Cannon Street
London EC4N 5BH
01-236 8761

Code of conduct: yes
Complaints procedure: yes
Complaint-handling charge: no
Disciplinary sanctions: legally binding monetary awards

POLICYHOLDERS PROTECTION BOARD
Aldermary House
Queen Street
London EC4N lTT
01-248 4477

Code of conduct: no
Complaints procedure: only complaints about insurance
companies in or on the verge of liquidation
Complaint-handling charge: no

SECURITIES AND INVESTMENTS BOARD (SIB)
3 Royal Exchange Buildings
London EC3V 3NL
01-283 2474

SECURITIES ASSOCIATION
see THE SECURITIES ASSOCIATION

SOCIETY OF PENSION CONSULTANTS (SPC)
Ludgate House
Ludgate Circus
London EC4A 2AB
01-353 l688

Membership: voluntary; corporate
Membership list: free on request from SPC office
Fee guidelines: no
Code of conduct: yes
Complaints procedure: yes
Complaint-handling charge: no
Disciplinary sanctions: rebuke; suspension; expulsion

THE SECURITIES ASSOCIATION (TSA)
The Stock Exchange Building
London EC2N 1EQ
01-256 9000

Code of conduct: yes
Complaints procedure: yes; only about TSA and ISE
(International Stock Exchange) members; Complaints and
Conciliation Bureau 01-588 2355
Complaint-handling charge: no
Disciplinary sanctions: de-authorisation of member firm

UNIT TRUST ASSOCIATION (UTA)
65 Kingsway
London WC2B 6TD
01-831 0898

Code of conduct: yes
Complaints procedure: yes
Complaint-handling charge: no
Disciplinary sanctions: yes

UNIT TRUST OMBUDSMAN
31 Southampton Row
London WC1B 5HJ
01-242 8613

Code of conduct: yes
Complaint-handling charge: no
Powers: monetary awards to complainant

Estate Agents

To find a buyer for your house, you do not need to use an estate agent, but it is generally the quickest and most reliable way.

The Estate Agents Act 1979

All estate agents are bound by this Act. Failure to comply with it may lead to criminal proceedings, usually by the Trading Standards Department of the local authority, which has the power to enter offices and to require the production of books or other documents. In some cases, a client may have a right to bring a civil (as opposed to criminal) action under the Act.

The Office of Fair Trading is responsible for policing the Estate Agents Act, and can issue warning or prohibition orders to estate agents. A prohibition order can ban someone from doing any estate agency work at all, so is a powerful weapon. Such an order is usually preceded by a warning order.

Anyone who is not a bankrupt can set up as an estate agent, and anyone (including bankrupts) can work for estate agents. The only restriction is that under the Estate Agents Act, the Director General of Fair Trading can ban an 'unfit' person from taking part in estate agency work; for instance, someone who has been found guilty of fraud, or of racial or sexual discrimination.

CHOOSING AN ESTATE AGENT

Estate agents are not obliged to belong to any professional body. If an estate agent decides to apply for membership of a professional body, it is most likely to be one of three: the

National Association of Estate Agents (NAEA), the Royal Institution of Chartered Surveyors (RICS), or the Incorporated Society of Valuers and Auctioneers (ISVA). To be eligible for membership of RICS or ISVA, he must pass their examinations. The RICS examinations include a test of professional competence; continuing membership requires continuing professional development, such as refresher courses.

NAEA also sets examinations, but passing them is not a prerequisite of membership, the emphasis being on practical experience, which is assessed at an interview.

As their names show, the emphasis of each professional body is different. NAEA is the only one of the three whose membership consists solely of estate agents. Being an estate agent is not necessary for membership of the other two: they have many members who are not estate agents. This does not mean that an estate agent who is a member of one particular professional body should be preferred to one who is a member of another; but it is advisable to choose an estate agent who is a member of some professional association. Look for signs on front of premises and on stationery.

NAEA, ISVA and RICS have all drawn up codes of professional conduct for their members which satisfy the requirements of the Estate Agents Act, and are on similar lines.

They include the maintenance of high professional standards and the duty of promoting a client's legitimate interests. The estate agent is required to avoid conflicts of interest between himself and the client, and to inform the client where such a conflict exists.

The member firms of all three organisations are required to have properly audited client accounts for holding money on behalf of clients: this money may be paid out only with the client's consent, to persons entitled to receive it. There are rules for the payment of interest on this money to the client.

The corporate members of all three organisations must have professional indemnity insurance, for claims against the agent for negligence, lost documents, and so on. They must also hold bonding insurance, which exists to compensate clients (within set limits) for financial loss through fraud or dishonesty on the part of a member.

Selling a house or flat

First, to find out what your home will sell for, ask several estate agents to give you an informal estimate of what would be an appropriate price. You should not need to pay for this. Make clear, however, that this enquiry is not an instruction to sell.

If you live in an area where there are a number of estate agents, choose ones who sell property similar to your own. This is particularly important if your property is at the upper or lower end of the market, or is a flat.

To handle your sale, do not necessarily use the estate agent who gives the highest valuation: he may not be able to find a buyer at that price. In order to decide what price would be reasonable, find out how much similar houses are selling for in your area by looking in estate agents' windows. At times when house prices are rising rapidly, those prices may be out of date; however, at such times there is a better chance that the agent who made the highest valuation will be able to find a buyer. You must also take account of how quickly you need to sell.

The next step in choosing an estate agent is to compare the commission charged by different ones; you may find considerable variations. The 1979 Act requires the agent to inform you of the amount of the commission, or how it is calculated, and to tell you about any 'extras', an estimate of which must be given, if the amount is not known before you enter into the agreement. Though this information should be in the contract, you may overlook it, or not understand it; so make sure you ask whether the price is all-inclusive, or whether there are additional charges for 'extras'. The most common 'extra', and vitally important, is advertising the house in the newspapers. Most vendors would not consider this an 'extra', and therefore may not realise until too late that they must pay for it. If your house takes a long time to sell, the cost of this 'extra' could be considerable.

Different customs tend to prevail in different parts of the country. In the North of England, many agents will insist on being paid their overheads (advertising, putting up 'For Sale' boards) in any event. By contrast, in the South of England most agents accept instructions on a 'no sale, no fee' basis, and absorb their overheads if there is no sale. The net effect of this arrangement is that the commission on a successful sale has to subsidise the transactions where the agent does not negotiate a sale or the seller withdraws.

The most difficult factor to assess when choosing an estate agent is how good and how conscientious he will be at selling your house. It is a good idea to ask people who have recently sold their house for personal recommendations. You may also be able to form a judgement from the attitude of the person who comes to value your house. Since the purpose of the valuation is to encourage you to use that agency, it is important to take warning if you gain an adverse impression on that occasion. You should also be able to form some impression from the estate agent's premises, and the attitude of the staff. Do not get the idea that an estate agent who is very forceful and persuasive is more likely to get you a buyer; he may, indeed, find you a buyer, but one who is more likely to back out. Under English law, an agreement for the sale of a house is not binding until there has been an exchange of contracts; that is, until both parties have signed that they agree to the transaction. Either you or the buyer can back out at any time before this stage, which usually takes months rather than weeks.

Entering into a contract with an estate agent

It is of the utmost importance that you never sign a contract which gives an estate agent the 'sole selling rights' – this means that you have to pay him commission or a fee even if you find a buyer yourself. This term must be distinguished from 'sole agency', which means that you should only use this one agent – if you use another agent who finds you a buyer, you may have to pay both agents.

The Estate Agents Act requires that the circumstances in which you will be liable to pay the agent must be specified in the contract.

You may think that you will sell your house more readily if you instruct several agents: if you do so, make it clear in your agreement with each that the commission will go only to the agent who introduces the actual buyer. This makes acting for you something of a gamble for each agent, as he may put in a lot of effort, only to see another agent scoop the pool; so he may not try so hard for you.

You may in fact do better to give one agent sole agency (not sole selling rights). Because he stands an excellent chance of getting the commission, he is likely to work harder to find you a buyer; and he may well agree to accept a lower rate of commission, because there will be less risk of his work going for nothing. However, if you yourself succeed in finding a buyer, you do not have to pay the sole agent anything.

If you do agree to appoint a sole agent, read the contract carefully to see whether there is any time limit on his agency. If there is not, make sure you insert one, so that if he does not produce results within a specified period, you can either go somewhere else altogether, or bring in an additional agent (or agents).

Though the law is, at present, silent on this point, the rules of NAEA and RICS require members to confirm their terms in writing. More likely than not, some of these terms will not have been discussed between you and the agent, and if you do not like them but fail to say so (preferably in writing), you will be accepting the agent's terms by default.

The rules of conduct of the National Association of Estate Agents provide that the terms of the agency must be fair and that clients must be made aware of them. The notes to the rules stress that this is particularly important where sole agency or sole selling rights are agreed; that the agent should explain the practical effect of such types of agency; and that the duration of these rights must not be excessive.

The rules of professional conduct of the Incorporated Society of Valuers and Auctioneers state that a member must ensure that his conduct is at all times of high professional and ethical standard, so terms of agency that are not fair would be a breach of the rules.

The rules of conduct of the Royal Institution of Chartered Surveyors state that the client must be notified of the terms and conditions on which the estate agent is to act. Although these rules do not say that these conditions should be fair, this could be interpreted as part of the general duty not to act in a manner unbefitting a chartered surveyor.

The rules of RICS contain a requirement that when members tout for agency work by, for example, writing letters to the occupiers of houses, they must warn in that letter of the possible liability to pay two commissions if a sole agent has already been appointed; and must also set out the terms on which commission will be payable if they are instructed. The rules of the two other professional associations contain similar provisions.

In any event, you should study the wording of the contract to see in exactly what circumstances you are bound to pay the commission. Do not assume that this will be only if the agent introduces a person who actually buys your property. The contract may say that you are obliged to pay if the agent has introduced someone who is 'ready, willing and able' to buy. In such a case, if you should withdraw from the transaction for some reason, you will still have to pay.

There might be several situations in which this could occur. Your own purchase could fall through; you could be made redundant, or suffer some other financial difficulties preventing a move; your reason for moving could cease to exist (say, because some noisy neighbours had themselves moved away). Although the 1979 Act states that the estate agent must tell you, before you enter into a contract with him, the circumstances in which you are liable to pay, this does not prevent him from inserting a 'ready, willing and able' clause into the contract, as that counts as telling you the circumstances; so be on the alert for this and do not accept this clause: insist on commission being payable only on the successful completion of a sale.

On a strict legal interpretation of the law of contract, an estate agent is entitled to his fee if he finds a buyer for a house, but is not actually obliged to do anything to bring this about. If he does not lift a finger to sell your house, you cannot sue him. Although he has a duty, under the Supply of Goods and Services Act 1982, to use reasonable care and skill, it would be difficult to argue that by not doing anything, he had failed in this duty. However, the professional associations' rules state that a member should use all due diligence in looking after your business, and should take reasonable steps to protect and promote your interests.

Although under the Estate Agents Act the estate agent must disclose to a buyer any link he has with the seller of a property, on a strict interpretation of the law he is not obliged to disclose to the seller any link he has with a buyer. However, the rules of the professional associations insist that where a link exists between a member and a prospective purchaser, it must be disclosed in writing to the vendor. In some circumstances, a failure to make such a disclosure might be actionable at law as a breach of agency duty.

Where such a link is put to fraudulent use the criminal law will step in, as happened when a dishonest estate agent persuaded his clients to sell cheaply to a nominal buyer (in reality the estate agent) and immediately resold the houses at nearly twice the price.

Buying a house or flat

Only the seller pays the estate agent, whose job is basically to find buyers, not sellers. As a buyer, you do not have a contract with the estate agent (unless you have employed him for a fee to find you a property). As it will not cost you anything, you should visit as many estate agencies as possible, and put your name down on their list. Make sure that you tell them the type

173

of property you are interested in, and your price range.

Under the 1979 Act, an estate agent must disclose any personal interest he or any of his employees, associates or relatives may have in the property; thus he may not sell you property of which he is the owner unless he discloses this fact. All the professional associations require that any conflict of interest should be disclosed in writing, and RICS and ISVA also require that the prospective vendor/purchaser should be urged to seek independent advice. Thus the rules of the professional associations are actually more demanding than the Act.

Complaints from buyers

The commonest complaints that buyers have against estate agents are misleading descriptions of properties, and to a lesser extent, tactics used to obtain a higher price.

Estate agents' jargon is not covered by the Trade Descriptions Act; therefore they do not commit a criminal offence by making a property sound more attractive than it really is, or even by giving exaggerated measurements. Not having a contract with the estate agent, you cannot sue him for misrepresentation. Moreover, most estate agents' descriptions include a disclaimer for inaccurate information. The agent often takes some of his information (and is expected to do so) on trust from his client, the vendor. This might be about the vendor's interest in the property (whether he has the freehold or a long lease), or about the benefit of a guarantee of works carried out on the property, such as damp proofing. These matters are usually left to the purchaser's solicitors to satisfy themselves about.

Since an estate agent's claims are made on behalf of the vendor, with whom you will have a contract if you buy the house, there exists a possibility of suing the vendor for misrepresentation, should these claims prove misleading. However, this would be fraught with problems. You must have been induced to enter into the contract as a result of the estate agent's representation; and, given that such descriptions are notorious for their unreliability, the court may not accept that this was the case. It is also likely that the misleading information was superseded at some later stage, for instance by information in the pre-contract enquiries your solicitor made (which you would have seen) or by information in the contract itself, making it obvious that the estate agent gave a false impression. You would not be able to rely on the fact that you did not read this later information.

The Advertising Standards Authority's Code of Advertising Practice requires all advertisements to be 'legal, decent, honest and truthful'; and so, in theory, you could complain to the ASA, and it could require the estate agent to withdraw the advertisement; if he refused, it could ask publishers not to publish his advertising material. However, you would need to complain about a particular advertisement, not about estate agents in general. That advertisement would have to be in a publication; the particulars you were given by the estate agent do not count for this purpose. Moreover, the details in an advertisement, although in estate agents' jargon, might not actually breach the code. In any event, a complaint to the ASA would not, of itself, result in compensation.

The rules of all three professional associations request members not to issue inaccurate or misleading statements, and generally urge them to maintain professional standards of behaviour towards prospective purchasers, as well as towards their clients. The estate agent's duty to protect and promote his client's interests should not involve improper conduct or unfairness to members of the public. However, the rules are purely internal, and do not give you a right of action against the estate agent.

The best advice is to check everything yourself, by taking measurements, and by asking questions of the seller. If the information he gives then turns out to be wrong, you may be able to sue him for misrepresentation, under the law of contract.

Gazumping

This occurs when a vendor, having accepted an offer subject to contract, subsequently accepts a higher offer from somebody else. He is entitled to do this: the first offer can be treated as merely a general indication of the sort of offer that the vendor might consider seriously.

Until the point of exchange of contracts, the vendor's agent (unless expressly told otherwise) is under an obligation to report all offers to the client; the decision whether to hold by the original offer or go back on it must be the client's. The frustrated purchaser should direct his feelings of grievance towards the vendor, not the agent.

But sometimes it is the (less reputable) agent who takes the initiative in gazumping, without the vendor's knowledge or agreement. Having received an offer, he invites the next 'offeror' to better it; then goes back to the first one, invites him to better the second offer – and so on. This is unethical, and if done without consulting the client, is against agency law.

It is therefore a good idea for the purchaser to keep in close touch with the vendor, to make sure that the agent is acting with his consent. Some vendors would find it hard to resist the extra money; but others might not authorise the agent's actions, knowing that they might find themselves on the receiving end of the same tactic in their own purchase.

If an agent has been practising unauthorised gazumping, he could be reported to his professional organisation – if he belongs to one.

An even more deplorable tactic used by less reputable estate agents is to tell a potential buyer that there is another offer, when this is not true. This can be used either to increase the offer, or to prevent the buyer making an offer lower than the advertised price.

The estate agent and your money

Once you decide to buy a house, the 1979 Act governs how the estate agent handles your money, i.e., the deposit(s) you pay.

You may pay a pre-contract deposit, as a sort of bond of good faith: an indication that you genuinely intend to buy. Under the law, you are not bound to buy the house at this point, because you have not exchanged contracts with the vendor. The estate agent holds the deposit on your behalf, acting as 'agent for the purchaser'. You may demand repayment at any time before contracts are exchanged, unless you have agreed that the seller may have your deposit if you do not purchase or do not complete the sale within a specified time.

Once exchange of contracts has taken place, if the estate agent still holds the deposit, he does so as a 'stakeholder' for both buyer and seller, and neither party is entitled to demand it until 'completion'.

Sometimes, for example when the agent is selling on behalf of a builder in a new development, the agent will take the 'good faith' deposit as 'agent for the vendor'. That means that you could lose it, together with any interest due on it. Do not agree to let your agent hold this deposit in any other way than as 'agent for the purchaser'.

The contract deposit is the one you pay through your solicitor to the vendor's solicitor on exchange of contracts. Although you do not become the owner of the house until 'completion', you have entered into a binding contract at this stage.

The estate agent cannot hold the contract deposit, unless both you and the vendor agree to this. It is much more common for the purchaser's solicitor to pay it to the vendor's solicitor. If the estate agent does hold the contract deposit, he will be doing so as stakeholder, that is, as a sort of referee, for the party entitled to claim it under the contract. Thus, if you back out, the vendor become may entitled to the deposit; if he backs out, you should get the money back.

Deposits must be kept in a client account, one that is separate from the estate agent's own account, and there are provisions for the payment of interest. As mentioned earlier, there are detailed provisions relating to the keeping and auditing of accounts, both in the Act and the rules of the professional associations.

COMPLAINTS FROM SELLERS AND FROM BUYERS

Whatever the reason for your dissatisfaction, your first step should always be to complain to the estate agent. If the person who dealt with you does not manage the firm, ask to see the manager or the owner. If this does not bring results, and the estate agency is a company, you should contact the managing director. It is becoming common for estate agencies to be part of a chain, and so the person in overall charge may not actually be on the premises.

The most common complaints from vendors are likely to be about high commission charges in relation to the work involved in finding a buyer; failing to sell a particular house; the wording of the contract (as when the vendor did not realise that he had to pay even if the sale fell through or the house was sold by himself or another estate agent); and undervaluing a house. The latter is an increasing problem when prices are escalating.

Under the Estate Agents Act, the agent cannot enforce his contract with you, the vendor if, before you entered into the contract, he did not tell you about the circumstances in which you were liable to pay him; how the fee would be arrived at; what 'extras' there would be, and how they would be calculated. However, because you agreed to a contract with those terms included, you are deemed in law to know about them: it does not matter that you might not have read or understood the contract. It also makes no odds that you did not actually sign a contract: spoken agreement is enough to make it valid, and most vendors never sign anything.

Thus the vendor can sue the estate agent only if he has been negligent, in failing to use reasonable care and skill; and the only one of the complaints just listed which may come into that category is undervaluing a house. The problem with the other complaints is that the vendor accepted these terms as being part of the contract, even if he did not read them. The Unfair

Contract Terms Act does not help, because, despite its misleading title, it only covers contracts where a party tries to exclude or limit liability, and the estate agent is not doing that with his terms. Even in the case of undervaluation, it must be the result of lack of reasonable care and skill, and not simply due to rapidly rising prices.

That does not mean that the estate agent can claim in defence that the valuation was accurate at the time he valued the house: his duty of reasonable care would extend to advising you to increase the price when it was clear that it was now out of date. However, if he had already found a buyer, a reputable estate agent might argue that it would have been unethical to increase the price.

The members of the three professional organisations are obliged to be covered by professional indemnity insurance for claims in negligence or other breach of duty.

If the property appears to have been grossly undervalued, this can give rise to another suspicion. When a house that has recently been sold is immediately put back on the market at a considerably higher price, it may sometimes be discovered that (as happened recently) the buyer was an employee or relative of the estate agent. There would then be a clear case for legal action. As mentioned earlier, the rules of all three professional associations require that the agent's own interest in a transaction should be disclosed in writing.

If your complaint is that the estate agent has dishonestly misappropriated your money, and that estate agent is a member of RICS, NAEA or ISVA, the firm will have been obliged to participate in a professional bonding insurance scheme. Therefore you would be able to apply to the relevant association for repayment, if you had suffered loss through this dishonesty. You would have to provide sufficient information and, if available, evidence to prove your loss. The Estate Agents Act provides for the introduction of compulsory bonding insurance for all estate agents, but this provision has never been implemented. Therefore, ironically, there is no compulsory insurance for the very estate agents from whom you are most likely to need protection: those who are not members of a professional association.

Criminal proceedings

Trading Standards Departments are responsible for enforcing the Estate Agents Act. You should therefore contact your local department if you suspect that there has been a breach of a specific provision of the Act; or simply send the department a copy of the agreement. They will see if any of it amounts to an offence under the Act, for which the penalty is a fine.

However, a Trading Standards Department must notify the Director General of Fair Trading if it intends to bring proceedings against an estate agent under the Act, including a summary of the facts, and it must then postpone proceedings for 28 days.

The Director General may decide to make a warning order or a prohibition order for failure to comply with certain provisions of the Act. A warning order will be made where the Director General does not consider the breach sufficient to ban the estate agent, but considers that a repetition of this behaviour would lead to a prohibition order: for example, not informing clients how much and when they will have to pay or not paying interest on clients' money. A repetition of the behaviour will be treated as conclusive proof that the estate agent is an unfit person, and a prohibition order may be made. If it is a question of dishonesty, violence or discrimination, a warning order does not have to be made before a prohibition order.

A prohibition order means that the agent must cease trading. Before making either order, the Director General must serve notice of the proposed order on the estate agent and give him at least 21 days to explain why the order should not be made. The Director General does not have to wait for cases to be referred to him from Trading Standards Departments: he can deal with cases on his own initiative. Therefore, you may complain directly to the Office of Fair Trading, if you wish.

Trading Standards Departments and officers acting on

behalf of the Director General have the power to enter estate agents' premises to inspect and seize documents if they suspect a criminal offence has been committed.

Disciplinary proceedings

Complaining to the estate agent's professional association, and thereby instituting disciplinary proceedings, will not necessarily result in any compensation. Also, as anyone can set himself up as an estate agent, it will not result in that person ceasing to trade as an estate agent, even if he is expelled from membership of his professional association, though his business may be affected if he ceases to be a member of such an association.

Unfortunately, the estate agents you are likely to have most cause to complain about are those who do not belong to any professional association. Therefore, assuming there has been no offence committed under the Estate Agents Act, you have no sanction, apart from telling all your acquaintances about your unfortunate experience, as a warning to avoid that agent.

If the estate agent is a member of NAEA, RICS or ISVA, make your complaint in writing to the association, giving full details. With your consent, the complaint will be sent to that agent, and you will receive a copy of his reply. If the complaint is not resolved by this reply, the matter will be dealt with by the relevant committee of the association. This has powers to reprimand, suspend or expel a member.

Future government intervention

The Estate Agents Act allows the government to prescribe minimum standards of competence, that is, to insist on certain qualifications, which could be obtained by passing examinations and/or practical experience. This provision, which has the support of the provisional bodies, has still to be implemented by the government.

Reputable members of the profession are also asking that estate agents should be liable under the Trade Descriptions Act 1968 for misleading advertisements and descriptions of property.

USEFUL ADDRESSES

INCORPORATED SOCIETY OF VALUERS AND AUCTIONEERS (ISVA)
3 Cadogan Gate
London SW1X 0AS
01-235 2282

Membership: voluntary; examination qualifications required
Style of qualification: ASVA (Associate); FSVA (Fellow)
Membership list: available from ISVA office
Fee guidelines: no
Code of conduct: yes
Complaints procedure: yes
Complaint-handling charge: no
Disciplinary sanctions: undertaking not to repeat offence; rep-
  rimand; suspension; expulsion

NATIONAL ASSOCIATION OF ESTATE AGENTS (NAEA)
Arbon House
21 Jury Street
Warwick CV34 4EH
0925-496800

Membership: voluntary; interview required
Style of qualification: ANAEA (Associate); FNAEA (Fellow)
Membership list: local lists free on request
Fee guidelines: no
Code of conduct: yes
Complaints procedure: yes
Complaint-handling charge: no
Disciplinary sanctions: reprimand; fine; suspension; expulsion

ROYAL INSTITUTION OF CHARTERED SURVEYORS (RICS)
12 Great George Street
London SW1P 3AD
01-222 7000

Membership: voluntary; only members may call themselves Chartered Surveyors; examination qualifications and professional experience required
Style of qualification: ARICS (Professional Associate); FRICS (Fellow)
Membership list: local lists free from RICS Information centre; individual enquiries answered as to someone's membership
Fee guidelines: not for estate agency or structural surveys
Code of conduct: yes
Complaints procedure: yes
Complaint-handling charge: no
Disciplinary sanctions: reprimand; suspension; expulsion
London telephone numbers

London telephone numbers

On 6 May 1990 the 01 telephone code for London will change to either 071 or 081, depending on the local code that follows it. From that date, people telephoning the 01 code will hear a recorded message telling them to re-dial using either 071 or 081.

Removers

Before anyone can set up a removal business, he must be granted an operator's licence by the local licensing authority. A prerequisite of the granting of this licence is that the firm should employ the holder of a 'certificate of professional competence' which is obtained by examination. This applies regardless of the size of the business – even if it consists of only one van. It is not necessary for the owner of the business to hold a certificate, provided he employs someone who does. The emphasis in the granting of the licence is on finance and transport, and the certificate is granted on the basis of ability to operate a fleet of vehicles; for instance, having a knowledge of the regulations governing drivers' hours and conditions. Therefore these requirements do not guarantee the standard of the actual removal.

CHOOSING A REMOVAL FIRM

Most established removal firms belong to the British Association of Removers (BAR), which is the only nationally recognised trade association for removers (757 UK members). It is not obligatory for removers to belong to BAR, and therefore the fact that a firm is not a member does not mean that it is not reputable.

Before being considered for membership of BAR, a removal firm must hold an operator's licence, must employ a holder of a 'certificate of professional competence', and must have been trading for at least 12 months. On applying for membership, the firm will be inspected by an area inspector, considered by local members who will take into account their local knowledge of the applicant, and finally considered by the national membership committee.

BAR has a code of conduct which stipulates, amongst other requirements, that quotations should normally be free of charge; that it is desirable for insurance to be provided (setting out minimum cover); that complaints should be dealt with promptly; that staff should be trained. Membership may be terminated if a member fails to maintain required standards.

BAR has an associated institute, The Institute of the Furniture Warehousing and Removing Industry, which sets examinations. An individual may belong to the Institute and sit its examinations whether or not his firm belongs to BAR. The Institute sets not only examinations which are recognised for the purpose of the certificate of professional competence, but also a range of other examinations, such as a certificate in removal estimating and a higher certificate in removal management. Associated with the Institute is the Removers Training Association, which provides a range of courses for anyone involved in the industry, whether in a manual, clerical or managerial capacity.

When choosing a removal firm, remember that you are entrusting to it your possessions, many of which will be irreplaceable and often of sentimental value. You should therefore try to obtain personal recommendations, ask how long the firm has been in business, and obtain several quotations. The cheapest firm may not necessarily be the best; you must balance the cost against the risk before making a decision. However, BAR's standard form of contract (see below) allows a firm to sub-contract your removal to another contractor; this right, if exercised, renders pointless any checks you have made, except to the extent that you trust the original contractor's choice of sub-contractor.

You should also consider whether you will require specialist services, such as having your belongings packed by the firm; storage facilities; removal abroad. In the case of storage facilities, you should inspect the premises, ask what security measures are taken and whether there are any restrictions on your visiting to check or even remove some of your possessions. In the case of removals abroad, BAR has an overseas group, members of which have been vetted as to both their facilities and their finances. All such members are guaranteed by BAR, and if the move runs into difficulties, BAR guarantees satisfactory completion at no extra cost.

Insurance

Inadequate insurance cover is a frequent problem in dealing with insurance firms. In all cases, you should check the insurance position carefully before entering into a removal contract. First, check whether insurance is included in the price quoted, and whether it is compulsory or optional. If it is not included in the price, find out how much it will cost and on what basis it is calculated. Then check what is included and excluded in the insurance policy. Look at your own insurance policies, and contact your insurance company to ascertain whether you are covered during a removal, and to what extent. Compare this with the insurance cover provided by the removal firm. You may be obliged to tell your own insurance company of your move in order to benefit from the cover in your policy.

BAR's minimum requirements are that there should be insurance to cover customers for losses incurred as a result of the following circumstances:

o   losses from unattended vehicles
o   remover's failure to maintain vehicles in a roadworthy condition
o   losses from warehouses
o   failure to set vehicle or warehouse alarms
o   remover's failure to obtain references on employees
o   collusion or theft by employees.

Such cover is valuable, and if your removal firm is not a member of BAR, make sure that its insurance policy provides equivalent cover. BAR also stipulates that the cover must be arranged for the benefit of the customer (the firm would be acting as agent). This means that you have a contract directly with the insurers and may make any claim yourself rather than going through the removal firm, which should make claims quicker and easier.

However, BAR's minimum requirements also provide that certain risks may be excluded, such as:

○ goods received in a packed condition from customers
○ jewellery, money, securities
○ wear and tear
○ claims relating to pairs or sets (where the item lost or damaged is one of a pair or of a set, you will not be able to claim for the replacement of the whole set)
○ consequential losses (further losses resulting from a loss or damage)
○ unexplained mechanical or electrical damage, unless as a direct result of external physical damage.

They also stipulate that any loss or damage covered by any other insurance policy may be excluded, and that there may be an excess payable by the customer of up to £50 for each claim.

Although these requirements are a minimum standard, and it is BAR's policy to encourage higher levels of insurance, the exclusions just mentioned may have serious consequences. Many people pack their possessions themselves. The removal will obviously cost more if the firm does the packing, and many people just do not want to entrust their most prized possessions to strangers. There is therefore a very strong chance that liability for the most common breakages, china and glassware, will be excluded. One compromise might be to entrust to the removal firm those items which can be replaced (assuming you can afford to pay the additional charge for packing) and to pack and possibly transport irreplaceable items yourself.

However, even if you allow the firm to do the packing, the exclusion clauses will bite in the case of broken china or glass if, as is likely, it forms part of a set; and if the rule about excess is invoked, you will have to pay up to £50 of each claim.

Jewellery or money are probably the most likely items to be stolen because they are easily taken and disposed of, but few people would trust them to a remover.

If the policy offered has the exclusions mentioned above, you should check whether your own policies (householders' or all risks) have similar exclusions. If they do, find out how much it would cost to extend the cover by removing the exclusions. Remember that liability may be excluded if the loss or damage is covered by another policy, so if your own policy gives you the cover you want, there is no point in paying for the cover offered by the firm. If it would be cheaper to extend the cover on your existing policy rather than take out or extend the firm's insurance cover, then do so. However, in this case you must check whether the firm's insurance is compulsory. If it is, try to negotiate for this not to be enforced in your case. If you do not succeed, try other removal firms.

Entering into the contract

Your contract with the remover may be oral or written. BAR has a standard form of contract which its members may use. BAR does not formally recommend its own contract to its members; it does not have the approval of the Office of Fair Trading because of its limitation of contractual liability.

Whether you are asked to sign a contract or not, there may be terms printed in a leaflet which you are given, or displayed on the wall or somewhere else in the firm's office. If these terms are in the contract that you sign, or if you are given them in a leaflet, or if they are displayed in a prominent place, they will be binding, whether you have read them or not. However, if the firm attempts to exclude or limit liability, such terms will be void under the Unfair Contract Terms Act 1977, unless the firm can prove they are reasonable. You may simply make your contract over the telephone, in which case there will be no terms binding on you, unless you were sent them before you agreed that the firm should do the job.

The price

If the firm does not have a printed contract, you should get confirmation in writing of certain details, such as the price; the day and time; exactly what you require to be done. Make sure that the price is a quotation, not an estimate. A quotation is binding, whereas an estimate is only a rough guide, and although the firm is not allowed to depart too far from that price, it is not binding. Make sure that the written confirmation states exactly what is being provided for the price: for instance, that you are expecting the firm to pack for you, or take up carpets, or dismantle and erect certain items of furniture.

Check whether the price is for the job, per hour, per day, or on the basis that the job will take a certain length of time, with an additional charge being payable if it takes longer. Make sure that both the time and the date are stipulated; and beware of saving money by booking the firm for a half-day only. If the van is due to go to or arrive from another job, you could have serious problems. For instance, if, as is common, you are completing on the purchase of your house on the day of removal, there may be some delay, perhaps of several hours; you will not be allowed to move your furniture into the new house until completion has taken place, and the van and crew will not want to wait around unless they were booked for the whole day.

Also check what the position would be if (for whatever reason) the job were to run into a second day.

Other contract terms

There may be other matters you will wish to cover in your contract, such as whether you can cancel the removal contract (for example, if the sale or purchase of the house falls through), how much notice of cancellation you must give, and whether you will have to pay a cancellation charge. The more of these matters you cover in writing, the more complicated the 'document' will be and it may seem better to choose a firm with a written contract. However, you must then scrutinise such a contract carefully to ensure that, in order to gain the advantage of terms beneficial to you, you do not acquire terms detrimental to you. In any case, the Supply of Goods and Services Act 1982 provides that the service must be carried out with reasonable care and skill.

It will be tempting not to read the contract carefully, because most standard contracts, including BAR's, are quite long and are in small close print. You must resist this temptation. With some contracts it is possible to cross out unacceptable standard clauses. However, BAR's contract stipulates that no employee or agent of the contractor has authority to alter or vary the standard terms. Therefore, if you do not wish to accept these terms, you must either go elsewhere, or persuade the contractor himself not to use or to vary the standard contract. If any employee who appears to have the authority agrees to amend the contract, it is possible to argue under the law of contract that this is binding, but as this would require a court decision, it is not advisable to take the risk.

BAR's standard terms

These cover:

- o   the circumstances in which quotations may be amended: these are, basically, where there is delay in accepting the quotation on the part of the customer, or in the completion of the work; where charges outside of the control of the firm are to be paid; where extra services are provided at the request of the customer
- o   the customer's responsibilities: being present or represented at the home; providing a schedule of items to be removed; providing protection for goods left on unattended premises; not submitting certain items for removal, such as jewellery or money
- o   payment: to be made without deduction or deferment by virtue of any claim against the contractor
- o   cancellation and postponement charges: there should be none if more than 10 working days' notice is given, and not more than 30% should be payable in the case of cancellation;

less may be charged, depending on how much notice is
given
o certain limitations on the contractor's liability (see 'complaints' below)
o arbitration
o third party claims.

COMPLAINTS

The most common complaint is likely to be regarding damage or
loss. The fact that an article is damaged does not necessarily
mean that the firm did not use reasonable care and skill. An item
may be so brittle or in such poor condition that it can suffer
damage despite reasonable care; it could have been your fault in
packing the article, or caused by a third party, for instance,
through involvement in a traffic accident which was not the
fault of the contractor's employee. If an article is missing, you
will have to be able to prove that it was actually packed, which
may be difficult.

Apart from this, your biggest problem is likely to be the
exclusion or limitation clauses in the contract. If the firm uses
BAR's standard contract, there are a number of such clauses.

Limiting liability

Liability is limited to the cost of repairing or replacing the article
or, at the contractor's discretion, to a figure based on the sum of
£4.50 per cubic foot, increased annually since 1st January 1983 in
accordance with the Retail Price Index. Even index-linked over
the last 7 years, £4.50 per cubic foot would in no way cover the
cost of many articles commonly transported by removal firms
and the value of an item is rarely directly related to its size. Nor
is it satisfactory to most people that the choice of compensation
or repair lies with the contractor. In the case of an article which
is part of a pair or set, the calculation is based on the cubic
capacity of that part and not on any special value as part of the
pair or set, since claims to do with sets are excluded.

Liability is excluded, amongst others, for wear and tear; for articles in wardrobes or drawers, packages or other containers not packed and unpacked by the contractor. Although all of these stipulations appear to be reasonable, they can give rise to disputes. Thus, there may be some dispute as to whether certain damage already existed and was wear and tear, or whether a piece of china or glassware was particularly brittle or simply normal for that type of article. The exclusion regarding articles in containers presupposes that the customer may not have packed properly; but what if the employees carrying out the removal are told that a particular container contains breakable articles, but are seen to handle the container in an inappropriate way for such articles?

The contract specifically requires customers not to submit jewellery, securities, etc., for removal or storage.

Liability is also excluded for removals from or to unattended premises, or where third parties are present. The reasoning behind this is that the remover should not be held liable for loss or damage which might have been caused by others. However, if the removal is over a considerable distance or the van has to make more than one trip, it is not always easy to comply with this, because a member of the family or a friend may have to be roped in to help at either end of the journey.

Damage to premises must be notified on the delivery receipt and confirmed in writing within 7 days. The contractor has the option whether to arrange for repairs or to meet the cost, subject to a limit of £200 (index-linked). It is not as easy as it might seem to notify damage on the delivery receipt; if the house is large and the damage in an out-of-the-way place, it may not be spotted for some time, and certainly not on the removal day when there is likely to be chaos. The monetary limit will not be adequate in many cases.

There is a time limit of 7 days for claims in relation to damaged or lost goods. Again, it takes a long time to unpack every box, especially if the customer is working and can only unpack in the evenings and at weekends.

If your removal work is being sub-contracted to another firm, the liability will be the main contractor's, as specified in the contract, unless he can prove that the sub-contractor was at fault: in that case, the sub-contractor will be liable on the same terms. In other words, if the contractor proves that the fault was the sub-contractor's, you will have no claim against the firm with whom you made the contract, and it will be the sub-contractor who will get the benefit of the exclusion and limitation clauses in that contract. You may rightly feel aggrieved, if you have gone to some trouble in choosing the contractor; and certain problems may arise – for instance, the sub-contractor may go out of business before settling the claim.

All of these exclusion/limitation clauses will be subject to the Unfair Contract Terms Act 1977 and will be void unless the contractor can prove them to be reasonable. However, when looking at limitation clauses, a court will take into account the charge for the work; therefore you cannot expect the contractor to take on unlimited liability for the sum he will normally receive for your removal . Nevertheless, it is likely that the contractor would not succeed in at least some cases, particularly in relation to clauses about the time limits and the compensation limits.

Contacting BAR

If you have not yet paid the bill, and you feel aggrieved by the service you received, it is a common tactic to withhold or make a deduction from the payment. However, BAR's standard terms state that the customer agrees not to do this. Moreover, the amount you want to claim may be in excess of the charge for the removal. You should first contact the removal firm and attempt to negotiate with the contractor. If you are not satisfied, and the firm is a member of BAR, you may complain to its consumer affairs department by telephone (01-861 3331) or in writing. All complaints are investigated.

Arbitration

If BAR fails to achieve a satisfactory settlement, you may agree to use its arbitration service. There are two main factors to take into account when deciding whether to use arbitration; it will be on the terms of the contract as they stand and therefore you will not be able to to challenge the validity of the exclusion and limitation clauses; and it may not be any cheaper than using the small claims procedure in the county court.

BAR's standard contract used to provide for compulsory arbitration; thus a customer who signed their standard contract was not allowed to take the matter to court instead. This arbitration could be expensive (it could cost £200 per day, and you would have to pay this if the arbitrator determined that the customer must pay the costs).

However, most compulsory arbitration clauses have now become unenforceable under the Consumer Arbitration Agreements Act 1988. The effect of this is that where a contract was made on or after 1st October 1988 and where the claim is for £5,000 or less, a consumer cannot be forced to use arbitration, unless he consents in writing after the dispute has arisen. Therefore, unless your claim is for more than £5,000, the compulsory arbitration clause is unenforceable.

If you are asked to sign one of these old contracts, you need not worry about it, because the clause will be ineffective; members of BAR are aware of this. BAR is currently looking at the implications of the Act for its contract. It is likely that in future it will provide for voluntary arbitration; and BAR is attempting to set this up at a lower cost than under the old scheme.

Deciding whether to bring a court action

Consider well the evidence as to whether the removal firm was at fault. If the amount involved is small, or you can claim against an insurance policy, it is unlikely to be worth bringing an action. However, many insurance policies have similar exclusions and limitations to those in the BAR contract; therefore your insurance policy may not cover your claim. If your complaint is against an exclusion or limitation clause, BAR arbitration will not help; but if these are not relevant in your case, check the cost of bringing the case in the county court, and compare this with BAR arbitration if the firm is a member. If you can limit your claim to £1,000, the case will automatically be referred to 'county court arbitration' under the small claims procedure, which will be cheaper and easy for you to handle yourself without a solicitor. If you can limit your claim to £5,000, you can bring the case in the county court and avoid BAR's compulsory arbitration (if you have signed such a contract).

USEFUL ADDRESSES

BRITISH ASSOCIATION OF REMOVERS LTD (BAR)
3 Churchill Court
58 Station Road
North Harrow HA2 7SA
01-861 3331

Membership: voluntary
Membership list: not available
Fee guidelines: no
Code of conduct: no
Complaints procedure: yes
Complaint-handling charge: no; charge for arbitration
Disciplinary sanctions: expulsion

Architects
and
Surveyors

When you are planning to rebuild or extend your house or have any major building work done, you may be involved with two different sorts of specialist. Broadly speaking, the designing, planning and supervising functions are the province of one set of professionals, mainly architects and surveyors, while the actual work is carried out by other specialists – builders, plumbers, electricians and so on.

'Architect', it should be noted, is a title protected in law, under the Architects Registration Acts; 'surveyor' is not so protected, so that anyone could call himself a surveyor. Hence, anyone employing a surveyor should ensure that he is a member of a professional association, such as the Royal Institute of Chartered Surveyors (RICS) or the Incorporated Society of Valuers and Auctioneers (ISVA). Whenever a surveyor is referred to in this chapter, it should be assumed that a member of a professional organisation is meant.

APPOINTING YOUR PROFESSIONAL
Before you begin to look for a professional to carry out your work, let alone appoint one, define what it is you actually want done. Doing this will help you to identify the sort of professional who should have the correct skills for your project and to appoint and 'brief' properly the person or firm you finally choose.

Many disputes originate from misunderstandings at this stage, so it is important to get it right.

Very early in the process you will have to outline your requirements to the professional. If you can be precise, there will be less chance of misunderstandings and problems later on. Frequent changes of mind, even at this stage, do not help anyone. For instance, if you want an extension built on to your house decide in advance how big you want it, what it will be used for, how much money you have got to spend on it, and so on. The professional can help you to refine your requirements in a way which may considerably affect the size of your proposed extension.

We can do anything

If you approach most professional firms in the property field, they will claim that they can carry out equally well the whole range of services that you might require. To some extent this may be true. Many modern firms have become multi-disciplinary and can take on a variety of jobs.

Architects and surveyors generally have their roots in a particular speciality, even though they may have moved into new areas of work. Their training and experience will generally reflect this expertise. For example, as a broad generalisation, architects will have the required design skills which can be applied to design problems, whether in new buildings or existing ones, while building surveyors are more accustomed to dealing with matters relating to existing buildings.

These are oversimplifications. Over the last few years, work to existing buildings has increased and more architects have specialised in designing schemes of work for such buildings. Surveyors, specialists when it comes to existing buildings, have been promoting themselves as being also able to design schemes for new buildings.

As a general rule, if your project requires a high level of design work, for instance a new building or a large extension, where you want some originality of appearance, then an architect will be more suitable. If the project demands alterations to an existing building, then a surveyor might be equally appropriate.

There is more to it than that. Someone may be on the Register of Architects of the Architects Registration Council of the United Kingdom (ARCUK) and a member of the Royal Institute of British Architects (RIBA), but may never have had the responsibility for the design of a new building since he qualified, or may have concentrated on commercial industrial buildings. A member of RICS may not have been near a drawing board or a building site for years. Some architects tend to specialise in larger-scale design work, such as commercial industrial buildings, and will not be prepared to take on a relatively small domestic commission. So a person's qualifications and/or status, although a good indicator of their training, do not provide enough information on which to base your selection.

Finding a professional

Most main public libraries have the appropriate directories, such as the RIBA *Directory of Practices*, and the *RICS Yearbook*, which contains a complete list of names, addresses and telephone numbers of chartered surveyors. Other professional bodies, such as the Royal Incorporation of Architects in Scotland (RIAS) and the Architects and Surveyors Institute (ASI), have similar directories.

RIBA offers a Clients Advisory Service through its regional branches, and will give a selection of names of architects who specialise in particular types of work. RICS publishes a *Geographical Directory*, which indicates which firms provide building surveying services; the RICS Information Service should be able to provide the names of such firms.

Most surveyors/architects will be in the Yellow Pages. It is one way of identifying potential professionals, but anyone you consider using should be vetted – by asking for references, and interviewing, and, if possible, looking at completed jobs.

It is generally best to follow personal recommendation from

friends. It is also possible to phone the professional's own institution, to ask which local people have experience in the type of work you are planning. Most professional bodies offer this type of service.

What to look out for

An important point to consider is the type of client the firm or person usually works for. Many firms prefer private and public institutions, because such clients provide larger and more interesting and profitable work than private individuals with relatively small amounts of money to spend. Some firms tend to see ordinary householders as high-risk work, 'uneducated' clients who take up a lot of time in return for a relatively small fee. They would much rather work with other professionals employed by the larger clients to carry out their projects. Despite this, many will take on smaller commissions when gaps appear in their workload. But they may switch their resources from your project if something better turns up, doing only just enough to honour their obligations.

Some firms, on the other hand, readily accept commissions to do work for householders. So, ask the professionals how much work they do for private individuals, and ask for references specifically from this group.

Most professionals will be happy to let you have a list of clients for whom they have recently done work. When you have found a person or a firm that seems suitable, contact one or two ex-customers: it can be very revealing.

It is wise to make yourself familiar at the outset with the structure of the firm you are appointing (whether sole practitioner, partnership or company) and with the status in it of your professional (whether director, partner or associate), so that if problems should arise, you will have some idea of where to take your complaint.

Insurances

The law with regard to liability of professionals has expanded over the last few years. In an attempt to protect their members against crippling legal action, the professions have set up their own companies providing professional indemnity insurance for their members. Most professional organisations insist that the members should carry such insurance. Ask what type of insurance the firm/person has and what sort of cover it provides.

Watch out for 'weekenders'

It is a tradition with many professionals, whether they work for private firms or public authorities, to carry out work for people 'on the side'. Done in their spare time, usually for cash, typical jobs might include drawing up plans for a new garage, house extension or loft conversion; or maybe a structural survey on behalf of a potential house purchaser. Sometimes these are friends or 'friends of friends'. They are known as 'weekenders' and also 'homers'. You should think very carefully before entering into an arrangement with such people, even if the charge seems very reasonable.

Such a 'weekender' may well not have any insurance cover so, if the design or survey is negligently carried out and you suffer substantial financial loss, it is unlikely that you will be able to obtain much compensation (if any).

One-man bands

Some professionals belong to the appropriate associations and have all the proper insurance cover, and so on, but through either necessity or choice, work on their own. Many 'loners' have excellent records and carry out good work; but if you should decide to engage one, you should ask about the arrangements if he should be ill or on holiday – who will look after his work? Also, there may be difficulties about contacting him. Find out if he has an office and a secretary – does he work from home with an answering machine? Talk to people he has worked for about this – better still, ask him.

Location

In many parts of the country, professionals will carry out work at great distances from their office base. If possible, however, it is best to employ a professional who is based locally, so long as he meets all the other requirements. It is easier for a local man to inspect the project. There is more chance of getting him to inspect if he only has to travel down the road rather than miles and miles. Moreover, for many types of projects, a separate charge is made for travelling expenses and other 'disbursements'. If the distances are so great that he has to take an overnight stop in a hotel, the cost of the service will be much higher.

Knowledge of the locality is useful: familiarity with features such as the type of buildings, local construction methods, local contractors, will prove valuable; also being known to the local authority planning department and to the building inspectors, and being aware of the local regulations.

ARRANGEMENTS ABOUT FEES

Before you enter into an agreement with the professional, you should discuss the fee or charges for his services.

Most professionals' charges are based on a percentage of the value of the building contract that they are designing, administering or inspecting. The actual percentage depends on the nature of the project and the value of the proposed work.

Most of the professional associations issue fee guidelines which have only the force of recommendations. RIBA, RICS, RIAS and ASI have very similar fee guidelines.

All the recommended scale of charges show that fees are higher for work to existing buildings than for new work, in the knowledge that there will be more work involved than in new buildings, and by its nature the risk will be higher.

In the RIBA classifications, new and existing work categories are further divided into building types or classes. RIBA, RICS and ASI indicate a higher percentage fee for work to private houses than, for example, estate housing or hotels.

However, not all services can be carried out on a percentage fee basis; in such circumstances, an hourly rate is applied.

Basic services

Supposing that you employ a professional to design, administer or inspect a building project on your house that involves extensive internal remodelling and the provision of an extension: RIBA, RICS and ASI all split their services for such a project into distinct stages.

Inception involves gathering initial information.

Feasibility usually relates to larger projects, and involves the evaluation of alternative basic designs and ideas.

Outline proposals deal with discussion of requirements, drawing up of outline proposals, and costs estimates. Be sure to allow in your budget for VAT on the work and fees, and any other inevitable costs.

Scheme design enables you to start taking decisions over sizes, materials and the appearance of the work; a cost estimate is prepared and possible start and completion dates suggested. Planning permission, if required, is applied for.

Detail design decisions are taken about the construction, type and quality of materials: the results of cost checks are reported to you. (These are normally carried out only on major projects and involve commissioning a quantity surveyor.) Applications for approvals under Building Regulations and other statutory requirements are made.

Production information involves the final drawings and the specification of the materials and workmanship to sufficient detail to go to contractors for an estimate. Any changes of mind at this stage are likely to prove costly.

Tender action: advice on the contractors who should be asked to quote (or 'tender') for the job. With your approval, the job goes out to tender and advice is given on the prices received. For a true comparison, it is important to supply all prospective tenderers with the same information (specification) and to notify any change proposed by one tenderer to all the others.

Project planning: general advice on contractual matters, and the signing of the contract between the contractor and yourself. The professional is not a signatory to the contract, but has duties under that contract.

Operations on site: when the building works are actually in progress, administration of the contract and inspection of the work; regular financial reports to you, particularly if the costs are changing.

Completion to ensure that the contract is finished properly; you should receive up-to-date drawings showing drainage and other services and be advised on maintenance afterwards. If you want a maintenance 'handbook', this can be provided as an extra.

These different stages are also used to apportion the payment of the professional's fee. A percentage of the total fee (varying from 15% to 25% depending on the stage) becomes due after each stage. In some cases, you will be asked to pay the appropriate percentage at the end of each stage, although you can agree on some other suitable arrangement.

This type of fee apportionment reflects the fact that by far the greater part of the professional's work is carried out before the builder is appointed. On small projects, it should be possible to adjust payment, say 50% at the halfway stage, and 50% at completion. This may give you more of a lever if the work is not to a good standard, or you feel that site inspection is not up to scratch.

At each interim payment of the fee, the total contract sum will be estimated to a greater or lesser extent. When the contract is complete and the final costs are known, the fee account will be adjusted accordingly. Remember, if the cost of the work rises while the work is being carried out, so normally will the fee of the professional, because he is working on a percentage basis.

One problem with the percentage basis of appointment is that it gives the professional an incentive to allow (or recommend) extra costs. A fixed fee (if you can negotiate it) may seem higher to start with but removes this incentive.

Other costs

The cost of employing a professional does not stop there. If your building project involves, for example, knocking out a few internal structural walls that hold up the rest of your house and you also require a special type of heating system, the professional may not have sufficient skills to carry out these specialist functions. He may therefore recommend that other consultants be employed – in this case, a structural engineer and a mechanical engineer. Substantial projects may require the services of a quantity surveyor, to control costs. The cost of their services will have to be paid by you in addition to the fee for the main professional.

Time charges

The percentage fee covers the 'normal' duties of the professional at various work stages (listed under 'basic services'). If you ask the professional to provide services that are not covered in the basic services, he makes additional charges, usually on a time charge basis (although a lump sum can also be negotiated). These special services vary widely in nature and, where possible, should be specified at the time of appointment.

Time charges are simply hourly rates. They vary considerably and depend on the complexity of the work, the qualifications, experience and responsibility of the professional, and the character of the negotiations. When a project is in its early stages, the cost is not known, and it may not go on at all. It is normal to base the fees for preliminary work on time charges of an agreed amount per hour; and this method can be used for the whole job. It is especially appropriate if you intend to manage the building work yourself. Ask your professional to send in his accounts as the job proceeds, so that you can check on progress.

Expenses

Unless otherwise agreed at the start, it is usual for you to have to pay the professional's out-of-pocket expenses and disbursements in connection with the service he is providing. These will include such items as printing and reproduction of all documents, maps, drawings, photos and other records; also, where necessary, hotel and travelling expenses.

If your project requires planning permission and building regulation approval, fees will be charged by the local authority which you will have to pay, although the applications are usually prepared by the professional.

The professional should keep an accurate record of the time spent on these matters and make it available for your inspection.

Yet other charges

RICS and ASI have a number of other standard scales of charges covering normal services. One of the most commonly used is the scale of fees charged for repair and maintenance of properties: RICS has a time charge for contracts under £25,000 and a l0% fee for contracts over that sum.

All the charges will be subject to VAT which will add considerably to the final bill. However, a small practice may be exempt from VAT registration.

Site inspection

The standard fee includes the inspection of the work while the project is 'on site'. The professional visits the site at intervals appropriate to the stage of construction. But the standard conditions of appointment state that the architect 'will not be required to make frequent or constant inspections'. If you do want such a service, it may be possible to get a clerk of works to visit the site, at an extra fee.

Letter of appointment

It is important to be clear about the terms of the appointment right from the beginning. When you have found a professional you are happy with, discuss with him the type of services required and the appropriate fees. If he does not confirm the terms to you in writing, you should write to him. The points to put into such a letter should include a reminder that:

o   the conditions of appointment will be in accordance with the current edition of the RIBA and RIAS *Architect's appointment* or the RICS *Conditions of Engagement for Building Surveying Services*

o   the services will be as described earlier under 'basic services'; the percentage fee will be based on the estimated cost of the work.

The other matters that should be mentioned are:

o   other services to be included (such as those of a structural or mechanical engineer chosen by the professionals) and the amount to be charged

o   negotiations with the local planning authority about the necessary permission, to be charged on an hourly basis (state the rate per hour and agree an upper limit)

o   when and in what proportions the fee is to be paid

o   what expenses and disbursements will be charged and in accordance with what guidelines

o   the mileage rate for transport.

Clients' money

RIBA, RIAS and RICS all have rules regarding clients' money entrusted to them: it must be kept in a separate account, and a complete record must be kept of all disbursements.

COMMUNICATION WITH THE PROFESSIONAL

One of the best methods of avoiding problems and misunderstandings between you and your professional is to make sure that you both communicate effectively. For instance, if you mention in passing that you would like your extension built of grey bricks and no one makes a note of it – when you see that it is being built in red bricks, you will have the makings of a quarrel with your architect. Because nothing has been committed to paper, such disagreements are difficult to resolve. The paramount rule is: *always get it in writing*.

Any architect or surveyor worth his salt should also be

following this rule; if you have formal meetings with him a written record covering the main points of discussion should be taken. When you receive these 'minutes', check them over carefully to make sure they are accurate. If something has been missed out or expressed in a way that you do not agree with, contact the professional and point out the mistake, and confirm this in writing as soon as possible.

You should make sure that all decisions, points of view, and soon, are put down in writing and communicated to the professional. Keep a notebook by the phone and make notes of any telephone calls made or received about your project. Take it to any meetings you may have. If important points have been agreed on, confirm this in writing as soon as possible.

When you write a letter, take a copy before you post it (it is not essential to type it) in order to make an accurate record. Ensure that all your letters are clearly dated, and if they are replying or confirming a telephone call or letter received, always make reference to it (mentioning the date) in your letter.

If you do get into a spoken disagreement with the professional, either on the phone or face to face, try to stay calm. Even if the other is being very unreasonable, you should not get abusive, storm out or slam the phone down. If you lose your temper, you will lose face even if you are in the right.

WHAT TO DO IF THINGS GO WRONG
The relationship between a client and the professional is expected to be one of trust. If, at some time during the life of the project, you begin to doubt the advice of the professional and do not sort the problem out quickly, it can affect the success of the whole venture.

The approach to take when things begin to go off the rails will depend on what type of project it is, what type of professional you have employed, the nature of the act or omission.

In the first place, contact the architect or surveyor himself and try to resolve the matter informally: sometimes it can simply be a misunderstanding. If you get no satisfaction, contact the professional's superior if he has one, depending on the type of firm this is. State your case calmly and clearly, referring to correspondence and/or incidents, as necessary. Be clear about what action you want taken.

If the company or firm gives you no satisfaction, there are a few remedies offered by several of the professional institutions and, when all else fails, a remedy may exist in either arbitration or litigation.

Complaining to professional associations

All professional associations have codes of conduct that their members have to abide by, and complaints facilities for the public. If a member contravenes the rules, he could be warned, suspended from membership or expelled. For some professions, expulsion is a very serious matter; for others it does not have such significance.

How extensive and effective the complaints procedures are from the public's point of view will vary from case to case.

Trying to resolve a dispute with a professional by appealing to that person's professional association raises a number of issues that you should think about carefully.

Most disputes with professionals require quick action for a successful resolution of the matter. For instance, if your architect is not inspecting work on your house extension properly, or your surveyor has missed out something on a structural survey of a house you are keen to buy, this could lead to your having a substandard building, or missing out on a house you really wanted. Complaints made to the professional organisations, if they are prepared to deal with them, will take weeks if not months to investigate; it will then be far too late to deal with the problems.

Professional organisations exist with one main objective – to promote the activities and protect the interests of their members. Part of this role involves making sure that these members do not act in an way that gives the professions a bad name; nevertheless, it is not unreasonable to suppose that their loyalty will lie with the professionals, rather than any member of the public. You are likely to find that the onus of proof will be squarely on you.

Even if the organisation finds against your architect or surveyor, the sanctions imposed on that member will have nothing to do with resolving your loss. Most organisations will say that they are not entitled to comment on or investigate cases where the law provides a remedy; and are usually unable to grant or enforce monetary compensation.

Despite these reservations, taking your case to the professional association could be a useful tactic in appropriate circumstances because it could be a relatively cheap and informal way of establishing responsibility for an act or omission. It could possibly strengthen your hand if you were to go to law. Moreover, the mere fact of your making a complaint to the professional's organisation may 'help' him to take your comments and complaints more seriously and to try and resolve the matter before it proceeds any further. In many professions, such complaints become common knowledge very quickly, and even if they come to nothing, they can still be bad for business or status.

Below is a review of the complaints procedure offered by the major institutions.

The Royal Institute of British Architects (RIBA)

Where a relationship between a RIBA member and a client which is based on *Architect's appointment* is giving rise to serious problems, it may be possible for a conciliator to be appointed through one of RIBA's Regional Secretaries: in which case, the conciliator will try to bring about a reconciliation between architect and client, in accordance with RIBA guidelines.

If the dissatisfaction has to do with the RIBA member's work, the RIBA Clients Advisory Service should be able to put the dissatisfied client in touch with other members who could be used to give the client a second opinion and, if necessary, act as expert witnesses.

If the dissatisfaction has to do with fees, and the appointment of the architect was based on *Architect's appointment* and confirmed in writing, RIBA is willing to give an opinion on the fees which should be paid, based on a 'joint statement of facts'. Before this is given, the parties must undertake to accept the opinion as final and binding. This service is free. Complaints about misconduct of RIBA members should be addressed to the Professional Conduct Secretary, and may include:

o dishonesty
o improper conduct of a client's affairs, or inadequate liaison with a client
o abuse of confidentiality or lack of discretion
o allowing other interests to conflict with those of the client without proper disclosure to the client
o improperly obtaining commissions.

Anyone who is considering making a complaint against an architect should ask the Professional Conduct Secretary for a copy of the document *Complaints about members of the Royal Institute of British Architects*. This outlines the presentation of a complaint and mentions the limitations on RIBA's powers: a very important one is that RIBA cannot enforce monetary compensation to a client (whatever disciplinary action it may decide to take against the member).

The Royal Incorporation of Architects in Scotland (RIAS) has a similar scheme for complaints.

The Royal Institution of Chartered Surveyors (RICS)
The Professional Conduct Department of RICS investigates complaints against chartered surveyors that relate to the following matters:

o unjustifiable delay in dealing with your affairs
o failure to reply to your letters
o disclosure of confidential information.

If a member is found to have breached one of the rules,

RICS can reprimand, severely reprimand, suspend or expel him. A surveyor who has been suspended or expelled from RICS membership could still carry on working but not call himself a 'chartered surveyor' and would no longer be covered by RICS professional insurance schemes. This could be important, especially in professional circles, but members of the public might not be aware of the difference.

Like RIBA and RIAS, RICS states that certain complaints cannot be considered where a remedy in law might be more appropriate. For instance, where it is a question of alleged professional negligence or breach of contract, or of assessing or awarding compensation, RICS will point you towards the courts.

USEFUL ADDRESSES

ARCHITECTS REGISTRATION COUNCIL OF THE UNITED KINGDOM (ARCUK)
73 Hallam Street
London W1N 6EE
01-580 5861

Code of conduct: yes
Complaints procedure: yes
Complaint-handling charge: no
Disciplinary sanctions: removal from register

ARCHITECTS AND SURVEYORS INSTITUTE (ASI)
15 St Mary Street
Chippenham
Wiltshire SN15 3JN
0249-444505

Membership: voluntary; examination qualifications required
Style of qualification: MASI (Member); AMASI (Associate Member); LASI (Licentiate; FASI (Fellow)
Membership list: free on request
Code of conduct: yes
Complaints procedure: yes
Complaint-handling charge: no
Disciplinary sanctions: expulsion

BRITISH CHEMICAL DAMPCOURSE ASSOCIATION (BCDA)
16A Whitchurch Road
Pangbourne
Reading
Berkshire RG8 7BP
07357-3799

Membership: voluntary; examinations and/or other tests required
Style of qualification: CRDS (for surveyors employed in industry)
Membership list: free on request
Fee guidelines: no
Code of conduct: yes
Complaints procedure: yes
Complaint-handling charge: no
Disciplinary sanctions: expulsion

BRITISH INSTITUTE OF ARCHITECTURAL TECHNICIANS (BIAT)
397 City Road
London EC1V 1NE
01-278 2206

Membership: voluntary; examination qualifications required
Style of qualification: MBIAT (Member)
Membership list: not available
Fee guidelines: yes
Code of conduct: yes
Complaints procedure: yes
Complaing handling charge: no
Disciplinary sanctions: removal from register

BRITISH WOOD PRESERVING ASSOCIATION (BWPA)
6 The Office Village
4 Romford Road
Stratford
London E15 4EA
01-519 2588

Membership: voluntary
Membership list: free on request
Fee guidelines: no
Code of conduct: yes
Complaints procedure: yes
Complaint-handling charge: no
Disciplinary sanctions: yes

BUILDING EMPLOYERS CONFEDERATION (BEC)
83 New Cavendish Street
London W1M 8AD
01-580 5588

Membership: voluntary; by subscription
Membership list: local lists free on request from BEC Building
    Trust Ltd., Invicta House, London Road, Maidstone, ME16
    8JH, and from BEC regional offices
Fee guidelines: yes
Code of conduct: yes
Complaints procedure: yes, under BEC Guarantee Scheme
Complaint-handling charge: yes, for conciliation/arbitration
Disciplinary sanctions: yes

DRAUGHT PROOFING ADVISORY ASSOCIATION LIMITED
PO Box 12
Haslemere
Surrey GU27 3AH
0428-54011

Membership: voluntary, by subscription
Membership list: free on request
Fee Guidelines: no
Code of conduct: yes (code of practice)
Complaints procedure: yes
Complaint-handling charge: no
Disciplinary sanctions: warnings (with pressure on member to
    put things right); expulsion

ELECTRICAL CONTRACTORS' ASSOCIATION (ECA)
ESCA House
34 Palace Court
London W2 4HY
01-229 1266

Membership: corporate membership only; proof of financial stability and technical competence required
Membership list: free on request from ECA head office
Code of conduct: based on the IEE Wiring Regulations
Complaints procedure: yes
Complaint-handling charge: no
Disciplinary sanctions: warning; expulsion

ELECTRICAL CONTRACTORS' ASSOCIATION OF SCOTLAND

23 Heriot Row
Edinburgh EH3 6EW
031-225 7221

Membership: voluntary; inspection of work and evidence of financial stability required
Membership list: local list free on request
Fee guidelines: no
Code of conduct: yes; also code of practice
Complaints procedure: yes
Complaint-handling charge: no
Disciplinary sanctions: suspension; expulsion

EXTERNAL WALL INSULATION ASSOCIATION

PO Box 12
Haslemere
Surrey GU27 3AH
0428-54011

Membership: voluntary
Membership list: free on request
Fee guidelines: no
Code of conduct: yes: code of professional practice
Complaints procedure: yes
Complaint-handling charge: no
Disciplinary sanctions: warning (with pressure to right any wrongs); expulsion

FEDERATION OF MASTER BUILDERS
Gordon Fisher House
33 John Street
London WC1N 2BB
01-242 7583

Membership: voluntary
Membership list: free on request from regional offices
Fee guidelines: no
Code of conduct: yes
Complaints procedure: yes; arbitration can be arranged
Complaint-handling charge: no
Disciplinary sanctions: expulsion

GLASS AND GLAZING FEDERATION
44-48 Borough High Street
London SE1 1XB
01-403 7177

Membership: voluntary; minimum of two years' trading and of
   three employees
Membership list: local lists free on request
Fee guidelines: no
Code of conduct: yes (code of ethical practice)
Complaints procedure: yes
Complaint-handling charge: no
Disciplinary sanctions: reprimand; termination of membership

GUILD OF MASTER CRAFTSMEN LTD
166 High Street
Lewes
East Sussex BN7 1XU
0273-478449

Membership: voluntary
Membership list: names of members with specific skills provided free on application; directory available

Fee guidelines: no
Code of conduct: yes
Complaints procedure: yes
Complaint-handling charge: no
Disciplinary sanctions: expulsion

GUILD OF SURVEYORS
61 Queens Road
Oldham OL8 2BA
061-627 2389

Membership: voluntary; examination qualifications or experience
    required
Style of qualification: AG of S; FG of S
Membership list: free on request
Fee guidelines: yes
Code of conduct: yes
Complaints procedure: yes
Complaint-handling charge: no
Disciplinary sanctions: suspension; expulsion

HEATING AND VENTILATING CONTRACTORS'
ASSOCIATION (HVCA)
ESCA House
34 Palace Court
London W2 4JG
01-229 2488

Membership: voluntary; sole traders or bona fide employers of
    labour; minimum of two years' trading plus references
    required;
Membership list: names of two local members supplied free on
    request by letter or telephone call to Home Heating
    Linkline, 0345-581158 (local call rates, regardless of location)
Fee guidelines: no
Code of conduct: yes (HCVA guarantee for central heating
    installation); code of fair trading (for other work)

Complaints procedure: free conciliation; low-cost arbitration
Complaint-handling charge: no
Disciplinary sanctions: reprimand;   suspension;   expulsion;
    reimbursement of HCVA costs

INCORPORATED ASSOCIATION OF ARCHITECTS AND SURVEYORS (IAAS)
Jubilee House
Billing Brook Road
Weston Favell
Northampton NN3 4NW
0604-404121

Membership: voluntary; examination qualifications required
Style of qualification: architects: MIAA or FIAA; surveyors:
    MIAS or FIAS; architects & surveyors: MIAA&S or FIAA&S
    non-chartered town planners: MIAS (TP) or FIAS (TP)

Membership list: free on request
*Fee guidelines:.*no
Code of conduct: yes
Complaints procedure: yes
Complaint-handling charge: no
Disciplinary sanctions: reprimand; expulsion

INCORPORATED SOCIETY OF VALUERS AND AUCTIONEERS (ISVA)
3 Cadogan Gate
London SW1X 0AS
01-235 2282

Membership: voluntary; examination qualifications required
Style of qualification: ASVA (Associate); FSVA (Fellow)
Membership list: available from ISVA office
Fee guidelines: no
Code of conduct: yes
Complaints procedure: yes

Complaint-handling charge: no
Disciplinary sanctions: undertaking not to repeat offence; reprimand; suspension; expulsion

INSTITUTE OF PLUMBING
64 Station Lane
Hornchurch
Essex RM12 6NB
04024-72791

Membership: voluntary; examination qualifications or 5 years' experience required
Style of qualification: AIP (Associate); MIP (Member); FIP (Fellow); RP (Registered Plumber)
Membership list: can be consulted at CABx, libraries, water undertakers
Fee guidelines: no
Code of conduct: yes
Complaints procedure: yes
Complaint-handling charge: no
Disciplinary sanctions: expulsion

NATIONAL ASSOCIATION OF PLUMBING, HEATING AND MECHANICAL SERVICES CONTRACTORS (NAPH & MSC)
6 Gate Street
London WC2A 3HP
01-405 2678

Membership: voluntary; appropriate training, experience and references
Membership list: free on request
Fee guidelines: no
Code of conduct: yes: code of fair trading (for domestic work)
Complaints procedure: conciliation; arbitration (for domestic work)
Complaint-handling charge: arbitration fee
Disciplinary sanctions: expulsion

NATIONAL ASSOCIATION OF LOFT INSULATION CONTRACTORS (NALIC)

PO Box 12
Haslemere
Surrey GU27 3AH
0428-54011

Membership: voluntary
Membership list: free on request
Fee guidelines: no
Code of conduct: yes (code of practice)
Complaints procedure: yes
Complaint-handling charge: no
Disciplinary sanctions: warnings (with pressure to right any wrongs); expulsion

NATIONAL CAVITY INSULATION ASSOCIATION (NCIA)

PO Box 12
Haslemere
Surrey GU27 3AH
0428-54011

Membership: voluntary; training and being in good standing required
Membership list: free on request
Fee guidelines: yes
Code of conduct: yes
Complaints procedure: yes
Complaint-handling charge: no
Disciplinary sanctions: warning (with pressure to right any wrongs); expulsion

NATIONAL FEDERATION OF ROOFING CONTRACTORS (NFRC)

24 Weymouth Street
London W1N 3FA
01-436 0387

Membership: voluntary; 2-3 years' trading record and inspection of work required
Membership list: free on request
Code of conduct: yes
Complaints procedure: yes
Complaint-handling charge: no
Disciplinary sanctions: termination of membership

NATIONAL HOUSE BUILDING COUNCIL (NHBC)

Information Department:
58 Portland Place
London W1N 4BU
01-636 3832

Membership: voluntary; proof of technical competence and financial stability required
Membership list: available
Code of conduct: yes
Complaints procedure: yes
Complaint-handling charge: no; returnable deposit demanded for investigating complaints
Disciplinary sanctions: caution; fine (as compensation or penalty); removal from register

NATIONAL INSPECTION COUNCIL FOR ELECTRICAL INSTALLATION CONTRACTING (NICEIC)

37 Albert Embankment
London SE1 7UJ
01-735 1322 (technical)
01-582 7746 (admin)

Membership: voluntary; members must conform to Council's rules and undergo regular inspection of work and resources
Style of qualification: NICEIC Approved Contractor; NICEIC Conforming Body
Membership list: may be seen at Electricity Board shops, CABx, libraries

Fee guidelines: no
Code of conduct: IEE Wiring Regulations and associated British Standards codes of practice
Complaints procedure: yes
Disciplinary sanctions: correcting faulty work; removal from Council's roll
Complaint-handling charge: only to contractor found at fault

ROYAL INCORPORATION OF ARCHITECTS IN SCOTLAND (RIAS)
15 Rutland Square
Edinburgh EH1 2BE
031-229 7205/75/45

Membership: voluntary; examination qualifications required
Style of qualification: ARIAS (Associate); FRIAS (Fellow)
Membership list: available
Fee guidelines: yes
Code of conduct: yes
Complaints procedure: yes
Complaint-handling charge: no
Disciplinary sanctions: suspension; expulsion

ROYAL INSTITUTE OF BRITISH ARCHITECTS (RIBA)
66 Portland Place
London W1 4AD
01-580 5533

Membership: voluntary; examination qualifications and practical experience required
Style of qualification: RIBA; but members elected before 1971 may use ARIBA (Associate); FRIBA (Fellow); LRIBA (Licentiate)
Membership list: available
Fee guidelines: yes
Code of conduct: yes
Complaints procedure: yes
Complaint-handling charge: no
Disciplinary sanctions: reprimand; suspension; expulsion

ROYAL INSTITUTION OF CHARTERED SURVEYORS (RICS)
12 Great George Street
London SW1P 3AD
01-222 7000

Membership: voluntary (only members may call themselves chartered surveyors); examination qualifications and practical experience required
Style of qualification: ARICS (Professional Associate); FRICS (Fellow)
Membership list: local lists free from RICS Information Centre; individual enquiries answered as to someone's membership
Fee guidelines: yes
Code of conduct: yes
Complaints procedure: yes
Complaint-handling charge: no
Disciplinary sanctions: reprimand; suspension; expulsion

ROYAL TOWN PLANNING INSTITUTE (RTPI)
26 Portland Place
London W1N 4BE
01-636 9107

Membership: voluntary (only members may call themselves chartered town planners); examination qualifications and practical experience required
Style of qualification: (corporate members only) MRTPI (Member); FRTPI (Fellow); LMRTPI (legal Member)
Membership list: not available (postal/telephone enquiries answered)
Fee guidelines: no
Code of conduct: yes
Complaints procedure: yes
Complaint-handling charge: no
Disciplinary sanctions: warning; reprimand; suspension; expulsion

SCOTTISH AND NORTHERN IRELAND PLUMBING EMPLOYERS' FEDERATION

2 Walker Street
Edinburgh EH3 7LB
031-225 2255

Membership: voluntary
Membership list: free on request
Fee guidelines: no
Code of conduct: yes
Complaints procedure: yes
Complaint-handling charge: no; arbitration fee
Disciplinary sanctions: suspension; expulsion

SOCIETY OF ARCHITECTS IN WALES

75A Llandennis Road
Cardiff CF2 6EE
0222-762215

Membership: voluntary; examination qualifications, practical training and ARCUK registration required
Style of qualification: RIBA; Associate of RIBA
Membership list: available
Code of conduct: yes
Complaints procedure: yes
Complaint-handling charge: no
Disciplinary sanctions: suspension and/or expulsion

SOCIETY OF SURVEYING TECHNICIANS

Drayton House
30 Gordon Street
London WC1H 0BH
01-388 8008

Membership: voluntary; examination qualifications and/or practical experience required

Style of qualification: MSST (Member); AMSST (Associate) not
   used since 1st Jan. 1987
Membership list: not available to public (but may be supplied at
   Society's discretion)
Fee guidelines: no
Code of conduct: yes
Complaints procedure: yes
Complaint-handling charge: no
Disciplinary sanctions: reprimand; suspension; expulsion

London telephone numbers

On 6 May 1990 the 01 telephone
code for London will change to
either 071 or 081, depending on the
local code that follows it. From that
date, people telephoning the 01
code will hear a recorded message
telling them to re-dial using either
071 or 081.

Essential Services

'Essential' services are those which every consumer has need of at some time: the supply of water, electricity, gas and coal; the postal services and telecommunications.

All of these were formerly national monopolies. Most are now either privatised (that is, owned by their shareholders) or will shortly become so, but are, by and large, bound to retain their monopoly status. In the case of telecommunications, an element of commercial competition has now arisen; the Post Office retains a virtual monopoly of letter deliveries, but its parcel delivery services are now open to competition. But except in these cases, the customer cannot choose the supplier, or secure a more favourable price.

Consequently, this chapter is chiefly concerned with telling people who have experienced problems with the essential services where to go for advice, and where to direct their complaints.

GAS

The supply of gas in Great Britain is governed by the Gas Act 1986 which enabled the privatisation of the British gas industry. British Gas retains a virtual monopoly over the supply of gas for domestic and other small consumers. The Secretary of State for Energy has appointed a Director General of Gas Supply with the duty of protecting the interests of such consumers of gas, through monitoring the prices charged, and the quality and continuity of supply. The Gas Act also provided for the formation of a Gas Consumers Council, to replace the National

Gas Consumers' Council and the Regional Gas Consumers' Councils.

The Office of Gas Supply (OFGAS)

This was set up by the Gas Act 1986 as an independent regulatory body. Its main duties are to enforce the conditions of authorisation given to British Gas plc by the Secretary of State, and to ensure that the company complies with its statutory duties.

Particularly significant is its responsibility of enforcing the price formula which governs the maximum average price that British Gas plc can charge its tariff customers; and also of ensuring that standing charges do not rise faster than the rate of inflation.

The authorisation given to British Gas contains conditions which the company is required to meet; the Gas Act 1986 also specifies certain duties. The Director General has the power to ensure that British Gas should comply with these obligations. The main areas in which he might exercise this power are:

○ in cases of disconnection, where British Gas has contravened its duty to give and continue to give a supply by disconnecting without legal justification

○ the failure of British Gas to meet a reasonable request from a potential customer for a supply of gas.

The Director General may also arrange for the publication of information and advice for gas customers, and fix the maximum price at which gas may be resold – for example, by landlords to tenants.

There are certain matters which the Director General and the Gas Consumers Council are obliged by statute to investigate if they are brought to their attention by interested individuals; or if they are referred to the Director by the Council, or to the Council by the Director. Such matters are, for example, queries about the cost of connection, or problems of meter tampering or disconnection for non-payment; but only the Director General has the power to enforce decisions on British Gas.

Gas Consumers Council (GCC)

This is an independent agency, set up to represent the interests of gas consumers. It serves all 17 million domestic and commercial gas users in the UK. The addresses of its regional offices are given on the back of gas bills, and displayed in all showrooms.

The Council's chief concern is the gas industry's policy as it affects the gas consumer. It represents the gas consumer in discussions with gas companies, manufacturers and suppliers and, if necessary, by approaching the Secretary of State for Energy and the Director General of Gas Supply or the Director General of Fair Trading.

The Gas Consumers Council is a completely independent agency. As well as dealing with complaints, it lobbies the government on matters relating to the supply or use of gas, and in some cases makes reports to the Director General of Fair Trading. It also works closely with other consumer agencies, such as the Citizens Advice Bureaux and Trading Standards Offices.

The Council also distributes free leaflets giving advice to particular groups, such as the elderly or disabled, on matters such as difficulties with reaching a meter or with using the handles of gas appliances or meters. For the blind, there is information about where to get special braille or studded controls for gas appliances.

Complaining about gas

The Council can handle most types of complaint, except for those to do with the level of tariff for domestic customers, which are handled by OFGAS. The aggrieved consumer should begin by contacting British Gas (if complaining about the gas supply) or the supplier (if complaining about a gas appliance). If still dissatisfied, he should then write to or telephone the head office of the Council, or one of the Council's regional offices. The complaint will be investigated without charge.

Once the facts have been established, the Council may refer

the matter to OFGAS, so that the Director General can use his powers of enforcement, should this become necessary. The complaint may also be referred to the Director General of Fair Trading. Complainants are advised to keep records of all their dealings with the Council and with British Gas and/or the appliance suppliers.

Paying for gas

British Gas provides information about easier ways of paying for gas. These include budget payments (in which the total annual gas consumption is estimated and the payments divided into 12 equal monthly instalments), and also savings stamps, £1 or £5 in value, which can be obtained from gas showrooms or post offices. Gas Regions and Electricity Boards have agreed to accept each others' savings stamps. Anyone who has difficulty in paying a gas bill is advised to consult staff at showrooms or gas offices without delay.

If bills are not paid, the gas supply may be disconnected. The gas industry (in association with the electricity industry) has for some years operated a code of practice which states that the supply will not be cut off in any of the following circumstances:

○ if the customer agrees to a reasonable payment arrangement that takes into account his circumstances and income
○ if it is safe and practical to install a slot meter
○ if all the people living in the house are retirement pensioners – but this applies only between 1 October and 31 March
○ if the debt is in the name of a past customer
○ if there is no adult at home at the time, unless the customer has been warned and an entry warrant has been obtained
○ if the debt is only for the hire purchase of an appliance.

Furthermore, the appropriate Gas Region should be told:

○ if the customer is getting income support or unemployment benefit, or if all the people in the house are retirement pensioners

o   if the customer is blind, severely sick or disabled
o   if there are children under ll years old, or if the family is getting family credit
o   if the customer is planning to contact the Department of Social Security or the social services department of the local authority.

Early in 1989 British Gas agreed to a modification to that part of its authorisation which is concerned with the methods to be adopted by the company for dealing with customers who have difficulty in paying their gas bills. Under the new system, British Gas has to offer such customers some arrangement for recovering the debt which is related to their ability to pay. Customers who cannot handle credit must be offered a prepayment meter rather than have the supply disconnected.

This modification gives legal backing to the terms of the gas industry's code of practice; but it is vital that a customer in financial difficulty should, in order to take advantage of the new arrangements, contact British Gas at the earliest opportunity.

Gas safety

The Gas Safety Regulations 1972 and the Gas Safety (Installation and Use) Regulations 1984 impose specific responsibilities on those who supply gas and install gas appliances. Only competent people are allowed to install or to service appliances.

A network of showrooms and British Gas Authorised Dealers is available for the sale and installation of appliances. Any gas appliances sold by British Gas must comply with the safety requirements of the British Standards Institution. People buying second-hand appliances should make sure to buy from a reputable dealer. For servicing, contract schemes are available, and British Gas recommends them to customers, to ensure that appliances operate safely and efficiently.

If a gas escape is suspected, it is vital to turn off the main gas supply, and the local Gas Service Centre must be told immediately. The number of the emergency service can be found under GAS in the telephone directory; and there is no charge for checking a suspected escape.

The Confederation for the Registration of Gas Installers (CORGI), established in 1970, has a register of firms which are certified as being competent to carry out safe gas installations, and have given a written undertaking that they will comply with Gas Safety Regulations. They are then termed CORGI Registered Installers and may display the CORGI logo in their advertising. CORGI carries out on-site inspection both of work being carried out and of gas safety procedures before granting registration, and at regular intervals after registration. It is therefore advisable, for reasons of safety, to make sure that any gas appliances should be installed by a CORGI registered installer. An unregistered installer may be cheaper, but may carry a risk too big to take.

A list of registered installers is available at gas showrooms, at some Citizens Advice Bureaux and some libraries. If a firm falsely claims to be a CORGI installer, it should be reported to the local Trading Standards Officer. Registered installers must comply with British Standards codes of practice and current Gas Safety Regulations: if a firm does not comply with CORGI requirements for registration, it can be removed from the CORGI register.

In disputes between customer and installer, CORGI can be involved only on gas safety grounds. In such cases a CORGI quality standards inspector may be called in to check a suspect installation and give advice: there is no charge for this service.

ELECTRICITY

At the time of going to press, a bill for the privatisation of the supply of electricity, which will greatly alter what is described here, is passing through Parliament. An outline of its provisions follows the account of the system as it is at present and will remain till the new statute has been implemented.

The electricity industry is also subject to statutory control, most significantly by the Electricity Act of 1947 and the Energy

Act of 1983. The 1947 Act is the controlling factor behind the tariffs which govern the price for electricity supplied by an Electricity Board.

These are the bodies chiefly concerned with the supply of electricity:

The Central Electricity Generating Board (CEGB) operates the power stations in England and Wales and the national grid.

It sells the electricity to the Area Electricity Boards. These are responsible for the distribution of electricity in their areas, selling it to households as well as to industry and commerce. They establish tariffs for consumers and collect payment. They also act as contractors, operating electricity showrooms and service centres.

The Electricity Council is the forum where general policy of supply is formulated, including finance, tariffs, presentation, marketing and demand forecasting.

Electricity Consumers' Council (ECC)

As well as providing regulations for the supply and safety of electricity, the 1983 Energy Act established the Electricity Consumers' Council, with a chairman appointed by the Secretary of State for Energy. The Council is required by statute to consider the following:

o any matter generally affecting the interests of consumers of electricity supplied by the Electricity Boards of England and Wales

o any matter affecting the interests of a particular category of such consumers

o any plans, arrangements or proposals of which it is informed by the Electricity Council, and in response to which it may make representations to the Electricity Council.

The Electricity Consumers' Council is required to report on any matters referred to it by the Secretary of State or the Electricity Council. At the end of each financial year it must report to the Secretary of State on its performance of its functions during the year.

The ECC has no power to deal with particular complaints. It is a national organisation, dealing with policy issues for the industry as a whole. Complaints from individuals are passed on to the appropriate Area Electricity Consultative Councils.

However, the ECC is able to help consumers in other ways: for example, by giving advice in conjunction with the gas industry on what you can do if you cannot pay a bill. It also issues some codes of practice, such as one on domestic electricity appliance servicing.

The ECC has also tried to help consumers with cashless prepayment electricity meters (operated by tokens). It has stressed that customers should have easy access to points of sale for tokens, and that the meter must allow for sufficient emergency credit supply to take a customer through the longest holiday weekend.

In cases of theft from prepayment meters, it has been the practice to disconnect consumers who could not replace the cash stolen by someone else. The ECC has encouraged a more sympathetic approach. In 1988-89, 78,000 domestic households were disconnected for non-payment of electricity bills. The ECC has helped to develop of a code of practice for disconnections, similar to that followed by the gas industry.

Area Electricity Consultative Councils (AECC)

There are 12 of these in England and Wales and two in Scotland, and they function under the aegis of the Department of Trade and Industry. They were established by the Electricity Act 1947.

The duties of an AECC are to consider matters to do with the distribution of electricity in the area (because consumers have complained, or because there appears to be a problem), and to report on them to the Area Electricity Board; to consider any matter referred to it by the Area Board; to consider and report on any matter concerning the variation of the charges; to consider and report on any matter referred to it by the CEGB; to consider and report to the ECC on any matter referred to it by the ECC.

In very general terms, the AECCs are concerned with the standards of service a consumer should expect; with representing the consumer in decisions on costs and prices; with improving the industry's arrangements for complaint handling; with providing a channel for complaints which have not been satisfactorily resolved by the industry itself.

Complaining about the electricity supply

Consumers in England and Wales with problems or complaints should first contact their own Area Electricity Board. If they receive no satisfaction there, they should contact their AECC, stating the complaint, preferably in writing. The addresses and telephone numbers of the AECCs are obtainable from local Area Electricity offices, and from complaint-handlers such as Citizens Advice Bureaux; and also appear on electricity bills.

The AECC will take up the problem with the Area Electricity Board. If it proves impossible to solve, the AECC has the right to refer the matter to the Electricity Council, and then to the Secretary of State. If the cause of complaint has bearing on matters affecting the whole country, it may be taken up by the Electricity Consumers' Council.

The future for electricity

The structure of the industry will be radically altered by its privatisation. The restructuring will probably start around the end of 1989, but may not be completed until 1991 or later. On completion, the industry will be structured and regulated in the following way:

A new regulator, the Director General of Electricity Supply, will be supported by the Office of Electricity Regulation (OFFER). This body will be responsible for the economic regulation and, where appropriate, the encouragement of competition, in all aspects of the industry. In addition, the Director General will have important powers to determine disputes between customers and the industry.

The Director General will set up Consumers' Committees (CCs) in each area covered by a Public Electricity Supply Licence. These Committees will take over from the existing AECCs. They will deal with consumer complaints and may, under some circumstances, take over the Director General's role in determining disputes.

The industry is also being restructured. Each of the current Area Boards will be replaced by a free-standing Public Electricity Supplier (PES). All the PESs will jointly own a company that runs the high voltage transmission system (the grid). This company will, however, run at arm's length from the PESs.

The current generating capacity of the CEGB is being split into two new companies – Power Gen and National Power. They will supply electricity under contract to the PESs but will be free to contract directly with final customers if they want to. In theory, at least, any other company that wants to will also be able to generate electricity and sell to the PESs or others on the same basis as Power Gen or National Power.

In actual fact, all domestic customers will take their electricity from the local PES, which will be under an obligation to supply any customer in its area. The conditions under which it does so will be laid down in a number of different ways – the Electricity Act 1989, regulations made by the Director General or the Secretary of State under the Act, the Public Electricity Supply Licence, various codes of practice which the licence will require and the conditions of the contract between the customer and the PES. At time of writing none of these are finalised.

However, some of their elements are complete, and it is likely that there will be some new consumer rights. For example, the quality of the service that the PES has to supply will be much more closely defined than now, and compensation will be payable if these standards are not met. The rules on disconnection in case of debt will be tightened up, and will be enforceable by the Director General.

These new rights will inevitably lead to more complaints

and disputes. Under the new system, complaints about the electricity supply will be made to the local Customers' Committee. This will take the matter up with the PES, or the Director General; or in some cases may actually be able to determine the dispute itself. How this will work in practice, remains to be seen.

COAL (AND OTHER SOLID FUELS)

British Coal, as it is now called, was originally set up as the National Coal Board by the Coal Industry Nationalisation Act 1946, Section 4 of which set up the Domestic Coal Consumers' Council (DCCC) to protect the interests of the domestic coal consumer. It checks on prices, carries out research (particularly into what solid-fuel users want for their money), enquires into safety aspects and is concerned with the quality both of the product sold and of servicing. It is completely independent – not part either of the coal trade, or of British Coal. Its funding comes from the Department of Energy.

Complaining about coal

One of the DCCC's major responsibilities is to consider any representation or complaint made to it by domestic consumers about the sale or supply of solid fuel. It can be written to at Freepost, London SWlP 2YZ. The address and telephone number can also be obtained from coal merchants, telephone directories and Citizens Advice Bureaux. No fee is charged for dealing with complaints.

As a first step, a reasonable attempt should be made to solve the problem with the merchant concerned: if this fails, the complainant should write to the Regional Secretary of the Approved Coal Merchants Scheme. If this also fails, he should then write to the DCCC, giving full details. However, the only disciplinary direction open to the DCCC is 'persuasive publicity'.

If the complaint has to do with alleged short weight, the local Trading Standards Officer should be told immediately: you can get his address and telephone number from your town hall, county council offices or the Citizens Advice Bureau.

The Approved Coal Merchants' Scheme (ACMS)

The scheme was jointly set up by British Coal, DCCC, the Coal Merchants Federation of Great Britain, the National Association of Solid Fuel Wholesalers and the Co-operative Fuel Trade Association. Its function is to promote a code of practice with which members are expected to comply: should a member fail to do so, he stands to lose his membership.

Members of the scheme must follow the Coal Trade Code and display a distinctive logo on their lorries, together with their name and address; delivery tickets, if they are for over 100kg, must carry the name and address and must describe the coal or smokeless fuel being sold, and its quality grade (group). Deliveries should be arranged to take advantage of summer discounts, where appropriate, and credit terms should be available for suitable customers.

A basic condition of membership is the duty to investigate promptly and sympathetically any complaint made about fuel supplied or service provided. Should a member of ACMS fail in this duty, a complaint should be made to the ACMS Regional Officer – to find him, look in the telephone directory under Approved Coal Merchants Scheme, or contact the national office. No charge is made for investigating complaints.

Coal safety

Another important concern of the DCCC is its safety code for consumers. It advises them to have the chimneys swept at least once a year, even if smokeless fuel is used; to remove ash and soot from pipes and throat plates at least once a month; to follow manufacturers' instructions and take care when lighting the fuel; to burn only recommended fuel; to guard the fire, particularly if children or elderly people live in the house.

Solid Fuel Advisory Service (SFAS)

The nearest office of this service can be found in Yellow Pages under 'Coal'. It is wholly owned by British Coal, and advises consumers about coal and coal fired appliances; for instance, about the most appropriate coal or smokeless fuel for a particular stove or fire. SFAS can also advise on choosing a new stove or boiler, cooker or fire and can help to solve problems with the fires or chimneys already in use. Its services are usually free. You can also order fuel through SFAS.

THE POST OFFICE

The Post Office consists of four separate but related companies: Post Office Counters Ltd, Royal Mail Letters, Royal Mail Parcels and Girobank plc. It holds a monopoly of some of the services it supplies; in the rest, it is in competition with other organisations, or is an agent for other organisations.

The Post Office is a public corporation established by the Post Office Act 1969 and has virtual monopoly of the delivery of inland letters. It is required by the British Telecommunications Act 1981 to provide throughout the UK satisfactory services for the handling and delivery of letters.

An order under this Act amends the letters monopoly (until the end of the year 2006) in several respects: an important one is the inland delivery of 'time sensitive' letters. However, other persons or bodies are permitted to convey letters only if a minimum charge of £1 is made for each letter conveyed.

In addition to the letter service, including recorded and registered letters, the Post Office monopoly services comprise the supply of stamps, some counter services, post offices generally, collections, deliveries and private boxes.

The Post Office does not have a monopoly of the conveyance of parcels: there are many private parcels service firms. The Post Office has many more 'acceptance points' than any of these, and offers delivery six days a week to virtually every address in the UK; but you may find that one of its rivals offers a service that is just as efficient, and, sometimes, cheaper.

It is best to telephone a number of these firms (many have Freefone facilities) and ask for a quotation, stating your exact requirements (for example, charges are higher for a 'same-day' service). Most of the major firms offer much the same services, so the cheapest is often the best; though this may not apply in the case of a single small parcel, for which the Post Office may be the better bet.

Post Office Users' Councils

The 1969 Act set up Post Office Users' Councils as independent bodies to represent the interests of the users of Post Office monopoly services. The Post Office Users' National Council (POUNC) monitors these, and ensures that customers have a voice in matters such as the quality of service, and the price charged for it.

The Post Office has a statutory duty to consult POUNC about changes proposed in the service, and in tariffs. POUNC is assisted by local Post Office Advisory Committees, and is in touch with other consumers' organisations; each year it publishes a report to the Secretary of State.

The POUNC report for 1988 stated that customers' protests about the quality of the mail service had resulted in the Post Office changing the basis for measuring its performance, since its aim to deliver nationally 9 out of 10 first-class letters the day after collection did not tally with POUNC's experience; POUNC had sent a batch of more than 7,000 letters, and found that only 79% arrived the next day. This has resulted in the phased introduction of change in the measuring system (from the time of posting to the time of delivery).

POUNC represents post office users generally: there are separate but similar Post Office Users' Councils for Scotland, Wales and Northern Ireland, the 'Country Councils', which are also represented on POUNC. The members of all four councils are appointed by the Secretary of State for Trade and Industry (the ministry which also provides their funding).

POUNC has no voice in the provision of the parcels and

express delivery services, Girobank, and counter services carried out on behalf of other bodies, such as social security payments and the sale of TV licences.

Post Office Advisory Committees

These voluntary local bodies, were established to represent Post Office customers at a local level and also to advise both POUNC and the Post Office itself, on a variety of questions, both local and national.

Complaining about the post

There may be a variety of problems: failure to redirect; failure to deliver mail early enough; difficulty in obtaining compensation; failure to provide posting boxes on new housing estates; collection tabs on posting boxes not being changed; and many others.

The Post Office has produced a code of practice, in consultation with POUNC and the Office of Fair Trading. Ask at your post office for a copy: it is a free, illustrated booklet, *The Code of Practice*, and includes a description of all the services available, and of procedures for complaining and claiming compensation. It contains a general statement of intent to provide a high quality of service, and to maintain and improve standards of service; to ensure that staff deal quickly, helpfully and efficiently with customers' needs, and to keep staffing levels high at peak times of business.

If you have a problem with counter services, complain first to the branch manager at your main post office. If not satisfied, contact the Customer Service Unit at your District Office. (If the complaint is about agency services, such as National Savings or DSS payments, where the post office is acting for another organisation, address your complaint to that organisation.)

Though in law the Post Office has no contract with its customers, it may, in many circumstances, be held legally liable for loss of or damage to letters or parcels, though not for delay. But there must be proof of posting (which you can ask for every time you post anything at the Post Office); and if you are claiming for damage, you should produce the wrapping, for your claim will depend on showing that the parcel was correctly wrapped and addressed. Claims should be made as promptly as possible.

Complain first to the Customer Service Unit. The Post Office tries to acknowledge complaints and compensation claims within a few days of receiving them, and to resolve them within six weeks in the case of inland mail (up to six months in the case of international mail). Ask for enquiry form P58, and return it, when completed, to the Customer Service Unit or any post office.

If you do not get a satisfactory response, contact your District Manager, or the Post Office Advisory Committee, if there is one in your area. However, you may do better to consult POUNC, or one of the Country Councils. Complain in writing, explaining the problem and perhaps enclosing photocopies of evidence, such as envelopes or proofs of posting, and also of any correspondence. POUNC has no actual sanctions to impose, but uses the influence it has with the Post Office.

If you still feel aggrieved, and your complaint is about inland post, your next step could be either an action at law, or arbitration. If you choose the latter, you must apply to the Chartered Institute of Arbitrators (75 Cannon Street, London EC4N 5BH, telephone 01-236 8761), which will send you forms to fill in. You will be asked for a fee (about £15) which will be refunded if the arbitrator finds in your favour. He will ask both you and the Post Office for a detailed statement of the case and all the evidence, and will decide on this basis whether to award compensation. His decision is legally binding (with no appeal) and so you cannot then take the case to court.

Even if the arbitrator considers that the Post Office is not legally liable, but there are extenuating circumstances in your case, he may suggest an ex gratia payment.

If the complaint has to do with overseas post, it can be put to an adjudicator appointed by the Chartered Institute of

Arbitrators: the procedure for applying is the same. In such cases the Post Office is not legally bound to pay compensation, but will consider itself honour bound to accept the adjudicator's decision.

Arbitration costs less than court action, the procedure is usually simpler and the process speedier; however, the award may be less, and there is no appeal.

TELECOMMUNICATIONS

Telecommunications were revolutionised in 1984 with the privatisation of British Telecom (BT) and the abolition of its (almost) exclusive right to provide telecommunication systems throughout the UK. Now other organisations have been licensed as Public Telecommunications Operators (PTOs).

Telecommunications are governed mainly by the Telecommunications Act 1984. Under it, a Director General of Telecommunications is appointed by the Secretary of State for Trade and Industry, and his duties include the promotion of:

○ the interests of consumers and other users of telecommunication services and equipment
○ effective competition between businesses related to telecommunications
○ efficiency and economy
○ research into and the development of new techniques.

The Director General also has a duty to monitor and enforce the licensing of telecommunication systems, to give information and advice, and to investigate complaints.

The Director General is the head of the Office of Telecommunications (OFTEL). This body has sole responsibility for the monitoring and enforcement of telecommunications licences and for ensuring that licensing conditions are complied with, or in some case, altered. OFTEL has the duty of ensuring that telecommunications services in the UK are sufficient to meet reasonable demands for them (including emergency services and services in rural areas). It is responsible for maintaining registers of approved apparatus and approved contractors. It is also responsible for the investigation of complaints about telecommunications, in liaison with the four national Advisory Committees on Telecommunications, and with local Telecommunications Advisory Committees (TACs) – voluntary bodies representing the interests of consumers in their areas.

Who provides the service?

BT is the largest of the PTOs, operating a network of 23 million telephone lines and providing more than 80,000 public call boxes. But since privatisation, it has had a rival: Mercury, which is a wholly owned subsidiary of Cable and Wireless, and was formed in 1986. Mercury's alternative national and international telephone service is now available to most business customers as well as more than 50% of domestic customers, and it has begun to provide its own public telephone boxes.

Business customers of Mercury who are large-scale users of telecommunications can be connected directly to the Mercury network. Smaller businesses and domestic customers are connected indirectly through existing exchange lines: so to become a Mercury domestic customer, you must already be renting a BT line.

You must have a standard BT square plug-in telephone socket and a modern telephone compatible with the Mercury system. You will be issued an authorisation code, which can be programmed into your telephone, and which distinguishes your Mercury calls from your BT ones. You can use Mercury for national and international calls, but local calls must be made through BT.

The only other supplier of telecommunications is Kingston Communications (Hull), formerly known as the Kingston-upon-Hull City Council Telephone Department, which has obtained a licence under the 1984 Act.

Codes of practice

All three PTOs operate a code of practice produced in consultation with OFTEL, for the benefit of consumers. The BT code of practice is the one most directly relevant to domestic telephone users. It includes the following points:

Bills

BT tries to ensure that bills are accurate. Any query should be addressed to the local BT office (its telephone number is on the front of the bill). BT will compare the meter readings with those of previous quarters, and will check a record of faults.

Customers who have difficulty in paying a bill are advised to contact BT as quickly as possible for advice on ways to pay. The service is likely to be disconnected if the bill is not settled, and a reconnection fee will be charged unless the late arrival of the payment was BT's fault. Anyone to whom the use of a telephone is essential should contact the local Department of Social Security or the social services department of the local authority, which may be able to help.

Faults

If a call you make is unsatisfactory (for instance, because the line is crossed, faint or noisy), call the operator who will arrange your account to be credited with the price of the call. Faults on the BT network which prevent you from making or from receiving calls should be reported to the BT telephone fault repair service (by calling 151). A fault may be reported at any time.

Under its Customer Service Guarantee, BT now pledges to repair line faults within two clear working days, and to pay compensation of £5 for every day that it fails to honour this pledge. The same conditions apply to appointments made to install a telephone. BT also offers, at additional cost, rather prompter servicing arrangements, with which the daily compensation starts to operate even sooner. It is paid in the form of a credit in the quarterly bill, or directly if it exceeds £25.

But if you are able to prove that you suffered actual financial loss through being deprived of your telephone, you may claim for this instead – up to £1000 for domestic customers, and up to £5000 per line for business customers (with an upper limit of £20,000). You must also be able to show that you did your best to minimise your losses. All claims must be made within two months of the incident.

If the fault is due to equipment which was bought from BT, then the terms of the contract of sale will apply. If the equipment is rented, it will be maintained free of charge.

Mercury's code

Mercury has produced, after consultation with OFTEL, a code of practice on similar lines. Domestic users, using BT lines, should report line faults in the same way as for BT. Directly connected business customers are promised repairs within four hours.

If the service fails due to a fault within the Mercury network, the customer will be credited with a rebate of rental charges for the period of the fault. Credit will also be given for misdirected calls. Telephones supplied by Mercury are repaired free of charge if they are rented, or are still within the one-year guarantee period.

Kingston's code

The Kingston Communications code of practice was produced in conjunction with OFTEL and is very similar to the BT code, except for the compensation scheme. If a fault remains unrepaired for more than two working days after being reported, a pro rata adjustment is made to the line rental in the next bill.

Complaining about British Telecom

All problems should first be taken up with the local BT office. Independent advice can be obtained from the local Telecommunications Advisory Committees (TACs), the voluntary bodies which represent the interest of telecommunications consumers at the local level. If there is one in your area, it will be listed in the telephone directory.

If not satisfied, you should approach one of the four Advisory Committees on Telecommunications (ACTs), which will, if necessary, seek advice from OFTEL. There are separate committees for England, Wales, Scotland and Northern Ireland. However, OFTEL can also be approached directly.

For most types of claim, BT offers arbitration through the Chartered Institute of Arbitrators, as an alternative to court action, provided the amount claimed is less than £5000. The Institute appoints an independent arbitrator whose decision is legally binding on both parties. All the evidence is submitted in writing. There is a registration fee of £15, which is returned if the arbitrator finds in the consumer's favour (or otherwise at his discretion). All claims should be submitted within 12 months of the cause of complaint, unless there are exceptional circumstances.

An alternative means of complaining about telecommunications is the Telecommunications Users' Association. Only members may use its facilities. It represents an amalgamation of the original Telephone Users' Association and another body which represented only the interests of large corporate bodies. It states its purpose to be that of ensuring that the UK telecommunications network matches the best of those overseas, and that full advantage is taken of modern technology; of ensuring that all those concerned with telecommunications become more responsive to the needs of users, particularly with regard to attachment and installation, pricing and service; and of providing expert advice and representation on all key regulatory committees.

It provides information, technical advice and consultancy, representation and negotiation, and a Helpline service. The subscription is £1 per £1000 of annual expenditure on telecommunications. Membership is largely corporate, and includes a variety of academic, commercial and voluntary organisations; there is also a small number of individual members.

The Association will negotiate with BT, Mercury or OFTEL on behalf of members who have a complaint. It has no disciplinary sanctions, but its negotiating strength with PTOs and manufacturers usually brings results. It is a lobbying body; it also runs seminars and conferences, and publishes a quarterly journal.

WATER

At the time of going to press, a bill for the privatisation of the supply of water, which will greatly alter what is described here, is passing through Parliament. An outline of the measures it contains follows the account of the water supply system as it is at present.

The Water Act of 1973 established an administration system for matters relating to water: water conservation, water supply, sewerage and sewage disposal, the prevention of river pollution, fisheries, land drainage and water-based recreation and amenity.

Consequently, the charge made for the supply of water covers at least three elements:

○ water supply: the collection, storage and supply of water
○ sewerage: the removal and treatment of waste water and rain-water
○ environmental services: water quality control, pollution prevention and the provision of leisure facilities.

The Water Act made it the duty of the Secretary of State for the Environment, together with the Minister of Agriculture, to promote a national policy for water.

England and Wales are divided into 10 Regional Water Authorities which are corporate bodies. The Water Authorities' Association is their central organisation. It advises any ministers on national policy for water, and assists the Water Authorities to carry out their functions efficiently. In Scotland, Regional Councils are in charge of the water supply; in Northern Ireland, it is the Department of the Environment.

All the Water Authorities publish leaflets which give

general information and advice, particularly about the payment of bills and arrangements for servicing equipment.

The 1973 Act required the water authorities to establish Consumer Consultative Committees (CCCs) and regional Recreation and Conservation Committees under the aegis of the Secretary of State for the Environment, to protect consumers' interests. Members of the public, together with representatives from local authorities, industry, commerce and agriculture serve on these committees.

CCCs are independent advisory bodies, whose terms of reference are:

○ to watch over the interests of the public with regard to water supply and public sewerage
○ to foster mutual understanding between the public and the Water Authority
○ to consider any matter raised with a CCC by a customer
○ to keep the handling of consumer complaints under review and to make reports and recommendations.

The Recreation and Conservation Committee has similar terms of reference to do with water- and land-based sports and other recreations within the scope of the Authority's functions, and conservation and amenities within the scope of the Authority's duties under the Water Act 1973 (as amended by the Wildlife and Countryside Act 1981). This includes the conservation and enhancement of natural beauty, the protection of things of archaeological interest, the conservation of nature, and the preservation of public access to the countryside.

Complaining about water

If your complaint is about a bill, write to your local customer accounts department; the address is on the bill itself. If the complaint is about the supply of water or about service, it should be made to the divisional office of your local water authority: look under Water in the telephone directory, or ask at a Citizens Advice Bureau.

If you feel that your complaint has not been properly dealt with, write to the local CCC. It cannot deal with an individual case, but only monitor the way in which the Water Authority is handling your complaint. For the address, look in the telephone directory under Water (CCCs operate under various names) or ask the Water Authority.

Your last resort is the local ombudsman (The Commissioner for Local Administration). He is an independent investigator of the local authority, police authority and water administration. His remit includes neglect, delay, failure to follow agreed policies, malice or discrimination, faulty ways of doing things and failure to use proper procedures when reviewing things.

You should ask a CCC member to send your complaint to the ombudsman, but if he refuses, you may send it direct. The Citizens Advice Bureau may help with this.

The complaint must not be about something that you knew about more than 12 months before telling the CCC member; nor a matter on which you have already gone to court. It must not be about contractual or commercial matters, or about docks or harbours.

If the ombudsman takes up your case, he may ask to discuss it with you personally. If he considers it necessary, he will make a formal report, and send you a copy. Any maladministration he may find will have to be made public, and the Water Authority will have to tell him what course of action it will take. If that course does not satisfy you, the ombudsman may issue another report, but cannot force the Authority to act.

Paying water bills

There is a code of practice for the payment of bills by domestic consumers. This states that a customer who has difficulty in paying a water bill should contact the Water Authority, which will want to know his circumstances: whether he has young children, is sick, blind, or disabled, is getting income support or unemployment benefit. The bill cannot be reduced but an agreement can be made to pay it in instalments; or the social security office or Social Services Department may be able to offer help.

A summons will be issued, or the water supply cut off, only if the customer does not pay the bill and does not agree to pay by instalments, and cannot be helped by social security or Social Services Department.

The future for water

The 1989 Water Bill makes possible the flotation and privatisation of the 10 Regional Water Authorities of England and Wales, as well as the conversion to public limited company status of the 29 Statutory Water Companies. It also establishes a new regulatory framework for the water industry in the form of the National Rivers Authority and a Director General of Water Services. Water in Scotland will be bound by some of the provisions of the Bill relating to water quality, but will remain in the public ownership of the 12 Regional Councils; in Northern Ireland, too, the situation will be unchanged.

The Water Authorities will become Water Service public limited companies (WSPLCs) and be responsible for the 'core' services of water supply and sewage disposal.

The regulation of other aspects of the former Authorities' duties will pass to the National Rivers Authority (NRA). These duties include the regulation and administration of water abstraction and conservation, the prevention of river pollution and the regulation of fisheries, land drainage and water-based recreation and amenity. These activities will be financed from directly imposed charges on polluters and other water users, government grant-in-aid and limited borrowing, which will replace the environmental service charge element in water prices. Regional advisory committees will be established for each of these areas of responsibility to advise on policy.

The quality of drinking water will continue to be monitored by local authority Environmental Health Officers, but will ultimately be the responsibility of a drinking water inspectorate within the Department of the Environment.

Each of the WSPLCs will be required to draw up an individual code of practice setting out the services it offers, its terms and conditions, and the mechanism for complaints. A Guaranteed Standards Scheme will provide an automatic £5 cash payment for each day that certain standards are not met, for instance when there is undue delay in dealing with a complaint. There are certain exemptions, however, for such things as failure of service due to industrial action. Codes of practice will regulate disconnections for non-payment of water charges and for leakage from metered supplies.

The Director General of Water Services will be required to regulate the relative performance and efficiency of the WSPLCs and take this into account when fixing the minimum prices the companies charge for water and sewerage services. In addition, WSPLCs will have to establish target standards of performance in various areas of their service, and the Director General will have the power to intervene, should these standards not be met.

The former Consumer Consultative Committees will be replaced by Customer Service Committees (CSCs) and are to form part of the Director General's framework of regulation. They will therefore be independent of the industry. The CSCs will have the power to look into consumer matters and to investigate and take up customer complaints about water companies and refer any such complaints to the Director General. CSCs will include representatives of domestic customers, industrial, commercial and farming interests and local authorities.

Future charges

At present, water is commonly charged for by an amount related to the rateable value of the property supplied. The replacement of rates by the community charge ('poll tax') will make new methods of charging necessary, and the Public Utilities Transfer and Water Charges Act (1988) has provided for regional water metering trials. It is as yet not at all clear which regions will adopt universal water metering and the different tariffs which can accompany it. However, a survey in *Which?* (May 1989) indicated that most people saw metering as the second-best option to charging by rateable values. Water metering has been criticised on the grounds that the poorest may pay more and that meters can inhibit use.

Water charges will be controlled by a formula called RPI + K. K is to be the adjustment factor by which charges will be allowed to increase, and will take account of several variables, including the cost of improving water and sewerage services to conform with EC and national standards. The K factor will be reviewable by the Director General after 10 years, or 5 if he or the WSPLCs should so decide. Each water and sewage 'undertaker' will have a different RPI + K formula and these formulae will be written into the individual conditions of appointment. There will also be a mechanism for cost pass-through, by which the Director may allow WSPLCs to pass on additional unforeseen costs to the consumer, over and above the price formula.

USEFUL ADDRESSES

ADVISORY COMMITTEES ON TELECOMMUNICATIONS (ACTs)
English Advisory Committee on Telecommunications (ENACT)
Atlantic House
Holborn Viaduct
London EC1N 2HQ
01-822 1650

Northern Ireland Advisory Committee on Telecommunications
Chamber of Commerce House (7th floor)
22 Great Victoria Street
Belfast BT2 7QA
0232-244113

Scottish Advisory Committee on Telecommunications
Alhambra House
45 Waterloo Street
Glasgow G2 6AT
041-248 2855 ext 253

Welsh Advisory Committee on Telecommunications
Caradog House (1st floor)
St Andrews Place
Cardiff CF1 3BE
0222-374028

Complaints procedure: yes
Complaint-handling charge: no
Disciplinary sanctions: representations to OFTEL

APPROVED COAL MERCHANTS SCHEME (ACMS)
Victoria House
Southampton Row
London WC1B 4DH
01-405 1601

Membership: coal merchants; voluntary
Membership list: local list free on request
Code of conduct: yes
Complaints procedure: yes
Complaint-handling charge: no
Disciplinary sanctions: expulsion from scheme

BRITISH TELECOM
81 Newgate Street
London EC1A 7AJ
01-356 5000

COMMISSION FOR LOCAL ADMINISTRATION IN ENGLAND
21 Queen Anne's Gate
London SW1H 9BU
01-222 5622

CONFEDERATION FOR THE REGISTRATION OF GAS INSTALLERS (CORGI)
St Martin's House
140 Tottenham Court Road
London W1P 9LN
01-387 9185

Membership: trade association members who form the CORGI council. (Registered gas installers are not referred to as 'members')
Membership list: register available for inspection at gas region showrooms
Fee guidelines: no
Code of conduct: no; standard codes of practice
Complaints procedure: yes, to do with safety of installations
Complaint-handling charge: no
Disciplinary sanctions: removal from register

DOMESTIC COAL CONSUMERS' COUNCIL (DCCC)
Dean Bradley House
52 Horseferry Road
London SW1P 2AG
01-233 0583
or Freepost
London SW1P 2YZ

Code of conduct: yes
Complaints procedure: yes
Complaint-handling charge: no
Disciplinary sanctions: persuasion; publicity

ELECTRICITY CONSUMERS' COUNCIL
Brook House
2-16 Torrington Place
London WC1E 7LL
01-636 5703

Complaints: handled by 12 Area Electricity Consultative Councils (AECCs)

GAS CONSUMERS COUNCIL
Abford House
15 Wilton Road
London SW1V 1LT
01-931 0977
and 11 country and regional offices

Complaints procedure: yes
Complaint-handling charge: no
Disciplinary sanctions: referral to OFGAS or the Director General
of Fair Trading

MERCURY TELECOMMUNICATIONS
90 Long Acre
London WC2 9NP
01-528 2000

OFFICE OF GAS SUPPLY (OFGAS)
Southside
105 Victoria Street
London SW1E 6QT
01-828 0898

OFFICE OF TELECOMMUNICATIONS (OFTEL)
Atlantic House
Holborn Viaduct
London EC1N 2HQ
01-822 1650

Code of conduct: yes
Complaints procedure: yes
Complaints-handling charge: no
Disciplinary sanctions: yes, but not usually applicable to in-
dividual consumer disputes

POST OFFICE USERS' COUNCIL FOR NORTHERN IRELAND
Chamber of Commerce House (3rd floor)
22 Great Victoria Street
Belfast BT2 7PU
0232-244113

Code of conduct: yes
Complaints procedure: yes
Complaint-handling charge: no
Disciplinary sanctions: reference to POUNC

POST OFFICE USERS' COUNCIL FOR WALES
Caradog House (1st floor)
St Andrews Place
Cardiff CF1 3BE
0222-374028

Code of conduct: yes
Complaints procedure: yes
Complaint-handling charge: no
Disciplinary sanctions: representations to the Secretary of State

POST OFFICE USERS' COUNCIL FOR SCOTLAND (POUCS)

Alhambra House
45 Waterloo Street
Glasgow G2 6AT
041-248 2855

Code of conduct: yes
Complaints procedure: yes
Complaints-handling charge: no
Disciplinary sanctions: none

POST OFFICE USERS' NATIONAL COUNCIL (POUNC)

Waterloo Bridge House
Waterloo Road
London SE1 8UA
01-928 9458

Code of conduct: yes
Complaints procedure: yes
Complaint-handling charge: no
Disciplinary sanctions: none

TELECOMMUNICATIONS USERS' ASSOCIATION (TUA)

48 Percy Road
London N12 8BU
01-445 0996

Code of practice: yes (British Telecom and Mercury codes)
Complaints procedure: yes, on behalf of members only
Complaint-handling charge: none to members
Disciplinary sanctions: none

Travel Services

This chapter deals first with transport in general: with air transport, and with rail and road transport in the UK. It then goes on to cover holiday travel, particularly in connection with travel agents and tour operators.

TRAVELLING BY AIR
Whether you buy an airline ticket through a travel agent or direct from the airline, the price is the same. By booking in advance you can get cheaper fares on scheduled flights (APEX or PEX), but with these, the flight times and dates cannot be altered, once they have been booked. Sometimes airlines have 'special offers' for some routes or some seasons.

'Bucket shops' specialise in cheap tickets which may be ones that the airline has failed to sell being sold off at a discount. However, the remarkably cheap tickets sometimes seen advertised in newspapers, magazines or shop windows may be a lure – not actually available when you try to buy one.

Whenever you buy a cheap ticket make sure to get the fullest information about the airline, the flight, and where it starts from (you may have to make your own way expensively to some distant airport). Do not part with your money until you have a ticket.

Even when buying your ticket from an established travel agent, or directly from the airline, read your ticket carefully and note any restrictions regarding the time of travel, changing or cancelling your flight, or breaking your journey. If there are things you are not sure about, check by telephoning the airline.

Not getting on the flight

If you buy a ticket on a scheduled flight, that does not entitle you to a seat on the aeroplane at the time stipulated. The ticket will state that it is issued subject to 'Conditions of Carriage', which include a statement that the airline will carry you 'with reasonable despatch'. Therefore you have no claim for breach of contract if you are 'bumped' from the flight because it was overbooked. You have a potential claim if you can prove that the overbooking was due to the airline's negligence, that is, failure to use reasonable care and skill. However, overbooking is usually deliberate, and not the result of negligence. The explanation normally given for overbookings is that a full-fare ticket is valid for one year, and the holder may cancel a seat on a particular flight at any time; therefore the airline has to overbook on the assumption that several full-fare ticket-holders will not turn up. The Air Transport Users Committee (AUC) has stated, however, that overbooking is more often caused by tour operators not releasing information about pre-booked seats in time, so the airlines have to guess how many of these seats will be taken up. Whatever the reason, the airlines cannot be held to be negligent for overbooking.

Some airlines, however, pay 'denied boarding compensation' if you should not arrive at your destination within four hours of your original arrival time as a result of being transferred to another flight (in the USA such payment is compulsory). The compensation is half the applicable one-way fare, up to a maximum of £150, plus incidental expenses, such as accommodation and meals. If you are bumped, find out if the line on which you were booked takes part in the 'denied boarding compensation' scheme and ask at the airport for a form to claim this compensation.

There is also no guarantee that your flight will depart and arrive on time. Again, it is unlikely that you could prove that the airline or airport had been negligent, and the provision of meals and, if necessary, accommodation, is at the airline's discretion. However, these are, in fact, usually provided.

Missing luggage

The other main complaint you are likely to have is about lost or damaged baggage. You should ask at the airport for a 'property irregularity form'. Complete this, and hand it in immediately. Do not allow yourself to be persuaded that your luggage will be sent on to you: if you leave the airport without filling in the form, liability may later be denied. Make sure that you keep the baggage claim check which was handed to you when you checked in your luggage.

If your luggage is lost on arrival abroad, ask for 'spot' compensation to cover the purchase of essential articles (such as toothbrushes and pyjamas) until the baggage is found. Airlines normally require baggage to be missing for 21 days before it can be classified as lost and compensation can be paid. Even then, the compensation is at a very low rate (9 US dollars per one pound of baggage) by international agreement; so you may do better to insure your luggage before you travel.

Complaining

Whether your complaint is about missing luggage or about facilities or service, you should first attempt to ascertain who is at fault: the airline, the airport, or if you are on a package tour, the tour operator. You should then complain to the customer relations department, or its equivalent, of the appropriate organisation. If a word-of-mouth complaint does not succeed, or does not fit the situation, complain in writing, enclosing copies of any evidence; but keep your original travel documents.

If that does not succeed, you can complain to the Air Transport Users' Committee. This is a non-statutory body, set up by the Civil Aviation Authority to represent passengers' interests. It cannot impose sanctions or arbitrate; it can, however, investigate complaints and make recommendations. You should write to the AUC, enclosing copies of any correspondence. The AUC's main term of reference is furthering the interests of air transport users by making reports and recommendations to the CAA; therefore its remit is much wider than the complaints mentioned above, and includes, amongst others, all aspects of safety and charges. It publishes a free booklet called *Flight Plan* which gives much valuable practical information for the air transport user.

If your complaint is about an airport in Britain, you could also complain to the airport's consultative committee. Again, it has no executive power, but will investigate complaints. It, too, has a much wider remit, which is to balance the needs of the community, air transport, the passenger and the environment. If you wish to complain, you can fill in one of the yellow comment cards available at airports.

If your tour operator is at fault, you should follow the complaints procedure described earlier.

TRAVELLING BY BRITISH RAIL (BR)

Your rail ticket is issued subject to the British Railways Board's 'conditions of carriage of passengers and their luggage' which can be obtained free on request from principal stations; copies of the bye-laws are available for inspection at booking offices and travel centres.

Some of these conditions are very wide-ranging. For instance, BR does not guarantee that any trains will start or arrive, and reserves the right to vary timetables without notice. Your ticket does not entitle you to a seat on a particular train, or in a particular class, or even to any seat; if the train is full, or does not run at all, or you cannot get a seat in the first-class area, or you have to stand all the way, the conditions will inform you that your ticket does not entitle you to these facilities in the first place. It would seem that you are not likely to succeed in a claim for breach of contract, nor in a claim alleging negligence, even if you can prove that the lack of any of these facilities was due to negligence on the part of British Rail.

It has generally been held that passengers are bound by these British Rail conditions (even if they have not read them – and they are most unlikely to have done so). But it now appears that some or all of these conditions could be found invalid under the Unfair Contract Terms Act 1977, on the grounds that they unfairly sought to exclude liability. There is, as yet, no case law on the subject, because the conditions have not yet been tested in the courts, but it is by no means certain that passengers are bound by them.

The conditions do not mean that BR will not compensate you. For example, if you bought a first-class ticket but there is no seat in the first-class carriages, you get the guard to endorse this fact on your ticket and you will obtain a refund; other cases, such as delay, are considered on their merits.

It is sometimes a good idea to get a seat reservation, although a charge is usually payable, because it should ensure that you are able to travel by the train in question *and* get a seat. Some inter-city trains are restricted to holders of reserved seats only (but when reservations are compulsory they are issued free of charge).

Complaints

If you have a complaint, you should always try to obtain evidence for it, preferably from staff on the spot; failing this, from fellow passengers. For certain complaints you would have a legal remedy: for instance, if you consigned your luggage or some other property to be delivered by BR and it was lost or misdirected; or if you were injured through the fault of BR. In the case of lost luggage or property, all you have to do is prove that you consigned the property to BR. It is for BR to prove that it was not at fault; that is, a court would assume that the loss was BR's fault unless BR could prove otherwise. This is because BR would be in breach of contract, by not delivering as and where expected. However, in the case of injury you would have to prove negligence on the part of BR.

BR has published a *Code of Practice and Guide to Customer Services* (now due to be reviewed) which states the aims of BR and gives information to the public about its services, and about making complaints. Amongst these aims are: that no-one should wait longer than five minutes to buy a ticket during busy periods; that 85% of inter-city trains should arrive within 5 minutes of the scheduled time; that BR should try to reply to requests for refunds within 14 days and to reply to any complaint within five working days (or acknowledge within five days and reply in full within four weeks).

If you have a complaint about any of these matters, or about matters such as catering, property missing from 'left luggage', reservations, the staff, the general quality of the service, complain first to staff who are on the spot at the time. If this does not resolve your complaint, you should contact the area manager, whose name, address and telephone number should be prominently displayed at each station. If you are still dissatisfied, you can complain to your local Transport Users Consultative Committee (TUCC); in London, it is the London Regional Passengers' Committee (LRPC). There are nine of these independent statutory bodies, appointed by the government and funded by the Department of Trade and Industry. Their national co-ordinating body is the Central Transport Consultative Committee (CTCC). This will take up your complaint with local officials, and has the power to make reports and recommendations directly to BR and to the Secretary of State for Transport.

You should contact the CTCC directly only if your complaint is about a matter of national policy. There are notices publicising the TUCCs (and the LRPC, where appropriate) at most stations, and these organisations publish leaflets explaining their role and work, in particular one entitled: *Complaints or comments about rail travel – what to do.*

Charges and fares are outside the remit of the TUCCs, but they do comment on fare structures, and the CTCC has had an undertaking from the government that this will become a statutory right.

Arbitration

If neither a complaint to the area manager nor one to a TUCC resolves the matter, rail users may have recourse to an arbitration scheme, which is run independently by the Chartered Institute of Arbitrators. You may use this scheme only if your claim is for failure by BR to carry out its contractual obligation to you, if the claim does not exceed £1,000 and if it is not connected with personal injury. Therefore it will not help you where BR claims to have no contractual obligation, as in some of the situations just referred to. There is a £10 fee, which is refundable if the arbitrator decides in your favour. You can obtain an application form and the rules from the Institute. You must apply within three months of receiving your last reply from BR. The Institute will send the form to BR for signature, as the case can only go to arbitration if both parties agree. The Institute will then notify you, and ask for a statement of your case in writing, with supporting documents.

The case will usually be decided on the documents alone, without a hearing. The decision of the arbitrator is binding, so that you cannot later change your mind and go to court: you must consider this before deciding to use the arbitration procedure. However, given the very low cost, this arbitration may be a desirable alternative to court proceedings.

The trouble with complaints against BR is not that the procedures available are inadequate, but that they apply to breach of contract and so many of the possible grounds of complaint are not classified under contractual obligations.

BUS TRAVEL

As you do not usually enter into a contract with the bus company until you buy or validate your ticket on boarding the bus, you are unlikely to be able to make any complaint against the company for breach of its contract. Your only claim for negligence would probably be in the event of your suffering injury through the negligence of the company's employees. The majority of complaints, such as those about the infrequency or late arrival of buses, the standard of the vehicle or the conduct of the staff, would not constitute an infringement of any legal rights. Nor is there any body to which you could make such complaints, except in the case of London and Northern Ireland. In London, consumer complaints are handled by the LRPC; in Northern Ireland, by the General Consumer Council for Northern Ireland (GCCNI).

The Traffic Commissioners are responsible for registering bus routes. Anyone with an operator's licence can register and operate a bus route, giving 42 days' notice. The Traffic Commissioners may refuse to register a route only on very limited grounds, such as safety.

If a local Passenger Transport Executive (PTE) or a local authority feels that a certain bus route which is uneconomic is required on social grounds, it may subsidise the route, but only if it is not in competition with a commercial route. Tenders must be sought for the route and the lowest tender must be accepted.

The PTE or local authority may consider complaints about such routes, but has no say about the commercial ones. For the commercial routes, complaints must be made to the operator. However, if you are desperate that something should be done, and can find a number of other people who feel as you do, you may complain to the Traffic Commissioner for your area. He will only entertain group complaints, not individual ones, not having enough staff for that.

Information about operators may be displayed on the bus stops. If there is none, you may find it hard to tell, for the purpose of complaining, who is operating a route. Ask the local authority (county council) first if it is one of its routes – if not, the Traffic Commissioner should be able to tell you whose route this is.

London buses all carry blue notices telling the public to complain first to London Regional Transport, and next to the LRPC, whose address is given on the notice.

The travel profession and your holiday

There is a difference between the travel agent and the tour operator. When you book an inclusive holiday through a travel agent, your contract for the holiday is always with the tour operator, not the travel agent. Even if the name of a travel agent is the same as the tour operator's (for example, Horizon) and if the tour operator's holidays can only be booked through that travel agent (for example, Thomas Cook), the two firms are completely separate in law, and you do not have a contract with the travel agent. Some travel agents, usually small local ones, also organise the holidays they sell, in which case you would have a contract with the travel agent, but check first rather than assume that this is the case.

Although the travel agent may give you advice, for instance, as to which tour operator or holiday is the most suitable, no contract exists between the travel agent and you for this advice, because the law requires 'consideration', which basically means payment, for a contract to be binding. The travel agent receives his payment from the tour operator, by way of commission, not from you. Although you could argue that this comes out of the price you pay for the holiday, a client who books directly with the tour operator pays the same as a client booking with the same tour operator through a travel agent. Any action against a travel agent for bad advice would have to be based on negligence, not on non-fulfilment of contract.

CHOOSING A TRAVEL AGENT

To most people who go on package holidays, choosing the right travel agent is not as important as choosing the right tour operator. However, having a good travel agent should reduce the chances of anything going wrong, because the travel agent should be able to warn you against poor tour operators or unsuitable holidays. However, for independent travellers, the choice of a good travel agent is more important.

Anyone can set up in business and call himself a travel agent. It is therefore important to ensure that you use only the services of a travel agent who is a member of the Association of British Travel Agents (ABTA).

More than 7,800 travel agents (including branch offices) are members of ABTA. Look for the ABTA logo, which is usually displayed in the window of travel agencies.

Travel agent members of ABTA are subject to the ABTA travel agents' code of conduct, which requires travel agents to ensure that accurate and impartial information is provided. This code was drawn up in consultation with the Office of Fair Trading (OFT). However, in July 1988 OFT published a report on both of ABTA's codes of conduct (there are separate codes for travel agents and for tour operators) which pointed out that most agents have their preferred suppliers of holidays, and recommended that where this is the case a notice should be displayed to potential clients.

Important factors in choosing a travel agent

Although the contract for the holiday is with the tour operator, you normally make the arrangements with and pay the money to the travel agent.

There must be at least one qualified person at each ABTA travel agent's office. The person will have qualified either by two years' practical experience or by a combination of practical experience and passing examinations, and is therefore considered able to give advice as to the choice of holiday or to arrange travel and accommodation for independent travellers. However, bear in mind that only one person at each office need be so qualified, and the person you deal with may not be the one. This may not matter if you know exactly what you want and simply need someone to make the booking: for instance, if you are using a tour operator you have used before and are going to a place you have visited before. However, if you have special requirements – perhaps you are disabled or need help with your travel plans – ask whether the person is qualified, or ask politely if you can see the manager, who is the member of staff most likely to be qualified.

If you wish to travel independently, you may find that although most ABTA travel agents will make the arrangements for you, some are more likely to specialise in such arrangements than others. A good way to make the choice is to ask people who have experience of independent travel for their recommendations. Failing such recommendations, ask the travel agent if he makes a speciality of advising independent travellers. Making such arrangements is more complicated and time-consuming than booking package holidays, so since this service is not charged for, travel agents who do not have expertise in this area are unlikely to claim that they have.

If you are booking a package holiday, you probably need little or no advice; shop around and choose the deal which suits you best.

TOUR OPERATORS

A tour operator can set up in business without being a member of any particular organisation. However, it is a legal requirement that operators who sell seats on charter flights, or charter blocks of seats on scheduled flights, whether as part of a package or not, must hold the Air Travel Organiser's Licence (ATOL) from the Civil Aviation Authority (CAA). This does not apply to seats booked on scheduled flights using published fares, nor to all cheaper fares, even though you may be able to obtain seats at less than the published price. The brochure, if there is one, should tell you whether your contract is with the airline (a scheduled seat); if not, the operator's registered name and ATOL number should be displayed in the brochure. If there is no brochure, ask the travel agent for the tour operator's name and ATOL number; or, if booking direct, ask the tour operator himself and check the number with CAA.

The protection given by an ATOL

If the company which is an ATOL holder fails financially, the claims of all customers will be met in full, out of the bond which an ATOL holder is required to arrange; or, if this is not enough, from the Air Travel Trust managed by trustees in the CAA. This bond is a guarantee or sum of money which the holder has to provide. Every ATOL holder is constantly monitored by CAA to ensure that the company is fit to hold a licence and is financially sound and unlikely to fail.

However, the possession of an ATOL does not guarantee quality of service; it cannot help where charter air travel is not involved; nor does it offer an arbitration scheme for disputes. These problems are more readily dealt with by ABTA (if the tour operator is a member) or organisations such as local Trading Standards Departments.

ABTA membership

Membership of ABTA is voluntary; although most tour operators are registered with ABTA, this does not mean that the non-members are necessarily less efficient. Some 825 tour operators (including branches) are members of ABTA, and all are required to make reference to their membership in their brochures and booking forms. There are no staffing rules for tour operators, unlike travel agents; they are, however, subject to the ABTA tour operators' code of conduct. ABTA tour operators are required to provide bonds, and there is a back-up from ABTA intended to ensure that customers will be able to complete their holidays or will be reimbursed in full in the event of a tour operator's financial failure. This scheme is wider than the ATOL one, in that it covers all overseas holidays rather than just those which involve charter air travel.

If the tour operator who fails is not an ABTA member, and your holiday does not involve charter flights, you are not covered, even if the travel agent is a member. Therefore both your tour operator and your travel agent should be members of ABTA, so that you are covered for the failure of either. If your holiday is a continental coach tour, the operator can be bonded either by ABTA or by the Bus and Coach Council. The Passenger Shipping Association also has a bonding scheme. If your journey travel is not covered by any of these bonds, there are a few travel agents who promise full reimbursement even where the operator is not bonded. But most travel agents who offer reimbursement restrict this to operators who are already bonded. A holiday insurance policy may cover the situation.

Neither the ATOL nor the ABTA bond covers claims relating to completed holidays by customers of failed companies. If the holiday was unsatisfactory and the tour operator fails before you can gain compensation, neither the ATOL nor the ABTA schemes can be called upon to settle outstanding payments. Such claims would more usually be made on the company in liquidation.

Choosing a tour operator

When comparing brochures, take into account how honest each appears to be; if one extols the virtues of every resort in the brochure, this may not be as reliable as one which gives a 'warts and all' description. A good way to check this is to look up the same resort or hotel in several different brochures and compare the descriptions. If still in doubt, ask your travel agent to look it up in the Agents Hotel Gazetteer which each travel agent should have, although it is not on public display. It describes 'holiday paradises' and 'luxury hotels' with a degree of frankness not to be found in most brochures.

When comparing prices, take account of all supplements and discounts, such as supplements for flying from provincial airports or at the weekend; airport taxes; supplements for full board or for sea view etc.; discounts for children or for travelling off-season; free or cheap rail travel, and so on. Not only does all this affect the price of your holiday, but practice among tour operators differs, so a basic price which seems lower in one brochure may not be so once supplements and discounts are taken into account.

Unfortunately, although having a tour operator who is a member of ABTA (and holds an ATOL, if relevant) will protect you in the case of financial failure, it does not guarantee that your holiday will be trouble-free, even to the extent of being the one you actually booked. Once you have narrowed down your choice to those tour operators who are offering the type of holiday you require, it is worth checking with friends and relations to see if they have used and can recommend that operator. *Holiday Which*? does a survey of tour operators each year, indicating those whose customers have been most and least satisfied. Similarly, the various holiday and consumer programmes on television and radio may draw attention to operators about whom they have received persistent complaints.

Booking direct

It is not necessary to use a travel agent; all holidays can be booked direct with the tour operator. Some tour operators do not use travel agents at all, and only accept direct bookings. Their prices are often lower, because they do not have to pay commission. However, check their prices against those of other tour operators, as this may not be the case for your particular holiday. You must also take into account any discounts or other incentives offered by the travel agents which may make a similar holiday cheaper.

If you book direct with a tour operator whose holidays can also be booked through a travel agent, there is no discount; you will pay exactly the same price as if you had used a travel agent. The overall cost will in fact be higher, because you will have to pay telephone charges for the calls to the tour operator which are likely to be long-distance; and if you do not get the first holiday you try to book, or if there are any problems, there may be a number of calls. You will also not be able to take advantage of the advice or any incentives offered by the travel agents.

Many people who book direct do so in response to advertisements in newspapers; these are often for flight-only deals, but can be for anything from accommodation only, to full package holidays.

If a charter flight is involved, the tour operator's name and ATOL number should appear in the advertisement. All ATOL holders are required by law to display their ATOL number and registered name in any advertising; if this is not shown, you should assume that you are dealing with a travel agent.

It is a requirement that in such circumstances the travel agent should include in his advertisement the phrase 'retail agent for ATOL holders'. Always ask the agent for the name and number of the tour operator with whom you will be booked. If he does not know, or will not tell you, inform CAA (or ABTA, if he is a member) and try another agent.

Booking through a travel agent

For most package holidays, the travel agent will telephone the tour operator, or make the booking by computer. You are usually asked if this is a firm booking, so it could appear that you have entered into a contract at that point. However, most brochures state that the contract is not actually made until your booking form has been received, and the tour operator has accepted it, confirming this by sending you a confirmation invoice. A tour operator may promise that the holiday booked over the telephone has been reserved for you: then you would have a case against the operator in the rare event that your booking was not confirmed. If there were no confirmation, you would be entitled to compensation, but not to the actual holiday.

If you have special requirements, such as vegetarian food or facilities for babies or the disabled, it is probably not enough simply to state these in the space reserved for special requests. A request is not at all the same thing as a requirement; the form or the booking terms will probably state that the operator will try to meet requests, but cannot guarantee to do so. If not having your special needs met would ruin your holiday – as in not having a ground-floor room for a person in a wheelchair – you must turn your request into a requirement without which you will not book the holiday.

You should therefore ask the travel agent to help you choose the most suitable holiday, and reserve the right to book it; but do not book it until the travel agent has communicated with the tour operator and has obtained written confirmation that the facilities you need will be available. If it should subsequently turn out that they are not, the tour operator will then be in breach of contract.

This approach may mean that the tour operator will refuse to confirm the booking, because he cannot promise to provide these facilities; and you may have to approach several operators before finding one who accepts your stipulations. On the other hand, there will be much less risk of disappointment, and should one occur you will have an excellent case for claiming compensation.

Terms of the contract

The contract, as explained earlier, is normally between the customer and the tour operator. Package holiday contracts are always 'standard form contracts'. This means that you will be asked to sign a form stating that you agree to the terms set out in the brochure, which are called standard terms because they are the same for everyone travelling with that tour operator. They will also be similar (though not identical) to those of other tour operators. When you have signed the form, these terms are part of your contract, even if you have not read them. You cannot later argue that they do not apply to you because you did not read them, nor will you be allowed to delete any of them. You must either sign the contract with all terms, or not at all.

It may therefore seem that there is no point in reading the terms, because they will apply whether you read them or not. However, you should read them before signing, for two reasons. First, you should compare them with those of other tour operators; although the standard terms tend to be similar, some are more generous than others, in offering more compensation for delays, or in not giving themselves such wide rights to change the holiday, for instance. Secondly, if anything goes wrong during the holiday, it is as well to know in advance how the company is likely to respond, so that you can be prepared. The ABTA code provides that the terms should not be on the booking form because you would then have no copy after sending off the form. Therefore you must look for them in the brochure. The code requires travel agents to draw clients' attention to these terms.

It also provides that booking conditions shall make clear the operator's policy with regard to alterations, cancellations, surcharges; and so on this allows the operator to make such alterations and charges and also allows some leeway for other exclusions and limitations. But the code provides that the booking conditions shall not exclude or limit the tour operator's liability for misrepresentations or his duty to exercise diligence. Thus, although the booking conditions are part of the contract, this does not mean that the tour operator will necessarily be able to rely on them in a court action.

You should check the booking form minutely, to see that you are booking the correct holiday: that is, the right hotel, departure time, airport, dates. The travel agent should go through this with you very carefully.

Booking on behalf of other people

Only one person signs the booking form, regardless of how many are travelling together. If you are that person, the form will state that you are signing on behalf of all members of the group, with their authority. This means that, provided this statement is true, the contract is binding on all of them. The other members of the group do not have to do anything formal to authorise you to make the contract on their behalf: simply asking you to go along and book the holiday is enough. However, make sure that you and they know exactly what you are booking, or there may be an argument later as to whether you were authorised to book that particular holiday, and they may refuse to pay. You will then be bound to pay the full cost of the holiday to the tour operator; it will be for you to sort out with your group whether you did or did not have authority, and to try to get the money from them. As such a group normally consists of family or friends, it is not easy to take them to court, either because the whole arrangement was rather informal there were no uninvolved witnesses and everyone is now disagreeing as to what was said; or because you are reluctant to take family or friends to court.

However, the fact that you sign on behalf of the whole party is normally advantageous rather than disadvantageous. It means that if anything goes wrong, you are *all* entitled to claim against the tour operator and to receive compensation, not just the one who signed the form (apart from children, who cannot claim in their own right, but will be taken into account when damages are assessed).

Methods of payment

Your choice of method of paying for your holiday may increase your rights of action if anything goes wrong with it. It is best to pay for your holiday by credit card. Make sure that this is a credit card (such as Access or Visa) under which you are allowed to pay off the balance in instalments, and not a charge card (such as American Express), under which you are obliged to settle in full every month. Credit cards are covered by the Consumer Credit Act 1977, and (under section 75), if you have a claim against the tour operator, you may also claim against the company which provided the finance.

It is not necessary to pay for the entire holiday by credit card; even if only the deposit was paid by credit card, a claim can be made regarding the entire cost of the holiday, provided the price of the holiday exceeds £100. However, there must be an arrangement between the credit card company and the tour operator for this holiday. This is a particular problem when booking holidays, because although the booking form usually has a space to sign for payment by credit card, normally it is the travel agent's name and number which go on the sales voucher. The arrangement is accordingly between the travel agent and the credit card company, and so you may lose any right of action against the credit card company. ABTA travel agents have special credit card vouchers which are made out to the tour operator; however, you must specifically ask for such a voucher to be used. If yours is not an ABTA travel agent, or has not got such vouchers, and you want to pay by credit card, you would do well to book directly with the tour operator.

The most obvious advantage of using a credit card in this way is that if the tour operator fails financially at a time when you have a complaint about your holiday, you will be able to claim against the credit card company. Even if the operator has not failed, you may choose to pursue your claim against the card company instead; and complaining to the card company will often result in an investigation by it which will put pressure on the tour operator.

Insurance

If you book a package holiday, the contract will probably make it a condition of booking that you are insured. Some tour operators insist that you take out their insurance, on which they will be getting commission from the insurance company; therefore you should not assume that this insurance is being imposed on you because it is the best available. Most operators do not, in fact, insist that you take out their insurance, but insist that if you do not use it, you must have other insurance, with equal or higher levels of cover. You may not realise this unless you read the form carefully.

The ABTA code requires a travel agent to draw the client's attention to insurance facilities to suit the client's requirements, and to indicate any exclusions or limitations, so that the client may seek additional or alternative cover; however, remember that the travel agent may receive commission if you use the insurance company he recommends. You should compare the cover being offered by the tour operator with that offered by the travel agent's insurers and your own insurers. Do not just pick the cheapest insurance you are offered: it may not give you sufficient cover.

277

Read the small print for exclusions or limitations in the policy. People rarely do this, because they first think about insurance when the travel agent is filling in the booking form, and they find it embarrassing to insist on reading all the small print there and then, even if the notion occurs to them.

There are a number of points you must particularly check:

○ Medical expenses cover: check both the amount and the extent, particularly if you are travelling to the USA.

○ You may not be covered in certain situations, such as accidents on motorcycles, or for pre-existing medical conditions, including pregnancy. You must always declare such a condition and may be required to pay a higher premium, but this is no hardship compared with that of having your claim turned down.

○ In what circumstances are you covered for cancellation or curtailment of the holiday, or for delayed departure? Does it include the tour operator failing financially?

○ If covered for delayed baggage, are you also covered for buying replacement clothing and other necessities?

○ Check what the excess (the part of the loss that you bear) is on claims for lost belongings and whether there are any conditions attached, such as reporting the loss to the tour operator's representative, or even to the police.

If you are not taking a package holiday, it is even more important that you take out adequate insurance, as you will not have the tour operator to assist you (or to claim against) if anything goes wrong. If you are travelling to a country within the European Community, you can obtain Form E111 from the DHSS (ask at any social security office) which will entitle you to the same medical treatment as a resident of that country. However, this is not as extensive as the medical expenses cover under an insurance policy: for instance, it does not cover bringing you back to the UK, and you might have to pay for all or part of the treatment (though you would be able to claim a refund later). Also, you would still need cover for a wide range of non-medical problems.

WHAT TO DO IF YOUR HOLIDAY GOES WRONG
Most people's holiday disappointments have to do with the resort, the accommodation, the food or the facilities not being of the standard expected, or being changed.

Problems with accommodation and other facilities
Whether you have any claim against the tour operator depends on what was stated in the brochure and on the booking form. You are entitled to what you were promised, and the operator is liable if you do not get this. It is not wholly determined (by the courts), however, whether strict liability in contract extends to the tour operator's independent sub-contractors and suppliers. The tour operator may not be liable if you did not get what you were promised, if it was not within his control, as long as he did not make any misrepresentations. For example, if the hotel was overbooked, the tour operator may not be held liable if it was the hotel's fault. This applies not only to the basics such as the resort and the hotel but to all facilities as well.

Moreover, the operator is not liable for what you were not promised, so, for instance, if the hotel staff are unfriendly and unco-operative, you will not have a case unless the brochure promised friendly staff. This often causes difficulty: for instance, if there is noise from building works nearby, you have no claim against the operator unless the brochure states that the location is quiet, or uses other words which would lead you to that conclusion.

In addition to what is stated in the brochure, the tour operator has a duty under the Supply of Goods and Services Act 1982 to use reasonable care and skill. Therefore if you could prove that, although there was no specific promise in the brochure, the operator failed in this duty, you would have a claim. This is a much more difficult area. However, you could succeed if, for example, a particular hotel was known to have poor standards of hygiene or safety.

The ABTA code requires that the brochure should contain clear, comprehensive and accurate information, to enable the client to exercise an informed judgement. However, the Office of Fair Trading (OFT) report published in July 1988 on ABTA's code of conduct (entitled *The Package Holiday Codes*) made 20 recommendations. These include greater accuracy and comprehensiveness of brochures; disclosure of noise levels at resorts and precautionary information about health matters; and that tour operators should accept responsibility for all the components of the package holiday. ABTA is currently reviewing and revising its codes.

Steps to take during the holiday

Do not wait until your holiday is over. Complain immediately to the operator's representative who is on the spot, and keep complaining if nothing is done to remedy your complaint. If there is a more senior representative or manager locally, complain to him. Put your complaint in writing at the time: tour operators usually have standard complaint forms for customers to fill in.

The form may have a disclaimer on it – this will usually be the case if you are being offered alternative accommodation. It may say, for instance, that the matter is beyond the control of the tour operator, who is nevertheless offering a remedy as a gesture of goodwill, and/or that you are satisfied with the alternative offered by the tour operator. If you can get the alternative you want without signing a disclaimer, do so. If not, do not worry; a disclaimer obtained under such circumstances will not be valid anyway.

Although it is depressing to embark on a holiday prepared for it to go wrong, it is advisable to take along the brochure, or at least the pages giving the description of the accommodation and other facilities, plus any guarantees given by the operator that you will receive the holiday you booked. Otherwise the representative may claim that you did get what you booked, and it may be difficult for you to be certain that the air-conditioning (or whatever) was actually promised, and to insist on this being provided.

Collect evidence at the time. Take photographs, if they might help to back up your complaint, say, of the hotel or the surrounding area. If you have incurred expenses, for example for journeys to a distant beach, or vegetarian food bought elsewhere (because the hotel did not provide this, despite your stipulation), keep the receipts. If other guests are dissatisfied, get them to put their complaints in writing, or at least take a note of their names and addresses. It is surprising how many people who complain bitterly throughout their holiday cannot be bothered to pursue the complaint when they get home. So, if you do not collect this information at the time, you may find that later on there is nobody to back you up.

Cancellation and alterations to your holiday

What has just been said covers the situation in which you are not notified of a change of resort, hotel facilities and so on, until you arrive. We are now concerned with the situation where you are notified in advance, whether at the last minute or not, of a change of resort, accommodation, flight date or time, and so forth, or even of the entire cancellation of your holiday.

The ABTA code of conduct for tour operators rules that holidays shall not be cancelled except in rare circumstances, such as political unrest, after the payment of the balance becomes due, which is normally 6-8 weeks before departure. On cancellation, the client is entitled to an alternative holiday, or a refund. The code makes no provision for compensation.

It does, however, permit the operator to make a material alteration after the balance becomes due, provided he pays compensation to the client. The level of compensation is set out in the brochure. However, overbooking is specifically excluded from the definition of material alteration.

If the alteration is caused by overbooking beyond the control of the operator, but known to him before departure, he should inform clients and give them a choice between an alternative holiday and a refund. If the overbooking is not known before departure, the client should be offered alternative accommodation and reasonable compensation for disturbance if the alternative is inferior to what was first arranged.

There are a several criticisms which can be made of these provisions. There is no compensation for early cancellation or early material alteration. The operator is allowed to make material alterations at a later time, subject to payment of compensation, which in most brochures is hardly generous and does not take account of the exact nature or effect of the change. There is no compensation for changes made because of overbooking, even if known just one day before departure; and there is otherwise compensation only if the alternative holiday/ accommodation/destination is inferior.

There are other criticisms: it is the tour operator who can choose whether to make a 'material' alteration or a cancellation; operators frequently do not notify clients of alterations which are known to them in advance; and the code does not apply to alterations which are not considered material, such as a change of flight time.

It is up to you, if you are notified of a cancellation or overbooking in advance, whether to accept the alternative or claim a refund. However, in either case do not meekly accept that you are entitled to no compensation, or, where compensation is due, only to what is set out in the brochure. These terms are subject to the Unfair Contract Terms Act 1977 and many of them are unlikely to be enforceable. When you accept an alternative or refund, make it clear (in writing) that you are doing so only under protest, and that you reserve your right to claim compensation.

Delays
Assuming the tour operator is not at fault, it is extremely unlikely that you could hold him responsible for the delay itself. If the delay is such that your holiday would be radically different

from what you bargained for, you can claim that the contract is 'frustrated'. However, the delay would have to be at least 24 hours, and probably considerably longer, before you could claim this, although it would depend on the type of holiday: clearly, a five-cities coach tour would more quickly become frustrated than a 14-day beach holiday.

If you do claim the contract is frustrated, the tour operator is allowed to keep back enough of your money to cover any expenses he has already incurred, and this could be considerable, in certain circumstances. You must take this into account before deciding not to take the holiday at all. However, most insurance policies provide for compensation for delays, and also for reimbursement of the cost of the holiday if you decide not to take the holiday after, say, 24 hours' delay.

Although you cannot hold the operator responsible for the delay, he does have a duty of care towards you. The extent of this duty has never been determined; it should certainly include informing you of the delay and updating this information. Many operators will provide meals and even accommodation, although this is done as a gesture of goodwill: the duty will be greater where the delay occurs at the end of the holiday, when the client has no accommodation and probably little money.

Surcharges

Most holiday booking terms give operators the right to make surcharges. However, the practice of levying surcharges has given rise to such dissatisfaction in recent years that pressure has been put on ABTA to remedy the situation.

As a result, its members have agreed that for holidays in the summer of 1989 and subsequently they will absorb an amount equal to 2% of the basic holiday price in respect of any increased prices charged to them by their suppliers after the brochures have been printed; and if the surcharge exceeds 10% of the holiday price, you are entitled to cancel and obtain a full refund. If you are asked to pay a surcharge because the increase is more than 2%, the ABTA code entitles you, on request, to a reasonable written explanation by reference to each main item of cost. Complain to ABTA if you are still not satisfied. ABTA is setting up a surcharge audit group to monitor the new policy; this group will include an independent representative. Before any surcharge can be levied, ABTA members must notify and obtain clearance from the Association's surcharge monitoring section. In theory, you could pursue the matter further by going to arbitration or taking court proceedings, but the amount involved is not likely to make these courses of action attractive.

COMPLAINING AFTER THE HOLIDAY

Although your complaint is against the tour operator, not the travel agent, you could start by complaining to your travel agent. The ABTA code of conduct states that the travel agent should use his best endeavours in acting as intermediary to bring about a satisfactory conclusion. Some travel agents will take up your complaint informally on your behalf, and provided the complaint is clearly justified and you are not claiming too much, this may produce results. However, many travel agents will suggest that you put your complaint in writing, and that they will see that this is passed on to the tour operator. In this case, there is no advantage over sending the letter direct.

Usually the first step is to write a formal letter of complaint to the tour operator. The booking conditions may state that complaints must be made in writing within 28 days. However, as this limit does not apply to arbitration or court proceedings, do not worry if you have not complied with this: it is not in the tour operator's interests to encourage you to start legal proceedings by refusing to consider a late complaint.

Make your letter clear and concise. Give the date of your departure, the name of your hotel and resort, and the booking reference number. Try to avoid getting emotional and, in particular, making insulting remarks: stick to the hard facts. If you find it difficult to be objective, get someone else to draft the letter for you, or at least to read your draft and delete anything which is inadvisable.

If you have a number of complaints, of which some are trivial or such as would be difficult to substantiate, do not include these at all. Tour operators have a tendency to answer the allegations which they can easily dismiss, making much of these, while ignoring or glossing over the other complaints. Include evidence, such as photographs or receipts, but make sure you keep copies of any letters you send, and send copies rather than the originals of any documentary evidence.

What to claim

You must state in your letter what you require as recompense. If you just complain without doing this, you are likely to receive either an explanation or an apology, but no compensation. It is particularly difficult to come up with a figure in a holiday case, as you are likely to be claiming more for disappointment than for actual expenses. You are entitled to compensation for loss of enjoyment, even though it is difficult to set a price on this.

However, a figure can be placed on some of your loss. If you have had actual expenses such as taxi fares because of the distance to the beach, you can claim these specifically, and the loss in value of your holiday can be calculated, albeit roughly, using the cost of the holiday as a starting point. If you can ascertain the difference between the cost of what you paid for and what you received, you can claim this; so if you book a 4-star hotel and are placed in a 3-star one, you can discover the difference in price from the brochure or, if it is not in that operator's brochure, from another one. Even then you are additionally entitled to claim for the inconvenience and disappointment of being in the wrong hotel.

Another way is to try to assess what proportion of the original holiday booked you have obtained, even if it is only the flight. However, if your holiday was genuinely such a disaster that you would have been better off staying at home, then you obviously would not deduct even the value of the flight. Finally, add on a figure for loss of enjoyment, even though you can only make a guess at a figure which seems reasonable. The amounts awarded for loss of enjoyment vary tremendously – from little more than a nominal sum, to awards of around £100.

Your total claim under all three headings (expense, inconvenience, loss of enjoyment) must be reasonable, otherwise your claim will not be taken seriously; however, pick a figure which is on the high side of reasonable, as there are bound to be negotiations and you are unlikely to get all you claim.

The ABTA code requires the operator to deal with complaints promptly and efficiently, and to settle disputes amicably and as quickly as possible. The OFT report recommends that ABTA should remind its members of this.

Persevere

Do not be put off by the reply to your first letter. This will probably be just a standard letter that is sent out to all who complain, or a standard letter which has been adjusted to fit your particular complaint. It may offer nothing at all, or offer a token amount without admitting liability, as a gesture of goodwill. This sum is usually £20-£30 per person. It is common practice nowadays to ask the customer to sign a disclaimer before sending this amount, in order to prevent the customer taking the money and then continuing to claim more.

Unless the amount offered or the explanation you have received is satisfactory, write a second letter. The tour operator may not have answered or will have glossed over parts of your complaint, or you may simply disagree with the explanation. Your second letter can therefore refer to these matters. In this second letter it is a good idea to state specifically that the tour operator had made misrepresentations in the brochure, or was in breach of contract. Do not be put off by the operator's saying that he cannot be held responsible because the fault lies with the hotel and is out of his control.

Similarly, do not be put off if the tour operator draws your attention to a particular term in the brochure which excludes or limits his liability. Although such a term is part of the contract, under the Unfair Contract Terms Act 1977 it has no effect unless the tour operator proves that it is reasonable. The stricter the term, the more difficult it will be to prove that it is reasonable; if the operator states that he is not liable at all for certain breaches of the contract, this is more likely to be considered unreasonable than if he offers compensation but limits the amount. However, if the amount is nowhere near adequate to recompense the average customer in that situation, it is still likely to be unreasonable.

You should normally end your second letter by stating that you will put the matter into the hands of your solicitor or will begin court proceedings (depending on which you intend to do) unless the operator responds to your satisfaction within a stated time (seven days is most common). You should not put this in your first letter because once you have said this, you must go ahead and do it.

If you do not, the operator will have called your bluff and will not take your complaint seriously. As it is obviously preferable to settle the matter without going that far, it is better to leave threats of litigation out of the first letter. If you are not just repeating yourself in your second letter, but have some very specific challenges to make to the operator's initial reply, you may even want to leave the statement about going to law until your third letter. There is no point in writing a fourth letter: at this point you must either take further action or give up.

Getting a solicitor's help
If at this stage you put the matter in the hands of a solicitor, this may have the desired result, as a solicitor's letter will not only make more impact, but will convince the tour operator that you mean business. However, although it is possible to reach a settlement under which the operator pays your solicitor's costs, it is more likely that a sum will be offered which does not include these. You may then be no better off, or even worse off than if you had accepted the previous offer. You must therefore consider how realistic the amount you are claiming is, and

weigh it against the strength of your case.

Some solicitors operate a fixed-fee interview scheme whereby they will give you up to half-an-hour of advice for a small fee, £5 plus VAT. You could use this scheme to get advice on whether to pursue the matter, but you must make it clear from the beginning that you want advice only under this scheme.

If you decide to take the matter further, you may be entitled to advice and assistance under the green form scheme (see 'Legal Services'). This depends on your means, which will be assessed there and then by the solicitor. If you are eligible, the solicitor will be able to do up to two hours' work for you; this may cost you nothing, or you may have to make a contribution towards the cost. If you are not entitled to green form advice, you will have to pay the solicitor yourself, although charges are normally quite low for advising and writing one or two letters: ask the solicitor at the outset how much it is likely to cost.

However, the costs will obviously mount quickly if you go to court. The green form scheme does not cover this, and you are unlikely to be granted legal aid for this type of case.

If you use a solicitor to write a letter for you, this does not mean that you must use a solicitor to take the matter further. Whether you bring a court action or pursue some other course of action, it should be cheaper to do so on your own and it is not difficult.

ABTA conciliation

ABTA offers a free conciliation service for dealing with complaints against ABTA members. This is to be used only when direct contact with the tour operator, as outlined above, has failed to resolve the dispute.

There is a form to fill in, which can be obtained from ABTA. The form will require the same information that you provided in your correspondence, copies of which should be enclosed, together with any photographs or documents (send copies rather than the originals; if they are unacceptable, you will be told). As in your letter, you should state what recompense you are seeking. The conciliator will consider the documents and the operator's brochure, and if he feels that you have cause for complaint, he will request the tour operator to review the case. ABTA cannot compel a member to agree to a settlement; however, the fact that an ABTA conciliator has become involved should be strong persuasion. The conciliation service is not available for claims involving injury or illness.

Your complaint will not be upheld if the events were beyond the control of the operator. Since ABTA is an association of travel agents and tour operators, its interpretation of what is beyond their control may be less favourable to you than a court's might be.

The conciliator will consider your complaint in the light of the brochure, and you will not be able to argue that any of the terms are unreasonable. The conciliator will accept all the terms as valid, so if your complaint is, for instance, that the amount of compensation laid down in the brochure is insufficient, conciliation will not help you.

The conciliation is on documents only. You will not be able to appear in person before the conciliator, or to telephone to explain anything. It is often difficult to get your point across with sufficient force in writing, and this is a particular problem if there is no documentary evidence, such as photographs.

Advantages of conciliation

o   The service is free.
o   Conciliation does not take away your right to legal action; if you are dissatisfied, you can still take the operator to court.
o   You do not have to go to the trouble – and perhaps anxiety – of appearing in person in court.

The disadvantages are that the conciliator is an appointee of the professional organisation of the person or firm complained of, and ABTA cannot enforce his recommendation against one of its own members. The service is worth using, however, to save you the trouble and expense of going to court. But if the conciliator has decided against you, or has set a lower amount of compensation than you will accept, you can still take the case to court.

ABTA arbitration

ABTA offers an arbitration scheme: it can only be used if both direct negotiation with the tour operator and conciliation have failed. The scheme is run independently by the Chartered Institute of Arbitrators; details are available from ABTA's conciliation department. Similar information is required to that required for conciliation.

Arbitration is not available for claims of more than £1,500 per person, or £7,500 per booking form. The fee is £23 for a single claimant, with a modest increase if there is more than one claimant. The fee is non-returnable, although the arbitrator has discretion to direct one party to reimburse the other's fee.

The customer is sent a copy of the tour operator's defence and is entitled to make written comments on it within 14 days of receiving it. If the arbitrator finds in favour of the customer, the tour operator is directed to make payment within 21 days.

Limitations of arbitration

o   You must apply for arbitration within nine months of returning from holiday.

o   Arbitration cannot be used for claims regarding injury or illness.

o   The arbitration is usually based on documentary evidence only.

o   You will not be able to challenge the validity of any of the booking terms.

o   The decision of the arbitrator is binding, and so you will not be able to bring a court action if you are dissatisfied with his decision.

○ The compensation awarded by arbitrators is on the whole lower than that awarded by the courts; you are likely to be awarded between one-third and one-half of your claim.

The other limitations must be viewed in the light of the last two: it now becomes more serious that the arbitration is on documents only, and that you are bound by the arbitrator's decision and cannot go on to court.

Advantages of arbitration

It is cheap: not only does it cost little to bring a claim to arbitration but also, if the claim does not succeed, the customer's liability to pay the operator's costs is limited.

What is more, 75% of claimants succeed. (However, you are as likely to succeed in court, in which case the sum awarded will probably be higher. If you lose, however, your costs could be higher unless you used the small claims procedure.)

Deciding whether to begin a civil court action

You should not do so until you have at least approached the tour operator directly and satisfied yourself that you can go no further along that line. You may consider first trying conciliation and/or a complaint to the Trading Standards Department, as explained later, or by arbitration instead.

Disadvantages of going to court

You will have to pay to bring your claim. However, if it is for under £5,000 you can take out a summons in the county court, and if it is under £1,000 you can use the small claims procedure (often referred to as county court arbitration). This is not very expensive and you can manage without a solicitor.

If your claim is for a sum in excess of £1,000 you will not be able to use the small claims procedure and will therefore have to use a solicitor. Because you are unlikely to be granted legal aid for a claim relating to a holiday, you will have to pay him yourself, which could be expensive.

If you use the small claims procedure and win, you will not be able to claim the cost of using a solicitor or your time and trouble in bringing the case yourself, although you will be able to claim the amount charged by the court to hear your case.

Advantages of a court action

If you use the small claims procedure, you will not have to stand up and represent yourself in a courtroom. The preliminary and final hearing will take place in an ordinary room, with a court official (registrar) who will be wearing ordinary clothes; and he will not insist on your following the same rules as lawyers. You will simply put your case, answer the registrar's and the tour operator's questions, and ask your own questions. You will probably find that the tour operator has sent a solicitor along to represent him. Do not be intimidated by this: the registrar will make sure this does not put you at a disadvantage.

If you use the small claims procedure and lose, you will not have to pay the other side's costs (unless the court decides you have acted unreasonably in bringing or pursuing the case, which is extremely rare).

It is possible that your case will not get as far as a full hearing. Many tour operators settle out of court, either after the summons has been served on them, or after the preliminary hearing the registrar holds in order to try resolve the matter, or just before the final hearing.

A majority of cases are decided in favour of the consumer; and, although there is considerable variation, the sums awarded by courts are generally significantly higher than when ABTA arbitration is used. However, this does not necessarily mean that you will be awarded the full amount of your claim.

The county court produces a free booklet entitled *Small Claims in the County Court* which is available from any court office, or from Citizens Advice Bureaux. You do not need to worry about filling in the forms: the staff at the court office are usually very helpful, and used to dealing with people who do not have solicitors.

Complaining to the Trading Standards Department

Under the Trade Descriptions Act 1968, it is a criminal offence knowingly or recklessly to make a false statement as to the provision of services, accommodation or facilities. The court has the power to make a compensation order under the Power of Criminal Courts Act 1973. Therefore, if your complaint is with regard to a misleading statement in the brochure, such as that the hotel is only ten minutes' walk from the beach (when in fact, it is more like half-an-hour), you can report the matter to your local Trading Standards or Consumer Protection Department – you can find the number in the telephone directory.

Limitations of the Act

o The prosecution has to prove that the operator knew the statement was false, or was reckless as to whether the statement was true. 'Reckless' means regardless of whether it was true or false; that is, although he did not have reason to think it was false, he did not bother to check whether it was true.

o If the case is brought in the magistrates' court, which is likely, the compensation limit is £1,000 for each offence. This might be all right if you were the only person who complained, but if there are others, you will have to share the compensation.

o The court is not obliged to award compensation, and is less likely to do so in a holiday case, where it is more difficult to quantify the loss than, say, if the mileage of a car has been misrepresented, where one can accurately state the loss of value. If the court does grant compensation, it is likely to award less than a civil court (allowing for the £1,000 limit).

o It is not you who decides whether to prosecute, and therefore it may be decided merely to warn the operator.

Advantages of a prosecution under the Act

○ It does not cost you anything, either in time or inconvenience.

○ It does not prevent you from bringing a civil action. Indeed, a successful prosecution can and should be used as evidence in your civil case.

Complaints against travel agents

In the unlikely event that your complaint is against your travel agent rather than your tour operator, any claim you have will be for negligence, as you do not have a contract with the travel agent. Negligence is much more difficult to prove. You would have to show that the travel agent did not take reasonable care, and that you suffered loss as a result. This should not be difficult if the travel agent forgot to book your holiday, or did not confirm an option you had taken out, or lost your tickets, so that you had to go to some trouble to arrange for replacements. However, if you feel that you were recommended a holiday which was totally unsuited to your requirements, it will usually be clear from the brochure that the hotel was not suitable for your purposes, in which case it is difficult to blame the travel agent; and even if the unsuitability is not clear from the brochure, it will be difficult for you to prove that the travel agent should have known.

Apart from the fact that the claim is for negligence, not contract, the advice given above regarding letters, conciliation, arbitration and court proceedings applies equally to travel agents, except that arbitration is not available. If it is a more general complaint about the standard of the service, then your complaint should be made to ABTA.

USEFUL ADDRESSES

AIR TRANSPORT USERS' COMMITTEE (AUC)
103 Kingsway
London WC2B 6QX
01-242 3882

Code of conduct: no
Complaints procedure: yes
Complaint-handling charge: no
Disciplinary sanctions: no

ASSOCIATION OF BRITISH TRAVEL AGENTS (ABTA)
55-57 Newman Street
London W1P 4AH
01-637 2444

Membership: by examination and/or practical experience
Membership list: available from ABTA head office
Fee guidelines: no
Code of conduct: yes
Complaints procedure: yes: conciliation; arbitration
Complaint-handling charge: conciliation free; fees for arbitration
Disciplinary sanctions: reprimand; fine; suspension; expulsion

CENTRAL TRANSPORT CONSULTATIVE COMMITTEE (CTCC)
Golden Cross House (1st floor)
Duncannon Street
London WC2N 4JF
01-839 7338/01-930 1304

Code of conduct: yes
Complaints procedure: yes
Complaint-handling charge: no
Disciplinary sanctions: no

CIVIL AVIATION AUTHORITY (CAA)
ATOL section
CAA House
45-59 Kingsway
London WC2B 6TE
01-832 6600

Code of conduct: no
Complaints procedure: limited; no arbitration available
Complaint-handling charge: no
Disciplinary sanctions: supension/revocation of ATOL licence

GENERAL CONSUMER COUNCIL FOR NORTHERN IRELAND (GCCNI)
Elizabeth House
116 Holywood Road
Belfast BT4 1NY
0232-672488

Complaints: about road transport in Northern Ireland

LONDON REGIONAL PASSENGERS COMMITTEE (LRPC)
Golden Cross House
London WC2N 4JF
01-839 1898

Code of conduct: BR yes; LRT no
Complaints procedure: yes
Complaint-handling charge: no
Disciplinary sanctions: no

TRANSPORT USERS CONSULTATIVE COMMITTEE (TUCC).

Eastern England
Midgate House
Midgate
Peterborough PE1 1TN
0733-312188

Midlands Area
Ladywood House (4th floor)
46 Stephenson Street
Birmingham B2 4DT
021-643 2144

North Eastern England
Hilary House
16 St. Saviour's Place
York Y01 2PL
0904-625615

North Western England
Boulton House (room 112)
17-21 Chorlton Street
Manchester M1 3HY
061-228 6247

Southern England
Golden Cross House
8 Duncannon Street
London WC2N 4JF
01-839 1851

Western England
Tower House (floor 13)
Fairfax Street
Bristol BS1 3BN
0272-265703

Scotland
249 West George Street
Glasgow G2 4QE
041-221 7760

Wales
St David's House
Wood Street
Cardiff CF1 1ES
0222-227247

London telephone numbers

On 6 May 1990 the 01 telephone code for London will change to either 071 or 081, depending on the local code that follows it. From that date, people telephoning the 01 code will hear a recorded message telling them to re-dial using either 071 or 081.

Driving Instructors

You are not obliged to undergo a course of professional instruction before taking your driving test: you could choose to be taught by a relative or a friend. However, you must consider not only your chances of passing with such an instructor, and the strain the driving lessons might place on the relationship, but also more practical matters, such as the increased risk of an accident, and the insurance position.

CHOOSING A DRIVING INSTRUCTOR

Under section 126(1) of the Road Traffic Act 1972, only (Department of Transport) Approved Driving Instructors (ADI) or legally authorised instructors (trainees) are allowed to give instruction for money or money's worth. You should check the windscreen of the instructor's car: there should be a green octagonal disc with a photograph of the approved driving instructor on the reverse. For a trainee driving instructor, it is a red triangle. In order to become an ADI, a person must pass both written and practical examinations set by the Department of Transport.

An instructor may, in addition, possess a Diploma in Driving Instruction awarded jointly by the Associated Examining Board and the Driving Instructors Association (DIA). Such an instructor will be entitled to use the letters DipDI. Instructors are not obliged to obtain the diploma, and those holding it are in a minority. An instructor with DIAmond status has passed a high-level driving test and further examinations in specialist aspects, such as skid pan or advanced driver training.

Only those instructors who give instruction in driving cars need be ADIs. There is no such requirement for motorcycle instructors; instruction in riding these is given by volunteers under the schools traffic education programme (usually by road safety officers), and there are some professional training establishments. Changes are expected soon, partly to comply with European Community requirements for 1992, but also in order to make some motorcycle training compulsory.

Heavy goods vehicle (HGV) and public service vehicle instructors, police instructors and off-road racing instructors need not be ADIs, but rally driving instructors must be ADIs. If you require instruction in specialist driving, consult the Driving Instructors Association which maintains a register of specialist instructors. For details of rally driving and skid courses contact the RAC.

It is not compulsory for a driving instructor to belong to a professional organisation. There are approximately 32,000 instructors in the UK, only one-third of whom belong to any association. There are numerous small professional organisations to which driving instructors may belong, but the two main ones are the Driving Instructors Association and the Motor Schools Association of Great Britain (MSA). The latter, as its name suggests, was set up for firms where there is more than one instructor, but now has individual membership. Instructors are frequently members of both associations.

Both organisations have professional codes of conduct which reflect their particular emphasis. The MSA's code of conduct covers similar matters to those in its standard terms of business (see below), the emphasis being on acting in a business-like manner and the provision of facilities. The DIA's code of professional practice applies only to DIAmond instructors, and is voluntary. It includes some of the same areas as the MSA's, but places considerable emphasis on ethics: for instance, avoiding improper language or physical contact; not discussing information disclosed by a client; not discussing the client's progress except for normal consultation within a school;

maintaining proper standards of hygiene and dress.

Apart from checking on the above matters, the choice of a driving instructor tends to be made from personal recommendation, publicity, and considerations of the cost of lessons and whether there are any special offers available, such as a number of lessons at a discount. Do shop around: there is considerable variation in the cost of lessons and discounts for block bookings. But do not agree to a block booking until you have had a few lessons with the school and satisfied yourself that it is suitable.

Other factors can be important; for instance, whether the instructor can collect the pupil from home or work. You should check whether the lesson is a full hour, or whether the travelling time is deducted: an important consideration if you live some distance away. Find out whether any of your lesson time will be taken up with taking the previous pupil home or picking up the next pupil. This can severely abbreviate your lesson time.

It is unwise to ask an instructor to give lessons in your own car; instructors are advised not to agree to this, because there may not be insurance cover. Some driving instructors offer intensive courses whereby the pupil attends for a whole day or a few days before a test. Some also offer free lessons if you do not pass your test after this form of tuition.

Entering into a contract

If your driving instructor is working on his own, your contract will be with him. If you book lessons through a driving school (that is, where there is more than one instructor, not merely where the instructor calls his business a school) your contract will be with the school and not the actual instructor.

Your contract may be oral or written. However, just because you have signed a registration form does not necessarily mean you are obliged to continue lessons with that instructor or school. Driving lessons are usually booked individually, that is, the pupil books the next lesson during the previous one, unless a block of lessons has been booked – but there is no point in doing that unless you are offered a discount.

The MSA has standard contract terms which are used by some of its members. These will usually be in the form of a brochure which pupils should be invited to study before signing on. Reasonable steps should be taken to draw these terms to your attention before you enter into the contract; otherwise, they are not binding on you. Provided such steps are taken, you will be bound by these terms whether you read them or not. If the terms are printed on the form you sign, this is considered sufficient to draw them to your attention, even if the instructor never points them out to you. However, if the instructor includes a term which excludes or limits his liability in any way, it would be binding only if he could prove that it was reasonable (under the Unfair Contract Terms Act 1977).

The MSA's standard terms cover matters such as postponement or cancellation of lessons by either pupil or instructor; a guarantee that instructors are qualified in accordance with legal requirements; change of instructors; duration of lessons; driving tests; insurance; standards of service; complaints; conciliation and arbitration.

Members of the DIA do not have standard terms. Whether the instructor is a member of the DIA or of another organisation or none, he may have drawn up his own terms, which will probably cover similar matters to the MSA's terms and will be binding in the same circumstances.

Just because you enter into a spoken contract does not mean that there will be no terms of contract. If your contract is spoken and there are no terms in any brochure or on the wall or a counter in the school's reception area (if there is one) which are clearly visible when you book your lesson, then the Supply of Goods and Services Act 1982 makes the assumption that the service (that is, driving instruction) is provided with reasonable care and skill. However, this will not cover such matters as postponement or cancellation of lessons. A court could assume additional terms if they are needed to make the contract effective, but it is too late to wait until a problem has arisen and then go to court to sort it out. Therefore you should avoid booking and paying for more than one lesson at a time if there are no terms covering this. If you wish to do so because there is a special offer, ask whether you will receive a refund if either you or the instructor cancels the lesson (for instance, because of bad weather) and preferably get the response confirmed in writing. If you do not have confirmation that you will receive a refund, you will lose any money paid in advance, unless you could prove in court that the instructor was in breach of contract.

COMPLAINTS
Complaints are unlikely to arise over the price of lessons, as you would be informed of the charges before booking and would simply go elsewhere if dissatisfied. However, 60% of complaints are about charges: money paid in advance for instruction not received, or money not refunded on cancellation.

Some 30% of complaints are about bad instruction and 10% about impropriety or physical harassment. In the case of impropriety, it is important to remember that in the close confines of a car innocent physical contact could be misinterpreted. Be sure of your facts before making a complaint which could affect an instructor's career.

Regardless of what your complaint is, if you have not booked a number of lessons in advance, the sensible thing to do is to go to another instructor or another school. It does not make sense to persevere when you are not contractually bound to do so; it could put you off driving for some considerable time.

MSA Members
If your contract is with a driving school, the terms provide that a pupil is entitled to change the instructor without having to give any reason, and will receive a refund if this request cannot be complied with. If you have booked in advance, the MSA terms provide for a refund if three clear days' notice of cancellation is given.

Despite the fact that you are unlikely to suffer financially as a consequence of your complaint, you may feel that it is serious enough to take the matter further. Under the MSA's terms, you must first notify the principal of the driving school, personally or in writing by recorded delivery, not more than seven days after the date on which the cause for complaint arose.

If this fails to resolve the dispute, the complaint may, with mutual agreement, be submitted in writing to the MSA's Complaints Committee for conciliation . The terms of the contract will form the basis of the conciliation; therefore you will not be able to challenge those terms. If either party does not accept the Committee's recommendation, the matter may be referred to the board of management for further consideration. The conciliation service is free.

The MSA does not provide an arbitration service; therefore, if you wish to take the matter further but do not wish to use the conciliation service or there is not mutual agreement to do so, you will have to take the matter to court. However, just because your driving school is a member of the MSA, this does not prevent you making use of the service provided by the DIA, or making a complaint to the Registrar of ADIs at the Department of Transport.

DIA Members

The DIA acts as a clearing house for complaints regardless of whether the instructor is a member of the DIA or not, and has a hotline (01-660 3333) for this purpose. You are not required to give your name or that of the instructor, although obviously you may do so if you wish. You will be given advice (usually by the General Secretary) on the substance of your complaint and how to proceed with it, including suitable wording for a letter to the instructor, if appropriate.

There are then three levels of action:
○ adjudication by the DIA's general purposes committee
○ advising the complainant to take the matter to court (including contacting the police if the impropriety or harassment appears to be a criminal matter)

○   reporting the matter to the Registrar of Approved Driving
    Instructors.

An adjudication can be made only if the instructor is a
member, and the DIA has no power to enforce the adjudication,
except by threatening to expel the member, which will not
prevent the member from continuing to work as an instructor.
Court action is normally advised for financial loss. If the
Registrar of ADIs considers an instructor not to be a fit and
proper person, he has the power to remove him from the
register, or give a warning that he may be removed, which
would prevent him from working as a driving instructor. You
make make a complaint directly to the Registrar but it is
advisable to seek advice from the DIA first.

Deciding on court action

As your claim is likely to be for less than £5,000, you can bring
your case in the county court; and, as it will probably be for less
than £1,000, you can use the small claims procedure in that
court. It will not therefore cost you much and it is not difficult
to bring a case without a solicitor.

However, it is unlikely that a dispute with a driving
instructor will end up in court, because there is likely to be little,
if any, financial loss involved. The most obvious situation in
which you would suffer loss would be if you were injured
during a driving lesson. However, that would not be dealt with
under the above procedure: it would be dealt with under the
instructor's insurance policy. If your complaint is that you did
not receive a refund on cancellation, you would not be entitled
to a refund unless the contract so stated. If the instructor has
disappeared with your money, in order to enforce a court order
you would first have to find him, and then he must have the
money to pay.

The only other situation in which you might feel you had
suffered sufficient loss would be if you failed your driving test a
number of times and had come to the conclusion that you had
been badly taught. The problem here is that it would be

extremely difficult (perhaps impossible) to prove that bad instruction was the reason for the failure and not your own general ineptitude or nerves during the tests. It would be still more difficult to prove if you had persevered with the same instructor for a considerable period of time.

USEFUL ADDRESSES

DRIVING INSTRUCTORS ASSOCIATION (DIA)
Lion Green Road
Coulsdon
Surrey CR3 2NL
01-660 3333

Membership: voluntary
Membership list: not available
Fee guidelines: yes
Code of conduct: yes (voluntary code of practice for DIAmond instructors only)
Complaints procedure: yes
Complaint-handling charge: no
Disciplinary sanctions: expulsion

MOTOR SCHOOLS ASSOCIATION OF GB LTD (MSA)
182 Heaton Moor Road
Stockport
Cheshire SK4 4DU
061-443 1611

Membership: voluntary
Style of qualification: MMSA (Member of the Motor Schools Association) ADDA (Approved Defensive Driving Assessor)
Membership list: local lists free on request
Fee guidelines: no
Code of conduct: yes
Complaints procedure: yes
Complaint-handling charge: no
Disciplinary sanctions: expulsion

Medical
and Paramedical
Services

The relationship between a medical or paramedical attendant and his patient differs in some important ways from that obtaining between other sorts of professionals and their clients.

The medical or paramedical person comes into a confidential and intimate relationship involving physical contact with the patient. Such people also have the power to influence their clients' well-being in particularly far-reaching ways.

Consequently they bear immense responsibilities. In carrying them out, they are governed by ethical principles expressed in the rules of conduct of their professional regulatory bodies. (They must also, of course, conform to the law of the land.)

Medical professional regulatory bodies are thus ethical associations; in some cases (such as the General Medical, Dental and Optical Councils) they have the sole power of controlling admission to the profession by granting or withholding registration. A practitioner whom the regulatory body finds guilty of a breach of professional conduct may have his registration suspended or withdrawn – which may prevent him from practising, temporarily or permanently. There are also other, less drastic sanctions.

THE PROFESSIONAL CONDUCT OF DOCTORS
The General Medical Council (GMC) has statutory disciplinary jurisdiction over doctors in relation to their professional

conduct. By the Medical Act 1983 it is empowered to lay down standards of professional conduct and ethical guidelines for doctors. The procedures outlined here are normally not intended to deal with complaints concerning hospital treatment, or treatment by general practitioners under the National Health Service. Where the complaint relates primarily to those services, clinical or otherwise, the procedures outlined later in this chapter may well be more appropriate. Certain forms of misconduct will be judged so serious that they may be taken to affect the ability of the doctor to practise in the profession. There may be an overlap between complaints about treatment and questions of serious professional misconduct. For example, neglecting a patient or failing to provide necessary treatment might form the subject of a complaint to a Family Practitioner Committee, but might also justify a complaint to the General Medical Council.

Misconduct?

Serious professional misconduct is not defined within the Medical Act 1983. Moreover, although the GMC publishes extensive advice for the medical profession on professional conduct in its pamphlet *Professional Conduct and Discipline: Fitness to Practise*, that pamphlet is not intended to contain a definitive list of the rules governing the profession. It follows that serious professional misconduct is simply a form of conduct which the GMC deems, after full inquiry, to have fallen seriously short of the standards of the medical profession. Beyond this, it is best described by giving examples. Certain forms of behaviour may cast doubt upon the doctor's professional competence: for example, gross neglect of duties to patients; breaches of professional confidence; sexual liaison with a patient which disrupts the patient's family life or otherwise damages or causes distress to the patient or to the patient's family.

A doctor will often carry responsibility for those working under him, and may fall short of professional standards in relation to the supervision of those people. There are also professional standards relating to advertising, breach of which may lead to disciplinary action by the GMC.

Complaints

The GMC complaints procedure is governed by statutory rules, and is therefore formal. You can initiate it by writing to the Registrar of the GMC, giving full details, including times and dates, and any evidence available to substantiate your complaint.

There is an initial filtering process carried out either by the President of the GMC, or by a designated Council member. The purpose of this is to eliminate complaints which do not seem to substantiate serious professional misconduct. If this decision is taken, you will generally receive a letter informing you of this, and offering you some form of reason why your complaint has not proceeded further.

Assuming the complaint goes further, you will be asked to make a sworn statement which, together with any response from the doctor, will be placed before a Preliminary Proceedings Committee. This committee has four options. It may

○   dismiss the complaint
○   warn the doctor that the conduct does not meet acceptable standards (but choose to proceed no further)
○   where the doctor appears to be suffering from some health problem which renders him unfit to practise, refer the case to the Health Committee for further enquiry
○   refer the case to the Professional Conduct Committee. This is done where the Preliminary Proceedings Committee takes the view that an inquiry is appropriate.

The Professional Conduct Committee undertakes a full investigation of the complaints, to which the complainant, together with the doctor and any legal representatives are invited. The doctor will almost invariably choose to be legally represented; the Council will usually arrange legal representation for the complainant, if required. The procedure is formal and public. Witnesses may be called and, as a complainant, you are likely to be questioned by both members of the Committee and the legal representative of the doctor.

If a finding of serious professional misconduct is sustained, the Committee has at its disposal a number of penalties, ranging from a warning through suspension to striking off the register. Although it is common to talk of doctors being struck off the register, in practice the doctor does have the right to apply for restoration to the register once ten months have elapsed from the date of the removal of his name. Moreover, the doctor (but not the patient) has a right of appeal to the Privy Council against any decision of the Professional Conduct Committee which affects his registration.

CONFIDENTIALITY AND ACCESS TO INFORMATION

According to the General Medical Council and the guidelines of the British Medical Association (BMA), any information which you impart to a medical practitioner must, as a rule, be treated in absolute confidence. However, there are some situations in which a medical practitioner may be considered to be acting within the course of his ethical duty in disclosing information. In general, these are:

o   if you have given your informed consent, or (in certain limited cases) if your consent cannot be obtained
o   if there is some overriding duty to society (for instance, if you constitute a danger to other people)
o   in certain circumstances, if the medical practitioner is taking part in legitimate medical research approved by an Ethical Research Committee
o   if the information is required as part of due legal process.

If a medical practitioner breaches the principle of confidentiality, he risks disciplinary action, as professional ethics place registered practitioners under a strict duty to refrain, in general, from disclosure to a third party of any information learnt directly or indirectly in a professional capacity. In addition (although this is a grey area of law), you may be able to obtain an injunction restraining disclosure of information about you, as being in breach of confidence. It is not clear whether you would be able to recover any damages.

Disclosing information

If you consent to information being disclosed about you, this releases the medical practitioner from obligations of secrecy. Make sure, however, that your consent is not assumed too readily: for example, even if you are a patient in a teaching hospital, the medical practitioner has no automatic right to discuss your case in the presence of a number of students. Patients sometimes unwittingly authorise third parties to have access to all their medical notes; they assume that when they sign an insurance application or authorise their lawyer to have access, only the information relevant to their claim or litigation will be given out. They should be careful to specify that they are not authorising their whole history to be passed on.

Some consent will generally be assumed. Thus, the general view is that a conversation between your practitioner and another doctor or a member of his health team concerning your case, with a view to assisting your treatment, will not be considered a breach of confidence.

More difficult is the question of whether a doctor can disclose to relatives information which he has not yet disclosed to the patient, possibly in the case of a terminal condition. The courts seem to have taken the view that a person of full maturity and understanding has a prima-facie right to information about his medical treatment, in advance of other interested parties.

On occasion, the medical practitioner's duty to society may override the patient's interest in keeping the information secret. An example would be patients who represent a danger to society by driving with epilepsy, inadequate vision or similar medical disabilities, or who are mentally unstable and in possession of firearms.

A doctor may be placed under a court order to disclose information about a patient. As medical practice does not enjoy the privilege of silence, it would constitute a contempt of court for the doctor to refuse to disclose that information. There have been cases when the doctor decided that his moral duty overrode any legal duty.

In general, if disclosure is obviously in the public interest, for instance, because drug trafficking is involved, the doctor will disclose. He will usually seek the patient's consent and if this is not forthcoming he will usually wait until a witness summons has been served before disclosing information about the patient.

However, much would depend on whether there was danger to the patient, or to anyone else. In cases of child abuse or serious crime against other people, the doctor would not necessarily wait for a court order obliging him to release information. A doctor is not legally obliged to release information without a court order, but might feel ethically bound to do so when others were at risk.

In relation to disclosure which is sought by a patient for the purposes of court action, detailed procedures have been laid down under the Administration of Justice Acts, to enable a party to obtain relevant medical information. These are mainly concerned with imminent legal proceedings (as for negligence), and it is unlikely that a patient would want to invoke these rights, except on the advice of a solicitor, in pursuing a claim against the doctor.

Access to medical reports

As from 1 January 1989, patients are allowed access to reports about them which medical practitioners have provided for employment or insurance purposes. In the case of employment, this covers situations in which a past or present employer, or a potential employer, requires a medical report about an employee. The insurance provisions cover, for example, situations where a medical report is required before an offer of life insurance is made, or where there has been a claim on a policy.

A patient's rights under the Access to Medical Reports Act 1988 apply at various stages in the process of obtaining the report. Before a report on you is sought, you have the right to be notified of the intended application, and to withhold your consent to it. The person seeking the report must inform you of your rights under the Act.

When you give your consent, you can demand the right to see the report in advance of the person seeking it, who must tell the medical practitioners of your interest; and the practitioner must allow you access.

After you have seen the report, it cannot be passed on, unless you have notified the medical practitioner of your consent. Before giving consent, you are entitled to ask for amendments to be made, if you find the report inaccurate or misleading. If the practitioner is not prepared to amend the report, you are allowed to attach a statement outlining your disagreement.

There are some exceptions. A doctor need not disclose information to the patient if, as a matter of clinical judgment, that disclosure is likely to cause serious harm to the physical or mental health of its subject (the patient) or would indicate the intentions of the doctor in relation to that person's treatment.

If an employer or insurance company uses a company doctor who is not responsible for the clinical care of the patient, the subject of the report does not have right of access to that report.

The Act gives you a right to apply to the county court to ensure compliance with its procedures. However, it does not provide any mechanism for compensation if those procedures are breached to your detriment. It is therefore a limited but none the less a welcome measure.

Another such measure is the Data Protection Act 1984. This is intended to prevent the holding of inaccurate information on computerised records or concealment of the existence of such records. It gives you the right to see records about you, and to ensure their accuracy. However, personal data held by a health professional about the physical and mental health of a 'data subject' may claim exemption from disclosure on the grounds that the information was likely to cause serious physical or mental harm to its subject, or would allow him to find out the identity of some other person, who had not consented to the disclosure.

Beyond these provisions, you have no actual right to see your medical records. Some doctors may allow this, but many do not. In law the view is that medical records are kept for the purposes of the general practice or hospital, in order to assist the staff in providing appropriate treatment. In this view, medical records are not owned by you, but by the general practitioner or the hospital. Therefore, you have no immediate access to your medical records, beyond the limited rights just mentioned. This is a matter which the Department of Health is pursuing with the professional bodies, and there may be some future change.

Confidentiality and the paramedical professions

A requirement of confidentiality is included in the codes of conduct of a number of paramedical professions coming under the supervision of the Council of the Professions Supplementary to Medicine. They are: chiropody, dietetics, occupational therapy, orthoptics, physiotherapy, radiography, medical laboratory scientific officers. It is a specific breach of their code of conduct for registered members of these professions improperly to disclose personal health data. It is intended that the specific rules governing improper disclosure of personal health data should be consistent between these professions and the medical profession, and between the NHS and the private sector.

Making the best of the NHS

There can be few consumer services as important as the National Health Service, as regards both the level of usage and the significance of the quality of service. While the NHS does not have a monopoly, for many people it does provide the single effective source of medical care. This ought to make people very familiar with the available medical services, and encourage them, if necessary, to make use of the complaint mechanisms, in the absence of other forms of protest, such as transferring to an alternative provider of medical services. In fact, users of the NHS tend not to think of themselves as consumers. They are not well informed about their rights of access to its facilities and, on the whole, they have tended to register few expressions of dissatisfaction, and even fewer formal complaints.

However, it is increasingly apparent that social perceptions of the NHS are beginning to change. The decisions of health care providers are less and less likely to go unchallenged. There has been an increased awareness of the problems of funding and the consequent difficulties.

What follows is a guide to making the most of medical services in the NHS. It attempts to explain what is available to you, and how to complain if you fail to receive what you require or if you are not satisfied with what you are given.

In writing about complaints, there is a danger of painting a very black picture of the available medical provision. This would be unfortunate: there is still good reason to be pleased with both the standards and the availability of this provision in the UK. However, such reassurances are worth little to people who have suffered unhappy experiences in health care; the aim of this section is therefore to help you not only to make full use of the services available, but also to take remedial action if those services break down.

Community Health Councils (CHCs)

Community Health Councils are statutory bodies which date back to the reorganisation of the National Health Service in 1974. In most areas there is one CHC for each District Health Authority, although there are rather more in Wales and some large urban areas. Each CHC consists of nominees from the local authority (one-half), voluntary organisations (one-third) and Regional Health Authority (one-sixth). There are different arrangements for Scotland and Northern Ireland.

Health Authorities and Family Practitioner Committees have a statutory duty to consult CHCs on plans to change local health services, and must provide CHCs with information about local services. CHCs have a statutory duty to monitor local health services and to recommend improvements. They also have the right to enter and inspect any NHS premises.

Each CHC has its own way of working, but generally the work will include assisting local organisations with health concerns; carrying out surveys to find out what local people want from the NHS; representing local interests when changes are proposed; advising on patients' rights; giving information on local services; and providing advice and support to people who want to complain about the NHS.

Although the investigation of individual complaints is a matter for other bodies, CHCs can, without prejudging the merits of individual complaints, give advice to potential complainants. They can also monitor such complaints so as to find out in more general terms why, in a particular locality, certain issues regularly give rise to dissatisfaction.

The activities of CHCs vary enormously, depending on local priorities, the type of area, resources and local demands. In relation to complaints, CHCs give advice on how to make complaints and ensure that complaints are properly followed up. In some cases, CHC staff will accompany complainants to any hearing. Even if the CHC is unable to act on behalf of a complainant (some Family Practitioner Committees will not allow CHCs to speak for complainants), it can be very reassuring for a complainant to be accompanied by some one familiar with the proceedings.

In Scotland, the equivalent of the CHCs are the Local Health Councils (LHCs). There are no Family Practitioner Committees: their functions are carried out by the Primary Care Division of the Health Board.

COMPLAINING ABOUT TREATMENT

You may have any of a variety of reasons for complaining about the treatment which you are receiving. The medication which you have been prescribed may be making you feel unwell; or you may simply wish to know just what it is. You may be unhappy about your GP's refusal to refer you to a hospital, or about the long wait for your hospital appointment or bed. Once in hospital, you may be aggrieved at the decision not to allow you to go home, or, conversely, feel that you are being discharged too early. For these and almost all other worries which you may have, there is one simple rule – ask.

If you are unhappy with any aspect of your NHS treatment, you should seek, at the earliest opportunity, to clarify the situation with the people responsible for that treatment. There are many reasons for this, but the best is that it might prove the quickest and simplest route to putting things right, formal complaint procedures being complex and time-consuming.

There are a number of basic principles which you would be wise to follow when pursuing any form of medical complaint.

o Resolve issues informally, if possible; but once you decide to embark upon a formal complaint, act quickly – within three months, at the latest. A long time-lag between the events about which you wish to complain and the date of the complaint may cause difficulties of evidence, and may lead people to doubt the seriousness of your grievance.

o Remember to keep copies of letters and written records concerning all aspects of your complaint.

o At any stage of the complaints procedure, do not hesitate to seek advice from a Community Health Council or any other body or pressure group which might be able to help you. (Some such bodies will be considered later.)

o Be persistent. Many people who embark upon complaints abandon them before the issue is resolved. Be prepared from the outset for a procedure which you may find frustrating and time-consuming.

Because there are many complaints procedures concerned with NHS treatment, before pursuing a complaint, ask yourself three questions: Who is the subject of the complaint? What is the substance of the complaint? What is the object of my complaining? Thus, if you feel that your GP has injured you by giving you the wrong course of treatment, and you wish to claim compensation, then you must proceed differently from the situation in which you felt that a hospital nurse had been intolerably rude to you.

What makes the greatest difference is whether the treatment you are complaining about was in or out of hospital, since there is a different process covering what is termed 'community (non-hospital) medicine'. Another important distinction is whether the subject matter of the complaint involves the exercise of the doctor's clinical judgment.

Finally, it is a good idea to ask yourself at the outset what it is that you hope to achieve by raising the matter – to receive an apology, or financial compensation, or change of treatment, or to make sure that what happened to you will not happen to anyone else. If what you are out for is 'revenge', you may find this counter-productive.

Hospital complaints

The Hospital Complaints Procedures Act 1985 places a duty upon the Secretary of State for Health to direct Health Authorities to ensure that for each hospital within their district there exist adequate arrangements for handling patients' complaints. These arrangements must receive adequate publicity. This limited measure does not institute any new complaints machinery, or make changes to existing procedures, and applies only to hospital complaints. However, it does mean that the hospital patient should be offered a simple outline of the relevant procedure and specific information on whom to approach.

The admission booklet which you are given on entering hospital often contains information about making a complaint. The hospital should also have a leaflet, available to patients, outlining complaints procedures; or there may be notices displayed in the hospital.

You should receive outlines of the different procedures for clinical and non-clinical complaints. A clinical complaint has to do with the quality of diagnosis or treatment received within the NHS at the hands of a doctor, surgeon or dentist. A non-clinical complaint may cover issues ranging from the standard of food or courtesy to errors on the part of the nursing staff which may rival clinical complaints in seriousness.

Each hospital has a complaints officer and the leaflets or notices should tell you where he is to be found. He is the person who will investigate your complaint and report on it.

Your local Community Health Council may be able to help you to present your complaint.

Non-clinical complaints

This simply means complaints which are not about your clinical treatment in hospital. For example, you may be unhappy about the attitudes of people who have treated you in hospital; you may have left in discomfort or pain due to poor administration or nursing provision on the wards; some of your property may have been lost or stolen. There are instances when the staff members welcome a formal complaint which highlights some defect of which they, too, are aware but have been unable to get anything done about. A written complaint from the patient may help to get something done.

The best place to clear up an area of complaint is the hospital itself. The speediest solution, as a rule, is to approach the hospital staff about any dissatisfactions which may have arisen. If you feel that you cannot speak to the particular nurse involved, there will generally be some opportunity to approach someone else – for example, the ward sister. All hospital staff will have been instructed to pay attention to patients' complaints, and to try and resolve them without delay, and that is what they will probably do.

If, however, you have some doubt as to whether your

complaint will be treated seriously, or if you have several complaints to make, it may be wise to complain in writing to someone in authority. You will need to use your discretion as to the seriousness of the matter. Sending a written complaint to a superior about some trivial issue will only serve to sour relations between yourself and the hospital staff. However, a more serious matter, or a complaint which is part of a long-standing chain of similar issues, might well merit a written record.

Formal complaint

If your problem is not dealt with to your satisfaction, you may decide to proceed to making a formal complaint. The difference is that a formal complaint has to be investigated by senior staff, and will generally result in either an explanation by an investigating member of the senior staff or a formal written reply from the authority.

It is not strictly necessary to make a formal complaint in writing, but it is usually advisable. You should emphasise the formal nature of the complaint. You should mention whether you have made any attempts to resolve the problem informally, and should give an account of the response to this.

By senior staff is meant someone above the level of a ward sister, such as a nurse manager; or, in the case of a doctor, a senior consultant. Such a member of staff will generally deal with the investigation right away. If there is any delay, you may expect to be fully informed as to the reasons; if you are not, you should persist in demanding some explanation.

The investigation may entail a meeting between yourself and the investigating member of staff, together with anyone on the staff who is the subject of your complaint. This may turn out to be a formal occasion. There are certain rules, based on what lawyers call 'natural justice', which mean that members of staff who are complained of have the right to know any allegations made about them, and also the right of reply to them. Moreover, they will, as a rule, be advised and assisted by their professional organisation. The hospital itself will be concerned that your complaint may lead to future litigation, and so the proceedings may take on a formal air.

You may have already decided to take legal proceedings against the hospital, whatever the outcome of the complaint. Alternatively, you may have decided not to bother to do so; or you may have been advised that you have no case in law. If you know that legal proceedings are not envisaged, it may be useful to say so to the investigator. This will ease the minds of other staff assisting with the investigation. In addition, professional organisations are often reluctant to advise their members to participate fully in the investigation of a complaint, a report from which may be later used as an aid in litigation.

At the conclusion of the investigation, the member of staff conducting it will produce a formal note of the discussions, together with an explanation to you, the complainant of the circumstances surrounding the complaint.

Further formal complaint

If you remain dissatisfied with the outcome of this process, you may decide to make a formal complaint – which should be in writing – to the chairman of the District Health Authority. This will institute an investigation by the district administrator or general manager. In some Health Authorities, and in cases of serious error or complaint, members of the Health Authority may be brought in to assist in the investigation.

You will eventually receive a letter from either the district general manager, or, in some cases, the chairman of the Health Authority. It should explain fully any action which has been taken as a result of your complaint; or if no action has been taken, why it was not felt appropriate to act. This letter is of considerable importance to the Health Authority, which is aware that you have a further right of complaint to the ombudsman that is, the Health Service Commissioner (whose function will be described later). Therefore you can expect that the Health Authority will have made considerable efforts to resolve the matter to your satisfaction.

There is one rather grey area concerning complaints about injuries suffered in hospital. Technically, such complaints may be resolved by resorting to legal action, and are therefore not within the formal ambit of the ombudsman. However, not all accidents which befall patients merit a legal action; it may be appropriate to register your complaint with the ombudsman if you are the victim of a minor but potentially more serious injury.

This does not apply to injuries received in the course of treatment. An accident resulting from some lack of care during an operation or other medical procedure would amount to a clinical matter.

Clinical complaints

These are complaints about the manner in which a medical practitioner has exercised clinical judgment and skill; that is, the complaint is one that concerns medical or surgical treatment.

You may complain orally or in writing, but should have a written record of the substance of your complaint. You may complain to the consultant in charge of your case, or to the Health Authority, or to any of the Health Authority officers. It may be best to approach the consultant directly, since he is responsible for your treatment while you are in hospital, and the initial investigation of the complaint will devolve on him.

First stage of clinical complaints

This is an attempt to resolve the problem speedily. The consultant should discuss the matter with any other doctors concerned, and should seek an early meeting with you, the complainant, to discuss the issue further and discover the causes of the grievance. As a rule he will record the discussion in the hospital notes, and you would be well advised to make your own record of it. If your complaint concerns a medical staff member other than consultants, then the consultant will bring that doctor concerned to the discussion.

There are two occasions when a consultant will not proceed

directly with a complaint. If he feels that there is a genuine risk of legal action, he is likely to refer the matter to the district general manager. If there are non-clinical aspects to the complaint, the consultant will likewise inform the district general manager, so that arrangements can be made to consider both the clinical and the non-clinical elements of the complaint.

If you choose to complain not to the consultant but to the Health Authority, the district administrator will simply refer the matter back to the consultant, for his comments. In response to your complaint, you will usually receive a written reply, with an accompanying letter from the district general manager. Any reference in this letter to clinical matters will have been agreed in advance by the consultant, in liaison with the district general manager; it may simply refer back to your own discussions with the consultant. This will be true particularly where the discussion with the consultant appears to have resolved the issue.

Second stage of clinical complaints
If you are not satisfied with the results of the first-stage procedure, you may pursue your complaint to a second stage. If you have not already put your complaint in writing, you should do so now, and send it to the Health Authority, demanding that the matter should be taken further.

At this stage, the Regional Medical Officer (RMO) will become involved: he will usually meet the consultant and consider what to do next.

The consultant may want another meeting with you; or he may have decided that this would be of little use. If he is willing to meet you, the RMO will arrange this; if he is unwilling, the RMO will consider whether to undertake an independent professional review – the third stage of the procedure.

Independent professional review
This is a review of your treatment, carried out by two independent consultants who work in the same speciality as the doctor by whom you were treated. It may not necessarily be as

useful as might at first appear, for two reasons. First, the independent professional review can only be invoked where, according to legal advice, the complaint is unlikely to be the basis of a formal legal action. Secondly, the complaints procedure stresses throughout that complaints which are subject to independent professional review should be of a substantial nature. This leaves room only for complaints which are serious, yet unsuitable for action before the courts. There are few complaints which fall into this category.

The consultants conducting the independent professional review will have access to all of your clinical records. They will discuss your complaint with your consultant, and with any other members of the medical staff involved. They will also have a meeting with you, at which you may wish to be accompanied by a relative or friend, if only to bolster your confidence.

The consultants should discuss fully with you the clinical aspects of your treatment. They may attempt to clear up any misunderstandings; or they may decide that there is some substance in your complaint. At this stage, they will report back to the RMO, in confidence. They may make recommendations about avoiding similar problems in the future; and will usually report back to you, telling you what they have recommended. This will not be a detailed report, but only an outline.

You will receive a formal report on completion of the independent professional review. The district general manager will write to you formally on behalf of the authority, explaining what action the authority has taken as a result of your complaint. Any comment on clinical treatment will be based on the RMO's interpretation of the independent professional review report.

The Health Authority will make no attempt to give your complaint wider publicity, and will confine its response to the letter to you. DHSS circulars show an awareness of the possibility that complainants may publicise the outcome of their complaints. This option is available to you, but you should pursue it only upon consideration.

FAMILY PRACTITIONERS

The term 'family practitioner' includes dentists, optometrists and ophthalmic general practitioners, pharmacists and doctors in general practice (GPs, also known as family doctors). All of these work under contract to the Family Practitioner Committee (FPC).

General practice

The provision of general medical services is administered by Family Practitioner Committees (FPCs); they oversee the patient list of the doctors in the district. A doctor must provide to patients on his list all necessary and appropriate personal medical services of the type generally provided by general medical practitioners. Services offered by GPs are free of charge, except where a patient cannot prove that he is on the list, and cannot produce a medical card. In such circumstances, the GP must offer necessary treatment, but is entitled to demand a fee. In general, most doctors know whether or not a patient is on the list; listed patients include the patients that they have accepted on the list either temporarily or permanently, and, in some cases, patients that have been assigned to them.

Treatment for patients on the list is generally provided at the doctor's surgery and, subject to the demands of an appointment system (if there is one), the doctor must treat patients who come in surgery hours. The doctor must also offer medical treatment outside practice premises, if a patient's condition so requires. However, this is generally confined to the doctor's practice area, so that the doctor would not necessarily be obliged to travel to the next town if, for example, the patient were taken ill while visiting relatives.

The general practitioner also acts as an intermediary for patients seeking access to other health and social service facilities. The GP has a duty to advise patients about these facilities and make referrals; he will also prescribe pharmaceuticals and issue medical certificates to patients. However, for certain services, particularly contraceptive and maternity medical services, the GP is under an obligation to provide these only if he has signified his willingness to do so. He is entitled to charge for some of the additional services, such as issuing vaccination certificates for overseas travel.

These duties are placed on a doctor personally, but in the case of general medical services a doctor has to take whatever reasonable steps are appropriate to ensure that treatment is always available from himself or another doctor acting as deputy. This may or may not be the doctor's partner or assistant; it has to be someone qualified, competent and capable of carrying out the appropriate treatment. Such delegation would not, however, absolve the doctor from the responsibility for the actions of a deputy doctor. The Family Practitioner Committee must be informed of assistants and deputies, and where a deputising service is used a GP must obtain the consent of the FPC.

Where a GP's absence or disability is likely to be prolonged, the FPC has the responsibility of arranging for the treatment of patients on that doctor's list for so long as the doctor is unable to carry out his obligations to the patients.

Changing doctors

How easy it is to change your GP may depend on the reason for that change. If you are moving house, you can simply write, enclosing your medical card, to any general practitioner in the area to which you are moving. The card will implicitly show your change of address, and if the practice has room you will be accepted. You should be aware, however, that there is a fixed number of persons to whom a doctor may provide general medical services, so a doctor may legitimately refuse to take you on to the list if it is full.

If your doctor has died or has been removed from the medical list, the FPC will offer you the right to apply to other doctors for acceptance on their list, and in the interim may arrange for a doctor to take over the existing patient list.

You may wish to change doctors because you are in some way dissatisfied with the service offered by your current GP. A change of doctor without change of address often indicates that the change is a form of complaint. If you do wish to change for that or any other reason, you could ask your current doctor to sign your medical card to indicate his consent, and you can then write to other doctors asking them if they would take you on, and mentioning your present doctor's consent to the transfer. There is, however, no need for this. You can simply give the FPC written notice of your wish to transfer and send your medical card. If you are refused by the doctor you are trying to change to, the FPC allocation committee will assign you to a doctor, but you will have no choice. A doctor may have a person removed from his list by requiring the FPC to assign the patient to another doctor.

General practitioners and complaints

The Family Practitioner Committee is a supervisory body. It has no formal link with the general practitioner, because the GP is an independent contractor, not an employee of the NHS.

This limits the subject matter of complaints which can be made to the FPC. Its role is to ensure that a GP fulfils the terms of service laid down in the contract between him and the NHS. The substance of the complaint may therefore only be that a GP has failed to fulfil the terms of service written into the contract.

Essentially, these terms consist of a duty to attend patients, and to provide to them all necessary and appropriate medical services of the type ordinarily provided by general medical practitioners. The treatment must be provided with the requisite degree of skill, knowledge and care, but the GP is not expected to observe a standard higher than that of general practitioners as a class.

The FPC is the appropriate forum for a complaint against a GP. The address of your FPC is on the front of your medical card, but you may also seek the assistance of other advisory bodies (for example, the Community Health Council). As soon as possible after the incident which gave rise to the complaint – and within two months of it at most – you should complain in writing to the administrator of the FPC. As a rule, some attempt will be made to resolve the matter informally, but not all FPCs attempt to do this.

Medical Service Committee

If the matter is dealt with formally, the administrator of the FPC will pass the complaint on to the chairman of the sub-committee which investigates this type of complaint – the Medical Service Committee.

Your report may be considered without a hearing, if the chairman of the sub-committee decides that the GP has not failed to comply with the terms of service. If you feel that you have further statements to make which would detail your complaint more fully, you should contact the FPC within 14 days of receiving notice that your complaint has been passed on. If you do not do so, there will be no opportunity for an oral hearing. The chairman will pass the papers to the members of the Medical Service Committee, which will report on the matter. In addition to the chairman there will also be three lay and three medical members.

The FPC will then send you a copy of the report with its decision. If the report states that there is no failure on the part of the GP, you will have the right to appeal. If your complaint is upheld at this point – that is, the report shows reasonable grounds to believe that the GP did not meet the relevant terms of service – then your complaint will be forwarded to the GP, who has four weeks in which to comment.

Many GPs will wish at this point to take advice from the medical defence societies, so it is usual for the Medical Service Committee to grant an extension to the four-week period.

When the GP makes an answer to your complaint, you have fourteen days in which to issue a response. If the GP has taken extra time to seek advice, you may also want to have the advantage of further advice and consideration. You should then also apply to the Medical Service Committee for an extension.

Once all comments are in, the Medical Service Committee may report. It can do this without a hearing, but generally it will decide that a hearing is necessary, especially if there is some factual disagreement between your account and that of the GP. The hearing is held before the full Medical Service Committee. The GP may be represented, but not by a lawyer or other paid representative.

The GP will present his case by putting forward his own testimony, asking you questions, and perhaps calling witnesses on his own behalf. You should invoke the same rights. Consider carefully whether you wish to be represented – the Community Health Council may help you in this. Prepare your own evidence carefully. Consider the witnesses that you may be able to call on your behalf. Plan what questions you will ask the GP, perhaps based on the comments made in the initial stages. As you are entitled to at least 21 days' notice of the hearing, you should have enough time for all this.

Following the hearing, the Committee will produce a report which will summarise the facts, draw inferences from them, state whether there has been a breach of conditions of service, and make recommendations (if appropriate) as to what should happen to the GP. This report will be sent to the FPC, which is obliged to accept the findings of fact; but, provided it gives reasons, it can choose not to adopt the committee's recommendations.

The FPC then reports formally to the Secretary of State, suggesting a course of action – such as that the GP should be warned to comply with the terms of service. The Secretary of State can order the GP to repay any expenses which you have been forced to meet as a result of the GP's breach of terms of service, and so you should make such expenses known to the Medical Service Committee.

Appeal

Either party has a right of appeal to the Secretary of State within one month of the date of receipt of the committee's decision. There is no particular form of appeal: you should summarise your case and outline the main arguments in support of your complaint. You will be informed whether you are to be granted an oral hearing on appeal. In general, the GP will at this stage be represented by a qualified lawyer, and you should do what you can to secure legal representation. The Secretary of State will convene a panel of three persons to hear your appeal: they will be a legally qualified chairman sitting with two medical practitioners, at least one of whom should be from a relevant medical discipline. This panel will have before it the full details of the case to date, including the FPC decision.

As the complainant, you will usually be asked to open the appeal, whether or not you instigated the appeal process. The panel will generally wish to hear the evidence again, so the appeal will involve the recall of witnesses and their cross-examination. The legal representatives are usually allowed to make final submissions before the panel retires to consider the issues.

The panel reports directly to the Secretary of State, in a manner similar to the report by the Medical Service Committee to the FPC. The Secretary of State considers whether to adopt the panel's recommendations; thereafter the DHSS notifies both parties to the appeal of the Secretary of State's decision, giving the reasons. There is often some delay between the appeal and the receipt of a decision, so you will need to be rather patient.

The Secretary of State has the jurisdiction to award you your costs, and your legal representative may wish to raise this matter at the hearing.

NURSES, MIDWIVES AND HEALTH VISITORS

The training of nurses, midwives and health visitors in Great Britain is under the supervision of National Boards for Nursing, Midwifery and Health Visiting. There are separate Boards for

England, Wales, Scotland and Northern Ireland, and they have the duty to ensure that the requirements of the registration body (the United Kingdom Central Council for Nursing, Midwifery and Health Visiting) are met as to kind, content and standard of training.

Nursing training can be for one of two levels of registration: as state registered or state enrolled nurse. Nurses can train in the care of adults with physical illness, children, the mentally ill or the mentally handicapped. Training to become a registered health visitor can be undertaken only by persons who are already registered nurses. Most people who train to become registered midwives first train as nurses and then take a shortened course; but a few people become midwives through a longer course for which nursing training is not required.

On successful completion of training, nurses (both registered and enrolled) are entered on the register of the UK Central Council for Nursing, Midwifery and Health Visiting (UKCC). Their professional conduct falls within the supervision of this Council, which is required to establish and maintain the standards of training and professional conduct for nurses, midwives and health visitors (in what follows, we shall refer to nurses only). Under its statutory authority, the council has produced a code of professional conduct, as well as supplementary advisory documents, the purpose of which is to maintain public trust and confidence in the nursing profession, and to ensure that all nurses uphold the good name of the profession by serving the interests of patients and those of society. The documents emphasise the primacy of the interests of patients and clients and the personal professional accountability of each person on the UKCC register.

Complaints against nurses
With comparatively few exceptions, nurses, whether in the NHS or the private/independent sector, and whether engaged in practice in hospitals, nursing homes, the community, occupational health or health promotion, are employees.

Complaints should, in the first place, be addressed to the appropriate employing authority.

Many of the complaints which patients may have concerning nurses within the National Health Service will be covered by the complaints procedures already outlined in relation to hospitals, or occasionally (for example in the case of health visitors attached to general practitioners) general practice.

The National Boards can provide a copy of the code of conduct and also details of complaints procedures. Each National Board is charged with an investigatory function in relation to alleged misconduct, and will undertake to investigate any complaint which you might choose to make. Although, in practice, most complaints emanate from patients, the complaints procedure is open to any person who feels that he can establish that a nurse is guilty of professional misconduct. All that is required is that you complain in writing to the appropriate National Board and accompany your complaint with a detailed statement and any supporting evidence you may have.

The board's investigating committee will first investigate on the basis of your complaint and will also hear the response of the nurse involved. It may find that no further action is necessary, or may adopt the intermediate response of not proceeding to a hearing, but none the less recording the complaint on the nurse's file. The final option is to refer the case to a hearing of the Professional Conduct Committee. Where an investigation indicates that a nurse might be unfit to practise because of ill health, the Board has the option of referring the matter to the health committee of the UKCC.

Once a complaint is received by the statutory bodies, the full costs of the investigation and hearings will be met by the UKCC unless the complainant chooses to prosecute the matter through his or her own solicitor.

The Professional Conduct Committee hears the most serious cases of alleged professional misconduct referred to it by the investigating committee. The procedures can be compared to those dealing with the professional misconduct of doctors, allowing for an oral hearing with legal representation. In the most serious cases, the professional conduct committee may order the removal of the nurse's name from the professional register.

The professional conduct committee may also change the status of the nurse: in the case of a midwife, for example, it may order that the nurse should no longer practise midwifery, but allow the nurse's name to remain on the professional register for general nursing purposes. This action has been taken very rarely and in quite exceptional circumstances.

Nurses who are removed from the register have a right of appeal to the relevant courts of appeal in different regions of the UK, if aggrieved by the decision.

DENTAL SERVICES

As with general medical services, general dental services are provided by general dental practitioners, under contract to Family Practitioner Committees. Many of the details which apply to the relationship between the FPC and the general practitioner apply also to the relationship between the FPC and the dentist, including supervision of treatment and deputising arrangements. A dental list is maintained by the FPC, and anyone requiring dental treatment can go to a listed dentist. It is easy to change dentists, and far more common than changing GPs. Although your dentist will generally keep your dental records together with any X-rays taken for a period of twelve months, and may send you reminders that a dental check-up is due, there is nothing to prevent you from simply consulting other dentists.

How much will it cost?

The charges for dental treatment and appliances are laid down by the Secretary of State. No charge can be made for treatment of expectant mothers or of mothers who have borne a child within the previous 12 months, of schoolchildren up the age of 18, and persons up to the age of 19 who are in full-time education. Certain forms of dental treatment are free, such as emergency dental treatment to arrest bleeding. The Health and Medicines Act 1988 introduced charges for some services previously freely available, including check-ups.

If you have not paid the dentist's bill, the dentist may discontinue your treatment, even though it is of a continuing nature.

If you want a form of treatment which is more expensive than that which is clinically necessary, such as gold fillings or inlays or certain forms of crowns, bridges or dentures, the dentist must offer you an estimate for your approval and then submit the estimate to the Dental Practice Board (DPB). The Board will determine how much the dentist may recover from you by way of additional charge. Also, the dental practitioner may be required to obtain the Board's approval before undertaking certain treatments.

The General Dental Practitioners' Association publishes a leaflet entitled: *Yes . . . But how much will it cost?* giving the current NHS charges for the most common forms of dental treatment. It can be found in libraries, and may be obtained from CHCs, FPCs and Citizens Advice Bureaux.

Professional organisations

There are a number of professional associations relating to dentistry. The British Dental Association (BDA) constitutes a pressure group which seeks to protect the interests of both dentists and patients in relation to dental services. The General Dental Practitioners' Association (GDPA) represents family dentists only and campaigns on issues involving members' interests and all matters of dental health. The GDPA has stated that it would attempt conciliation in the event of a complaint against a member. The British Dental Hygienists Association (BDHA) is a professional body for which only dental hygienists are eligible. Dentists and dental surgery assistants may become associate members. It will advise on complaints against members if these are addressed to the Council of the BDHA.

Complaints about dentists

Complaints about dental treatment provided under the NHS General Dental Services should be made to the Family Practitioner Committee, in the same way as complaints about medical treatment.

The General Dental Council (GDC) has a disciplinary function in dealing with allegations of professional misconduct made against registered dentists and auxiliary staff (such as hygienists and therapists). The Council was set up in 1956 and now derives authority under the Dentists Act 1984.

The Council in general prefers disputes as to fees to be pursued through the civil law; other complaints can be made in writing to the registrar of the GDC. Where it appears that there is a prima-facie case of serious professional misconduct, the council may ask the complainant to swear a statutory declaration or affidavit covering the facts. The dentist will be given the opportunity to explain the background to, or make observations upon the complaint. After that, the President of the Council decides whether the matter should be referred to the preliminary proceedings committee, which decides whether the matter should proceed to an inquiry before the professional conduct committee.

This committee meets twice each year, to enquire into serious professional misconduct in a formal legal setting. It takes evidence on oath and examines witnesses, with a legal assessor present. It may decide to suspend a dentist or to erase his name from the register. A dentist may appeal to the Judicial Committee of the Privy Council against such a decision.

The professional conduct rules of the GDC also cover matters relating to qualifications and to drug misuse, canvassing, advertising, and all other matters which might render a dentist unfit to practise.

OPHTHALMIC SERVICES

Any registered medical practitioner may test sight. Among non-medical practitioners, only optometrists (also known as ophthalmic opticians) may test sight. Only ophthalmic medical practitioners are on the registers of Family Practitioner Committees.

Anyone who wishes to have a sight test can simply go to an optometrist or ophthalmic medical practitioner. The Health and Medicines Act 1988 introduced charges for eye tests, but these do not apply in the case of sufferers from glaucoma, or people over 40 whose parents or siblings have had glaucoma; registered diabetics; schoolchildren under 16 or students under 19 years of age; or people on low incomes, receiving income support or family credit.

The provision of an eye test cannot be made conditional on buying any required spectacles from that particular practitioner. If you have a prescription for spectacles, you can take it to any registered optician (or unregistered spectacle seller) to have the spectacles made up – except for children under 16 and those who are partially sighted, who must go to a registered optician. A prescription is valid for two years.

The fee for an eye examination is a matter between the patient and the practitioner: it is not fixed. At the end of the examination the practitioner should give the patient a copy of the prescription and a statement of the result. The ophthalmic practitioner has a duty to exercise proper care and attention and to inform the patient's GP if he detects any sign of injury, abnormality or disease.

Professional organisations

The professional bodies concerned with ophthalmic services include the Association of British Dispensing Opticians (ABDO), which deals, as the name suggests, primarily with dispensing opticians, although some optometrists are associate members. Opticians may call themselves 'dispensing opticians' only if they are registered by the General Optical Council (GOC). They may fit and supply spectacles to the prescription of an optometrist or an ophthalmic medical practitioner; some may fit contact lenses also.

Dispensing opticians are subject to the supervision of the GOC in relation to their qualifications and professional conduct; the GOC also lays down rules on publicity.

Optometrists, in addition to testing sight and issuing prescriptions can, like dispensing opticians, dispense spectacles and contact lenses. One of their professional bodies is the Association of Optometrists (AOP), previously called the Association of Optical Practitioners. This is the negotiating and representative body for the profession. Members are registered by the GOC, and registration depends on a relevant degree in optometry together with clinical training as required by the British College of Optometrists. The College is the academic and examining body for optometry, and lays down the rules which the AOP expects all members to follow.

Dispensing opticians may also join the AOP as associate members.

Complaints about ophthalmic services

ABDO offers a complaints service in relation to professional misconduct by members which does not, however, cover simple consumer complaints (for example, about spectacles).

The Consumer Complaints Service (CCS) is situated at the AOP address but is an independent organisation. It will handle complaints if the complainant writes to it, setting out briefly the basis of the complaint, and giving the full name and address of the practitioner concerned. After an enquiry, the CCS will write to the aggrieved patient with an explanation, in an endeavour to reach a speedy and amicable resolution of the complaint. The CCS makes no charge to the patient. It deals with the majority of disputes relating to ophthalmic services.

The British College of Optometrists deals essentially with ethical and professional matters in relation to optometrists. College rules require an optometrist to place the welfare of the patient before all other considerations, and to ensure that his behaviour towards patients and professional colleagues is such as not to bring the profession into disrepute.

The General Optical Council is the body charged with the task of enforcing professional discipline, and investigating complaints of serious professional misconduct. The GOC has a statutory footing and operates under a statutory rule book. If you wish to make a complaint, write to the registrar for advice on how best to proceed.

As with some other professional bodies, when making a formal complaint, the facts must be submitted in the form of a statutory declaration. Once the complaint is accepted, it is processed by the Council's investigating committee, prior, if necessary, to reference to a disciplinary committee. Such a committee, if finding the case proven, has the power to suspend or erase the registration of the practitioner involved. As with the other disciplinary bodies, a decision of the disciplinary committee may be the subject of an appeal to the Judicial Committee of the Privy Council.

Orthoptists

Orthoptists are concerned primarily with the diagnosis and treatment of squints and other disorders of vision and eye movement. Most patients are children, but a number of adults are referred, because of the orthoptist's ability to diagnose complex disorders of eye movement which are often first noticed by neurologists or neuro-surgeons. Orthoptists qualify by three years of academic study culminating, if successful, in the Diploma of the British Orthoptic Society (BOS). There are approximately 1,000 practising orthoptists within the BOS, working alongside NHS practitioners or in community work, or private practice. Private practitioners are allowed to inform medical practitioners of their services and to charge such fees as they choose for their work.

In relation to complaints, orthoptists fall within the ambit of the Council for Professions Supplementary to Medicine (CPSM) dealt with elsewhere in this chapter. However, the British

Orthoptic Society will also consider any letters of complaint. It is concerned with the maintenance of professional standards, particularly by education and training.

PHARMACEUTICAL SERVICES

To become a pharmacist, a person must obtain a degree in pharmacy, undertake one year's pre-registration experience and register with the Royal Pharmaceutical Society of Great Britain. Only registered persons are allowed to use the title 'pharmacist' (also known as 'chemist').

All pharmacies, that is, chemist shops, have to be registered, and are required to have a pharmacist in control and supervising the dispensing or sale of restricted medicines. 'Drug stores' are not pharmacies; they do not have a pharmacist and may not sell restricted medicines or use the title 'chemist'.

If, like many people, you seek medical advice from a chemist, be sure to consult the pharmacist himself, rather than one of the (probably) unqualified salespeople. The pharmacist should know whether he should supply you with an appropriate product or suggest that you seek medical advice.

The dispensing of NHS prescriptions is governed by District Health Authorities and administered by Family Practitioner Committees. These have lists containing the names, addresses and opening hours of dispensing chemists in their districts who have undertaken to provide pharmaceutical services. Under the terms of service with the health authority, a chemist has to provide medicines, appliances and other medical necessities on the presentation of a prescription. Complaints with regard to NHS services can be made to the administrator of a Family Practitioner Committee or, on professional matters, to the Royal Pharmaceutical Society.

The Royal Pharmaceutical Society is charged under the Medicines Act with enforcing the law relating to the sale of medicines, wherever it takes place. The Society's 19 inspectors regularly visit pharmacies to ensure that standards are maintained, and to investigate any complaints. The Society has a code of ethics governing the conduct of pharmacies; any breach of this code may come under the consideration of the Society's statutory committee, and may give rise to the risk of removal from the register and thus the loss of the right to practise.

Retail pharmacies, except for some of the larger multiples, usually belong to the National Pharmaceutical Association (NPA), membership being accorded to each pharmaceutical outlet. The NPA provides an indemnity scheme in respect of the potential liability of its members but does not handle customer complaints. It is a trade association concerned with the business of running a pharmacy, and provides a professional pressure group.

CHIROPODISTS

Chiropody is very much accepted as a paramedical profession in its own right. It specialises in the care and protection of the foot.

Chiropodists are employed – in the NHS and private practice – in a variety of settings such as hospitals, health centres, mobile clinics, schools. They may also be employed by athletic and sporting teams.

Chiropodists are commonly engaged to deal with short-term foot problems, alleviating pain and discomfort caused by deformities and dysfunctions of the feet; but they also deal with more long-term problems, using curative foot-care involving therapeutic techniques, massage and exercise therapies and ultrasonics. Chiropodists may perform minor surgery, for example, to remove verrucae or treat ingrowing toe-nails (under local anaesthesia).

Another important function is the diagnosis of medical conditions which manifest themselves in the feet, including diabetes, ulcerable conditions, varicose veins and other circulatory problems.

Chiropodists under the NHS
To obtain NHS chiropody treatment, you would need a referral from your GP.

Chiropodists practising under the NHS or Local Authority Social Services (LASS) must be state registered (SRCh) and have trained at a school of chiropody recognised by the Chiropodists Board of the Council for Professions Supplementary to Medicine (CPSM). The duties of the Chiropodists Board are to establish and maintain a register of state registered chiropodists, to promote the highest standard of professional conduct among such chiropodists and to maintain high standards of chiropodial education.

All state registered chiropodists are required to abide by codes of conduct governing matters of ethics, conduct and relationship with patients. These codes have the sanction of formal disciplinary action, if breached.

State registered chiropodists are permitted to advertise. The Chiropodists Board stipulates that the advertising must be accurate and restrained in nature (as well as meeting any other legal, voluntary and statutory requirements). It prohibits outright canvassing for patients, or selling to the public any aids connected with chiropody.

Complaints about state registered chiropodists

The Chiropodists Board has issued a statement of conduct and set up investigating and disciplinary committees. It handles complaints from members of the public alleging breaches of the statement of conduct.

The investigating and disciplinary committees of the Chiropodists Board do not deal with allegations of professional negligence as such. Their remit covers only 'infamous conduct in a professional respect' and any complaint must be judged to have met that condition if the committees are to be able to consider and deal with it. This is not meant to deter genuine complaints properly made to the Board; but a potential complainant should seek advice on whether the matter is one best dealt with through the employer, the professional association, the state registration body, or the ordinary process of the law (whether criminal or civil).

The Society of Chiropodists is the only professional organisation exclusively for state registered chiropodists. It deals with complaints from members of the public, which must be submitted in writing and are referred for comment to the chiropodist complained of. The matter may then be referred to the ethical committee of the Society, or, exceptionally, to the Council of the Society. Termination of membership is the ultimate sanction.

The Society arranges third party professional indemnity insurance for its members, but it is not compulsory for them to have this.

Chiropodists in private practice

Chiropody is an unregulated profession: there is no statutory requirement that chiropodists practising outside the NHS or LASS should be state registered. People at varying levels of formal training (from none at all up to postgraduate level) can practise privately.

Qualified chiropodists may or may not choose to be state registered – though most private sector medical employers choose to operate within the state registration system. Thus the absence of registration does not, in itself, tell you anything about a practitioner's competence; what you should check is whether he is a member of a reputable professional association.

There are a number of regulatory bodies in the field of chiropody which do not require their members to be state registered chiropodists.

The Institute of Chiropodists requires those who apply for membership either to be state registered or to have satisfied the Institute in some other way of their competence to practise chiropody. The General Chiropodical Board of the Institute maintains a register of schools which it recognises as places of instruction in chiropody.

All members must abide by the Institute's code of conduct; the Institute will consider complaints from members of the public. These should be made in writing and addressed to the secretary of the Institute.

The English Chiropodists Association also does not require that its members be state registered. The Association does not actually carry out any training, but applications for membership will be accepted only if the applicant holds a diploma from a recognised school.

Members must abide by a code of ethics; complaints from patients will be examined if they relate to contraventions of this code or to other unprofessional conduct.

The British Chiropody Association is a large organisation with more than 9,000 members. Its members must complete the training course offered by the SMAE institute at its training school, which leads to a diploma in chiropody and full membership of the School of Surgical Chiropody (MSSCh). The course is longer and more advanced than that for state registration; state registered practitioners who wish to become members of the Association must undergo further training. It runs its own course at its training school leading to a Diploma in Chiropody.

Members must abide by the Association's code of conduct. Complaints by consumers should be in writing and will be dealt with by the Association's disciplinary panel, which may take action ranging from compensation of the complainant to termination of membership.

A word of warning

Owing to the absence of statutory regulation for the whole profession, it is possible for a totally unqualified person to set up as a chiropodist. If someone is neither state registered nor a member of a reputable professional organisation, this should be taken as a warning sign.

In view of the risk of cross-infection with hepatitis B, AIDS and other diseases, a reputable chiropodist will follow scrupulous guidelines in treatment, including thorough sterilisation of all instruments, the use of disposable needles and safe disposal of all waste material. You cannot be sure of these precautions with a practitioner whose training is an unknown quantity.

PHYSIOTHERAPY

Physiotherapy is a term that was coined to embrace the therapeutic use of physical means such as massage, manipulation, medical gymnastics and all forms of electrotherapy. Physiotherapists use these techniques to activate and stimulate a natural process of healing and repair. They may be able to help with problems as diverse as prolapsed vertebral discs, fallen arches, sinus problems and bad headaches. The profession of physiotherapy has a long and reputable history.

Physiotherapy under the NHS

Only state registered physiotherapists can work within the NHS or LASS. Training for the appropriate qualifications is offered at the schools of physiotherapy attached to hospitals, polytechnics and universities. The course must be validated by the Chartered Society of Physiotherapy and the Physiotherapists Board of the Council for Professions Supplementary to Medicine. Having passed the relevant examinations, students are eligible for membership of the Chartered Society of Physiotherapy and registration with the Physiotherapists Board of the CPSM.

Physiotherapists work in hospitals, in local authority clinics, in the community, in industry, and also in private practice. All Health Authorities provide physiotherapy services. Patients are referred to them from a wide variety of sources: medical practitioners (including GPs), nurses, other paramedicals and, increasingly, self-referral.

The rules of professional conduct of the Chartered Society of Physiotherapy deal with matters such as confidentiality, relationships with patients on a basis of mutual trust and respect, relationships with medical colleagues and other health and allied professions, and professional standards. They allow advertising, so long as it is accurate and professionally restrained.

Complaints about state registered physiotherapists

Any formal complaint should be addressed to the Chartered Society's Director of Professional Affairs, who reports to the Preliminary Committee. The member complained of is invited to reply to the complaint. The Preliminary Committee can decide to take no further action, or refer the complaint to the Professional Conduct Committee. The sanctions of that committee are admonishment, probation, suspension or deletion of the registration. There is also an Appeals Committee to which a deleted member may apply after one year to be restored to the register.

The Council for Professions Supplementary to Medicine, through its Physiotherapy Board, exercises the same supervisory and disciplinary functions towards physiotherapists as it does in the case of chiropodists.

Physiotherapists in private practice

Most members of the Chartered Society who are in private practice belong to the Organisation of Chartered Physiotherapists in Private Practice (OCPPP). It is an occupational group within the Society, and therefore comes within the control of the rules of professional conduct; but complaints, in the first instance, should be referred to the Honorary Secretary of the OCPPP.

The SMAE Institute, mentioned earlier in connection with chiropody, also offers a postgraduate course in physiotherapy; it concentrates on massage to a greater extent than the training for state registration.

OCCUPATIONAL THERAPY

Occupational therapists assess and treat people through the use of purposeful activity to prevent disability and develop independent function.

There are many ways of becoming a qualified occupational therapist; they include three- and four-year degree courses, three-year diploma courses, four-year in-service training courses and two-year accelerated courses for graduates.

The majority of occupational therapists, who need to be state registered, work within the National Health Service but a significant number are employed with social services departments. A small but increasing number work in private practice.

Occupational therapy is the fastest growing profession allied to medicine, showing a growth from about 100 to 10,000 during the past 50 years.

The British Association of Occupational Therapists maintains a code of conduct for its members which is additional to that maintained by the Council for Professions Supplementary to Medicine for state registered therapists.

The Health Service Commissioner (ombudsman)

Ombudsmen are independent investigators who explore allegations of maladministration and produce reports on them, particularly in relation to central and local government but also in connection with an increasing range of other services. Although these reports do not offer formal legal remedies, they carry great persuasive and moral force.

A Health Service Commissioner has existed since 1973, with a brief to investigate claims that an individual has suffered injustice or hardship through maladministration in the health services or through their failure to provide necessary treatment or care. The Commissioner's jurisdiction does not extend to matters which might form the subject matter of a complaint against a GP, dentist, optician or pharmacist under contract to the Family Practitioner Committee. This restriction extends to complaints procedures which involve a formal complaint against a GP.

There are two other significant limitations. The Commissioner cannot investigate issues concerning the professional or clinical judgment of medical staff. Nor can he investigate matters which have a readily available legal remedy. In practice, the Commissioner may occasionally intervene where a legal remedy technically exists but the complainant cannot reasonably be expected to pursue it. A complainant may be asked to give an assurance that it is not his intention to resort to law. Such assurances, if given, are not legally binding, but if they are frequently breached, they may lead to a cautious and more restrictive approach by the Commissioner.

Approaching the ombudsman

In one way, the jurisdiction of the Health Service Commissioner is wider than that of his central government counterpart. He may investigate complaints received directly, and without their having to be filtered through a Member of Parliament. You can complain simply by writing to the Health Service Commissioner for England, Scotland or Wales (depending on where the incident occurred).

If you have difficulty in formulating your complaint, ask your Community Health Council to help you: the Commissioner will accept your complaint through the Council. However, he will want to know what steps you yourself have taken with the Health Authority to resolve the matter, and so an approach to him should be considered as a last, rather than a first, resort.

You should have already pursued the matter with the Health Authority – either by writing to the general manager yourself, or with the assistance of your Community Health Council. If this did not produce a satisfactory result, you may approach the Commissioner, including copies of the earlier correspondence with your letter of complaint. Sending these copies has a number of advantages: it shows the reasonableness of your position; it helps to provide background information on the facts of the case, and makes your letter of complaint easier to write; if there were long delays in replying to your letters, or abrupt and incomplete responses, this may help to establish your complaint of maladministration.

In addition, be sure to provide all other relevant information on names, places and dates relating to the incident which is the subject of the complaint. Give precise details of where you can be contacted. All these things will hasten the consideration of your case. Complaints should be made within one year of the incident in question. The Commissioner will not investigate complaints which go back further than this, unless he considers that it is reasonable to do so. If your correspondence with the Health Authority has dragged on for so long that more than a year has passed, do not be deterred from applying, as it is still possible that the Commissioner will investigate. Nevertheless, register your complaint promptly, to be on the safe side.

The Commissioner must first decide whether his office has the jurisdiction to handle your complaint: you will be informed of his decision. Many complaints have to be rejected each year. If in doubt, go ahead and hope for the best.

If your complaint is accepted, the Health Authority will generally be given the opportunity of a written response, and a member of the Commissioner's staff will then begin to investigate. This will usually involve a discussion with you and separate interviews with the Health Authority staff concerned. Later on, when the Commissioner has prepared a draft report, the Health Authority may be allowed to read this and comment on the factual accuracy of its staff's evidence before the finished product is sent to you, to the Authority concerned and to the next senior Authority.

The report will not receive any wider circulation, but the press may be interested if you feel strongly that your complaint deserves a wider airing. There is nothing to stop you disclosing the report to whomsoever you please. Bear in mind, however, that although the publication of reports by the Commissioner is covered by absolute privilege for defamation liability, their publication by a complainant would not be.

The Commissioner's report will not provide you with any remedy as such. A report usually contains certain recommendations, and although many of these will concern procedural changes within the Health Authority or hospital, some may make suggestions concerning your own case: for example, the report may recommend that you should be reimbursed for any expenses caused by the Authority's maladministration. However, these recommendations carry no legal force, so if the Health Authority refuses to pay you, there are no legal mechanisms to ensure it does. It will follow such recommendations, as a general rule, but if it does not, you may wish to resort to publicity for your case, or perhaps consult your Member of Parliament.

Other help for patients

The Patients Association is an independent organisation offering advice to patients and representing their interests. It is financed by donations, by a government grant, and by members' subscriptions. The Association produces information leaflets and a directory of self-help health organisations and will answer queries, by letter or telephone, on health service or private problems.

THE NHS AND PRIVATE PRACTICE

When the National Health Service was created in 1948, most private medical practice which had existed to that date was incorporated into the new state system. Most general practitioners agreed to contract for the provision of general medical services, and entered into a contract for services with the NHS. Any general practitioner has the right to treat private patients who are not on his or her list, but many general practitioners choose not to do so.

Hospital doctors (and dentists) who work within NHS hospitals as consultants can treat private patients, who may use the hospital's accommodation and facilities. Those patients are eligible for NHS treatment but prefer to make arrangements for private treatment while using, at full cost to themselves or their insurers, the facilities of the NHS.

The consultant provides at the same time services for the NHS under a contract for private patients. The Secretary of State has wide powers to prescribe charges for the use of NHS facilities by private patients. The fact that you are a private patient will mean that you have a contractual relationship with the consultant and, should it prove necessary, you will be able to sue on the basis of that contract.

Legal remedies

If you wish to pursue a claim about health services, the initial question which may determine your course of action will be whether or not you have paid for them. If so, your claim may be dealt with as a contract claim, whereas if you have received free treatment you may have to rely on making a claim on the grounds of negligence. Most NHS treatment is free (that is, not paid for individually), so there will be little scope for a breach of contract claim. However, in relation to the provision of treatments for which you pay there is a contractual arrangement between yourself and the supplier of the particular service. Although in such situations there may be scope for the application of negligence principles it is likely, as a broad rule, that you would sue on the basis of your contract.

Rights under the law of contract

A contract does not have to be a written document – a spoken agreement to provide health care for payment constitutes a contract which may contain implied as well as express terms. In general, you would sue the provider of health services upon the express terms of your contract – that is to say, the oral or written promises which were made to you. Even if at the time at which the contract was concluded there was very little discussion of what you were entitled to expect from the supplier, there will nevertheless be terms which are implied by statute. Section 13 of the Supply of Goods and Services Act 1982 states that 'in a contract for the supply of a service where the supplier is acting in the course of a business there is an implied term that the supplier will carry out the service with reasonable skill and care'. Whether that supplier has actually exercised reasonable skill and care is largely a question of fact which the courts may ultimately have to decide. This is, however, not a very strict standard, and it is diluted by other legal principles.

The law takes a common-sense approach. If you go to a jeweller to have your ears pierced, you cannot expect the same quality of service as if you had gone to a surgeon. The test in law is whether the person in question has held himself out as having some particular skill or competence. If so, the test of whether the service has been adequate is based on the standard of the ordinary skilled person exercising and professing to have that particular skill. Therefore, in the example, the requisite level of skill will be that of an ordinary competent jeweller professing to be able to pierce ears. The level would not be pitched at the highest possible level of expertise on the part of a jeweller, nor at the very lowest. In other words, 'reasonable skill and care' is just an objective bench-mark used by the law.

A practitioner would clearly fall short of the requisite level of skill if, for example, he did not follow the accepted practice within the specialism, or if he had failed to keep up to date with developments in a particular specialism. One problem is that there are often shades of medical opinion, and the fact that a practitioner belongs to one school of thought rather than another does not in itself amount to a breach of the requisite standard of skill and care.

If you are warned of certain possible side-effects of treatment, your consent to such risks may go some way towards restricting your contractual remedies. This does not mean to say, however, that the provider will be able to restrict liability in relation to medical accidents or other injuries which you may suffer in the course of treatment. Your own contract may have included warranties to a stricter standard than those implied under the 1982 Act and if they are broken you may be able to sue on them.

When you have to buy goods in the course of your medical treatment – these may range from dentures to pharmaceutical products – you have the benefits of rights under the Sale of Goods Act 1979 and the Consumer Protection Act 1987.

Rights under the law of tort

Tort law is the law of civil wrongs, and in general your remedies for medical accidents will lie in the tort of negligence, irrespective of whether you made any payment for your treatment.

In order to show negligence, you have to meet certain basic requirements, namely, that you are owed a duty of care; that that duty was breached; and that the breach of that duty caused you damage or loss.

There will generally be very little problem about the first of these. In relation to the NHS, once you are accepted by a doctor for treatment, or are admitted into hospital, or gain access to the accident and emergency unit of a hospital, a duty of care is owed to you.

That duty will be breached if the medical practitioners who are offering you treatment do not meet the requisite standard of care. In essence, this is the standard previously outlined in relation to implied contractual duties. It is the standard of the reasonable medical practitioner of a particular calling. There may be situations in which greater or less care will be expected of the practitioner. For example, if knowledge of a particular medical condition on the part of the patient would cause the ordinary competent doctor to take particular precautions, then these precautions must be followed. Or if it is necessary to take a risk during treatment in an emergency in order to attempt to save the patient's life, a surgeon's action may be justified where ordinarily it might not be considered good practice. So the degree of precaution taken by a medical practitioner will vary in accordance with the risks being faced by the patient, and the importance of the doctor's action in saving the patient's life or health.

Remember that you have a say in the medical treatment given to you. The doctor is required to obtain your consent to all treatment. Where the doctor fails to obtain consent, the courts would consider the question of negligence. They would ask whether an ordinary competent medical practitioner would have obtained the patient's consent to the particular form of treatment, or would have disclosed inherent risks in a particular form of treatment, or would have disclosed the inherent risks in a particular course of treatment. For example, the courts may allow that once the patient is under anaesthetic the doctor may outstrip the bounds of the patient's formal consent if it becomes necessary to undertake more extensive surgical intervention in order to preserve the patient's life. In general, the courts would assume that the patient's consent would be implied, and that good medical practice would require a surgeon to act in this way. Similarly, the law allows that the doctor need not disclose every risk inherent in treatment. It adopts the rather paternalistic approach that the doctor may choose not to mention minor risks, or risks the knowledge of which, he considers, would be detrimental to the health of that patient (for example, because the patient was especially nervous of the proposed treatment). Full and informed consent on the part of the patient is not at present required by English law.

In cases of alleged negligence, the duty principle extends to all aspects of breach of the duty in medical treatment, including misdiagnosis, clinical and non-clinical injuries, failure of communication between medical practitioners, delay in treatment, and so forth. Note, however, that you will receive compensation only for negligently inflicted harm. When you are admitted into hospital, or when surgery is performed on you, you cannot claim to have been harmed just because you have not been cured. Indeed, even using their best endeavours, the medical practitioners might render your condition worse, without acting in a negligent manner.

If you succeed in establishing a breach of duty – and this is rarely an easy task – the medical authorities will be liable for resultant damage. However, the amount of this damage may be reduced if you are yourself in part to blame by your own contributory negligence. Thus, notwithstanding that the medical practitioners were negligent, if you failed to follow medical advice and rendered your condition worse, the amount of your damages would be reduced. Medical practitioners are liable only for harm which they have caused. Thus, even if doctors are negligent, for example by failing to treat a patient immediately upon arrival at the accident and emergency unit, if it can be shown that it was too late to save the life of that patient, the hospital authorities or the doctors concerned cannot be said to have caused the death of the patient.

It may be that a number of people have been negligent in relation to your treatment. The issues may become complicated, because the hospital doctors may be working as independent contractors, while the nurses are the employees of the Health Authority. Technically, this means that you ought to sue both the doctor and the Health Authority. In practice, the actions tend to be defended by the Health Authorities on behalf of all parties, and then, if damages are paid out, the Health Authority seeks a contribution from the relevant medical societies. This is not something with which you would need to deal, however, as in practice any action which has got to this stage should be dealt with by a solicitor.

Seek legal advice

You will not wish to sue on every occasion when things go wrong. You may be satisfied simply to register a complaint, and you may be happy with the outcome of the complaints procedure. On the other hand, you may wish to sue as well as complain; or the complaints procedure may fail to satisfy you. It may even be that your injuries are so extensive that you badly need the compensation which only legal action will bring. It is not easy to sue medical professionals, if only because the issues involved in deciding whether a doctor was negligent are inevitably technical and often far from clear-cut. Actions against medical professionals have a far lower success rate than other personal injury claims. You will therefore need expert legal advice if you are going to bring a case to court, or to threaten court action in order to recover a sum of money by way of settlement.

If you would like to have some initial advice before consulting a solicitor, you should consult Action for Victims of Medical Accidents (AVMA). This is a pressure group devoted to reforming the law in order to help victims of medical accidents to obtain compensation. It offers support and advice to such people, and thus constitutes a major source of assistance to a would-be plaintiff. AVMA will advise you whether you have a case worth pursuing and will recommend a solicitor who is competent in medical negligence cases.

You could also ask advice of your Community Health Council, or Citizens Advice Bureau.

Actions against medical professionals are on the increase. They present a grave worry to many health professionals, to the point where it is claimed that in some disciplines, such as obstetrics, the fear of legal action inhibits recruitment. The BMA is actively pressing for a quick and easy system of no-proof-of-fault compensation for victims of medical accidents.

Not every person who suffers a medical accident goes on to sue the health professionals involved. Many people choose not to sue, and the complexity, delay and cost of the present system act as an obvious discouragement (though there may be other reasons as well). If you do intend to sue, you should therefore seek advice, in particular from solicitors with some experience in handling medical negligence problems: the average High Street solicitor will have little experience of that sort of work.

USEFUL ADDRESSES

ACTION FOR VICTIMS OF MEDICAL ACCIDENTS (AVMA)
Bank Chambers
1 London Road
Forest Hill
London SE23 3TP
01-291 2793

ASSOCIATION OF BRITISH DISPENSING OPTICIANS (ABDO)
6 Hurlingham Business Park
Sulivan Road
London SW6 3DU
01-736 0088

Membership: voluntary for dispensing opticians; optometrists may be associate members: examination qualifications and training required
Style of qualification: FBDO (Fellow)
Membership list: not available to the public
Fee guidelines: no
Code of conduct: no; registered members are expected to follow the General Optical Council rules
Complaints procedure: yes, for complaints of misconduct.
Complaint-handling charge: no
Disciplinary sanctions: in cases of misconduct only, reprimand, fine, compensation, suspension, expulsion

ASSOCIATION OF COMMUNITY HEALTH COUNCILS FOR ENGLAND AND WALES (ACHCEW)
30 Drayton Park
London N5 1PD
01-609 8405

Membership: Community Health Councils
Code of conduct: yes: Guide to Good Practices
Complaints procedure: yes; only for complaints to do with the
   NHS
Complaint-handling charge: no
Disciplinary sanctions: no

ASSOCIATION OF OPTOMETRISTS (AOP)
Bridge House
233-234 Blackfriars Road
London SE1 8NW
01-261 9661

Membership: voluntary; examination qualifications and training
   required
Membership list: not available to the public
Fee guidelines: no (NHS fees are fixed)
Code of conduct: no; members are expected to follow that of the
   British College of Optometrists and the rules of the General
   Optical Council
Complaints procedure: yes
Complaint-handling charge: expulsion

BRITISH ASSOCIATION OF OCCUPATIONAL THERAPISTS/COLLEGE OF OCCUPATIONAL THERAPISTS (BAOT/COT)
628 Marshalsea Road
London SE1 1HL
01-357 6480

Membership: voluntary; occupational therapists require exam-
   ination qualifications; OT helpers and technical instructors
   may be associates
Membership list: not available
Fee guidelines: no; most members are employed by the NHS
Code of conduct: yes

Complaints procedure: yes
Complaint-handling charge: no
Disciplinary sanctions: termination of membership

BRITISH CHIROPODY ASSOCIATION

The New Hall
149 Bath Road
Maidenhead
Berkshire SL6 4LA
0628-32449

Membership: voluntary; examination qualifications and training
    required
Style of qualification: MBChA (Member); MSSCh (qualification
    in surgical chiropody); FSSCh (Fellow of the School of
    Surgical Chiropody)
Membership list: not available
Fee guidelines: yes
Code of conduct: yes
Complaints procedure: yes
Complaint-handling charge: no
Disciplinary sanctions: removal from register

BRITISH COLLEGE OF OPTOMETRISTS (BCO)

10 Knaresborough Place
London SW5 0TG
01-373 7765

Membership: voluntary; open to optometrists on qualification
Style of qualification: MBCO (Member); FBCO (Fellow)
Code of conduct: yes
Complaints procedure: yes
Complaint-handling charge: no
Disciplinary sanctions: suspension from or termination of
    membership

358

BRITISH DENTAL ASSOCIATION (BDA)
64 Wimpole Street
London W1M 8AL
01-935 0875

Membership: voluntary; open to registered dentists
Membership list: not available
Fee guidelines: no (NHS fees are fixed)
Code of conduct: guide to professional ethics; adherence to rules
   of General Dental Council
Disciplinary sanctions: termination of membership

BRITISH DENTAL HYGIENISTS ASSOCIATION (BDHA)
The Ridge
Yatton
Avon BS19 4DQ
0934-833932

Membership: examination qualifications required
Style of qualification: EDH (Enrolled Dental Hygienist)
Membership list: not available
Fee guidelines: no
Code of conduct: yes
Complaints procedure: no; complaints should be referred to the
   General Dental Council
Complaint-handling charge: no
Disciplinary sanctions: no

BRITISH MEDICAL ASSOCIATION (BMA)
BMA House
Tavistock Square
London WC1H 9JP
01-387 4499

Membership: medical practitioners only
Membership list: not available
Complaints procedure: no

BRITISH ORTHOPTIC SOCIETY (BOS)

Tavistock House North
Tavistock Square
London WC1H 9HX
01-387 7992

Membership: voluntary; orthoptists only; examination qualifications required
Style of qualification: DBO (Diploma); DBO(D) (Demonstrator's qualification); DBO(T) (Teacher's qualification); FBO (Fellow)
Membership list: not available
Fee guidelines: yes, for private practice
Code of conduct: yes
Complaints procedure: yes; complaints may also be directed to the Council for Professions Supplementary to Medicine
Complaint-handling charge: no
Disciplinary sanctions: admonishment, termination of membership

CHARTERED SOCIETY OF PHYSIOTHERAPY (CSP)

14 Bedford Row
London WC1R 4ED
01-242 1941

Membership: qualified physiotherapists; examination qualifications
Style of qualification: MCSP (Member)
Membership list: not available
Fee guidelines: no
Code of conduct: yes
Complaints procedure: yes
Complaint-handling charge: no
Disciplinary sanctions: admonishment; probation; making registration conditional; terminating registration

CHIROPODISTS BOARD
Council for Professions Supplementary to Medicine
Park House
184 Kennington Park Road
London SE11 4BU
01-582 0866

Register: published; updated annually
Code of conduct: yes
Complaints procedure: yes, about professional conduct only
Complaint-handling charge: no
Disciplinary sanctions: removal from register

ENGLISH CHIROPODISTS ASSOCIATION
42 Velsheda Road
Shirley
Solihull
West Midlands B90 2JN
021-745 1552

Membership: chiropodists holding recognised diploma
Style of qualification: MEChA (Member); AEChA (Associate member); FEChA (Fellow)
Membership list: not available
Fee guidelines: no
Code of conduct: yes (code of ethics)
Complaints procedure: yes
Complaint-handling charge: no
Disciplinary sanctions: yes

ENGLISH NATIONAL BOARD FOR NURSING, MIDWIFERY AND HEALTH VISITING
170 Tottenham Court Road
London W1P 0HA
01-388 3131

GENERAL DENTAL COUNCIL (GDC)
37 Wimpole Street
London W1M 8DQ
01-486 2171

Code of conduct: yes
Complaints procedure: yes
Complaint-handling charge: no
Disciplinary sanctions: suspension or termination of registration

GENERAL DENTAL PRACTITIONERS ASSOCIATION (GDPA)
152 Maldon Road
Colchester
Essex C03 3AY
0255-861829

Membership: voluntary; restricted to qualified dentists
Membership list: not available
Code of conduct: no; adherence to the rules of the General
   Dental Council
Complaints procedure: yes
Complaint-handling charge: no
Disciplinary sanctions: expulsion

GENERAL MEDICAL COUNCIL (GMC)
44 Hallam Street
London W1N 6AE
01-580 7642

Code of conduct: no; statutory rules
Complaints procedure: yes
Complaint-handling charge: no
Disciplinary sanctions: warning; imposition of conditions on
   registration; suspension; termination of registration

GENERAL OPTICAL COUNCIL (GOC)
41 Harley Street
London W1N 2DJ
01-580 3898

Code of conduct: no; statutory rules
Complaints procedure: yes; complaints against opticians (not consumer complaints)
Complaint-handling charge: no
Disciplinary sanctions: fine; suspension or termination of registration

HEALTH SERVICE COMMISSIONER (OMBUDSMAN)

England:
Church House
Great Smith Street
London SW1P 3BW
01-276 2035/3000

Scotland:
Second floor
11 Melville Crescent
Edinburgh EH3 7LU
031-225 7465

Wales:
4th floor
Pearl Assurance House
Greyfriars Road
Cardiff CF1 3AG
0222-394621

Code of conduct: yes
Complaints procedure: yes
Complaint-handling charge: no
Powers: ombudsman may recommend compensation

INSTITUTE OF CHIROPODISTS
91 Lord Street
Southport
Merseyside PR8 1SA
0704-46141

Membership: voluntary; restricted to qualified chiropodists
Style of qualification: LCh (Licentiate in Chiropody); FInstCh
    (Fellow); HChD (Diploma in Higher Chiropody Therapy)
Membership list: not available
Fee guidelines: no
Code of conduct: yes
Complaints procedure: yes
Complaint-handling charge: no
Disciplinary sanctions: removal from register

NATIONAL BOARD FOR NURSING, MIDWIFERY AND HEALTH VISITING FOR NORTHERN IRELAND
RAC House
79 Chichester Street
Belfast BT1 4JE
0232-238152

NATIONAL BOARD FOR NURSING, MIDWIFERY AND HEALTH VISITING FOR SCOTLAND
22 Queen Street
Edinburgh EH2 1JX
031-226 7371

NATIONAL PHARMACEUTICAL ASSOCIATION (NPA)
40-42 St Peter's Street
St Albans
Hertfordshire AL1 3NP
0272-32161

Membership: voluntary; retail pharmacy proprietors only
Membership list: not available

OCCUPATIONAL THERAPISTS BOARD
Council for Professions Supplementary to Medicine
Park House
184 Kennington Park Road
London SE11 4BU
01-582 0866

Register: published; updated annually
Code of conduct: yes
Complaints procedure: yes, about professional conduct only
Complaint-handling charge: no
Disciplinary sanctions: removal from register

ORGANISATION OF CHARTERED PHYSIOTHERAPISTS IN PRIVATE PRACTICE (OCPPP)
855A London Road
Westcliff-on-Sea
Essex S50 9SZ
0702-77462

Membership: voluntary; restricted to chartered or other approved
    physiotherapists
Membership list: may be consulted in libraries or doctors'
    surgeries
Fee guidelines: yes
Code of conduct: that of the Chartered Society of Physiotherapists
Complaints procedure: complaints should be made to the CSP or
    the Hon. Secretary of the OCPPP

ORTHOPTISTS BOARD
Council for the Professions Supplementary to Medicine
Park House
184 Kennington Park Road
London SE11 4BU
01-582 0866

Register: published; updated annually
Code of conduct: yes
Complaints procedure: yes about professional conduct only
Complaint-handling charge: no
Disciplinary sanctions: removal from register

PATIENTS ASSOCIATION
18 Victoria Park Square
Bethnal Green
London E2 9PF
01-981 5676/5695

Complaints procedure: yes
Complaint-handling charge: no

PHYSIOTHERAPISTS BOARD
Council for Professions Supplementary to Medicine
Park House
184 Kennington Park Road
London SE11 4BU
01-582 0866

Register: updated annually
Code of conduct: yes
Complaint-handling charge: no
Disciplinary sanctions: removal from register

ROYAL COLLEGE OF NURSING OF THE UNITED KINGDOM
20 Cavendish Square
London WlM 0AB
01-409 3333

ROYAL PHARMACEUTICAL SOCIETY OF GREAT BRITAIN
1 Lambeth High Street
London SE1 7JN
01-735 9141

Membership: compulsory; examination qualifications and experience required
Style of qualification: MR PharmS (Member); FR PharmS (Fellow)
Membership list: may be consulted free of charge at the Society's office
Fee guidelines: no
Code of conduct: code of ethics
Complaints procedure: yes
Complaint-handling charge: no
Disciplinary sanctions: removal from register

SCOTTISH HOME AND HEALTH DEPARTMENT
St Andrews House
Edinburgh EH1 3DE
031-556 8400

SOCIETY OF CHIROPODISTS
53 Welbeck Street
London W1M 7HE
01-486 3381

Membership: voluntary; examination qualifications or state registration required
Style of qualification: MChS (Member); FChS (Fellow)
Membership list: available from the Society's office

Fee guidelines: no
Code of conduct: yes
Complaints procedure: yes
Complaint-handling charge: no
Disciplinary sanctions: removal from register

UK CENTRAL COUNCIL FOR NURSING, MIDWIFERY AND HEALTH VISITING (UKCC)
23 Portland Place
London W1N 3AF
01-637 7181

WELSH NATIONAL BOARD FOR NURSING, MIDWIFERY AND HEALTH VISITING
Floor 13
Pearl Assurance House
Greyfriars Road
Cardiff CF1 3AG
0222-395535

London telephone numbers

On 6 May 1990 the 01 telephone code for London will change to either 071 or 081, depending on the local code that follows it. From that date, people telephoning the 01 code will hear a recorded message telling them to re-dial using either 071 or 081.

Alternative and Complementary Medical Services

In recent years, one of the most rapidly growing forms of health care has been alternative/complementary medicine. These terms embrace a wide range of theories and practices existing alongside the mainstream health care offered by the NHS and private medicine schemes. 'Alternative' is the name given to remedies and treatments for disease that are not included in conventional medical practice, or that have not undergone the rigorous controlled tests, both laboratory and clinical, which are required for conventional drugs and treatments. Therapies are referred to as 'complementary' when they are intended to reinforce, not replace, conventional therapy. The burgeoning of alternative medicine has provided the consumer with a wider choice than was previously available and has also emphasised the benefits of preventive health care. However, such unparalleled growth has created a number of problems for the unwary consumer.

Alternative medicine has tended to be represented in many quarters as a field crowded with cranks and charlatans, failing to live up to outlandish claims. It has also encountered suspicion verging on hostility from some members of the medical establishment, by which 'fringe' medicine has been widely regarded as likely to do harm. However, many of the alternative therapies have a long pedigree, and in recent years they have gained greater acceptance from conventional medical practitioners – to the extent that some types of complementary medicine, such as acupuncture and homoeopathy, are now available under the NHS.

Some organisations practising alternative medicine, such as the British Osteopathic Association (BOA), insist on their members being trained in conventional medicine. Others, such as the General Council and Register of Osteopaths and the British Chiropractic Association (BCA), strive to be regarded as complementary to the mainstream of medical practice. Conversely, bodies such as the Incorporated Society of Registered Naturopaths perceive their aims and methods as being truly alternative to and radically different from those of mainstream medicine.

There are no state registers for alternative/complementary practitioners, so the public has no readily available source of verifying the credentials of such health practitioners.

There is, moreover, no statutory regulation of the non-orthodox medical professions. They are governed solely by the common law. This has led to the present unacceptable situation whereby anyone can set up as a practitioner in any branch of alternative medicine, regardless of whether or not he has received any training. It appears that there is little any of the reputable associations and bodies can do to prevent the public from being misled.

However, for each therapy there is at least one professional body which regulates the qualifications and conduct of its members; thus, provided they are aware of its existence, members of the public may contact it for lists of its members. However, even where reputable practitioners are concerned, consumers are faced with a bewildering array of initials and subtle distinctions in title.

Fees

Alternative practitioners generally operate outside the NHS, and must be paid by the patient. However, some forms of complementary medicine are increasingly coming to be covered by private health insurance schemes. Homoeopathy, and to a lesser extent acupuncture, are the only alternative therapies generally available on the NHS. A small number of GPs and health centres employ complementary practitioners, which enables patients to receive free treatment from the practitioner, who is paid by the doctor in the practice.

The scale of fees charged for alternative treatment is generally not controlled by the professional bodies. Where guidance on fees is provided, there is generally no mechanism for ensuring that this is complied with.

Testing the theories?

One problem is that some alternative practitioners claim that scientifically accepted research methods (such as animal experiments) are often ill-adapted for testing non-orthodox theories and therapies, particularly as most branches of alternative medicine adopt a holistic approach, which claims to treat not just the disease, but the whole of the individual patient and every aspect of his well-being. This notion of treatments tailored to the needs of the individual patient makes controlled tests very difficult.

Other practitioners of complementary techniques, particularly those who are medically qualified, feel that vigorous scientific testing is the only way to discover which techniques have real value and to assure their general acceptance by the medical and scientific establishment.

Alternative medicine is, however, gradually gaining converts, many from amongst those dissatisfied with the inefficacy and harmful side-effects of some modern drugs. At the very least, it is coming to be considered as a valuable adjunct to modern scientific medicine.

HOMOEOPATHY

Homoeopathy is based on the principle that 'like should be treated by like', so that agents which cause certain symptoms in a healthy person will cure those symptoms in an unhealthy person. The substances which cause the symptoms are diluted, which is said to release their healing properties (this is called 'potentisation'), and shaken ('succussation') before being administered to the patient.

Treatment is tailored to suit the individual patient, rather than merely to fit a given set of symptoms. Initially the smallest effective dose is administered, to see how the patient responds. It is claimed that homoeopathic remedies do not give rise to side-effects, though some patients may experience a reaction, or 'healing crisis'.

Homoeopathy is usually carried out in private practices but is available under the NHS in the out-patient departments of some hospitals; there are even two homoeopathic hospitals. Homoeopathic remedies may be dispensed by chemists, so they can be viewed simply as an alternative to pharmaceutical remedies within the conventional health care system. There are also many non-medically qualified homoeopaths, whose treatments are not available on the NHS.

Doctors who offer homoeopathic treatment must be fully qualified medical practitioners who have taken a postgraduate course at the Faculty of Homoeopathy. A list of these may be obtained from the British Homoeopathic Association (BHA) by sending a stamped addressed envelope. It indicates which doctors treat patients under the NHS or one of the medical insurance schemes, such as BUPA. You must send for this information, as medical ethics do not allow it to be given out on the telephone.

The British Homoeopathic Association is not a professional association but a charity, founded with the aim of promoting the cause of homoeopathy. Membership is open to all sympathisers, whether these are medical or paramedical practitioners or ordinary members of the public.

The Society of Homoeopaths keeps a register of therapists who are not medically qualified, but have either graduated from a recognised college or have passed examinations set by the Society itself and can show a required number of case records.

However, some practitioners who are not registered with the Society, nevertheless call themselves registered homoeopaths; it is therefore advisable to check their credentials with the Society of Homoeopaths.

NATUROPATHY

Of all alternative medical treatments, naturopathy is perhaps the furthest removed from the orthodox concept of medicine. Not only is it holistic in its approach, it is essentially a philosophy or way of life, rather than simply a medical treatment. Indeed, in many respects the naturopath is a teacher rather than a doctor. His basic concern is to discover and eliminate the root cause of the disease and to educate the patient into a better way of life.

This means that naturopathy may not provide immediate physical relief from pain, because the naturopath believes that certain manifestations of disease, such as coughs, colds, fevers, diarrhoea, have eliminative and stress-reducing functions, which should not be prevented or masked by the use of drugs. Hence naturopathy does not aim to be a substitute for medication, and it is not primarily for ill people.

Naturopathic treatment demands from you, as patient, a commitment to changing your life style. To that end, on your first consultation the naturopath will take a detailed medical and personal history, concentrating on certain aspects of your physical and mental well-being. The starting-point is generally diet. The naturopath also considers external physical functions, such as posture and exercise. He may use osteopathic techniques: many naturopaths are also trained osteopaths. Naturopaths also use modern diagnostic techniques, such as x-rays and blood and urine tests.

Even though most naturopathic treatment is educational rather than medicinal, and therefore ought to be, at least, physically harmless, it is still advisable to consult only registered naturopaths.

The training and registration of naturopaths is chiefly in the hands of the General Council and Register of Naturopaths, which offers a four-year full-time course at the British College of Naturopathy and Osteopathy, and of the Natural Therapeutic and Osteopathic Society and Register (NTOS), which requires its members either to have completed the course at the London School of Osteopathy or another approved school, or to have sat the Society's external examination. The Incorporated Society of Registered Naturopaths has members who have been trained and examined in basic and clinical sciences and are entered on the British Register of Naturopaths.

Members of the Osteopathic and Naturopathic Guild must have completed a practical and theoretical training course, partly by correspondence. They are entitled to designate themselves 'incorporated osteopath' and/or 'consulting naturopath'.

These naturopathic practitioners tend to emphasise the part that diet and mental attitude play in our health, and may recommend changes to alleviate stress. They adopt a holistic approach. They believe that it is not just the symptoms that need to be treated – the underlying causes of these must be traced, and the body's framework is only one element.

MEDICAL HERBALISM

This is a therapy based largely on substances extracted directly from plants: any part of the plant may be used medicinally.

Many conventional drugs are also composed of plant extracts, but the difference is that they consist of isolated ingredients extracted from plants to treat specific symptoms. Herbalists believe this to be dangerous: it may produce side-effects, because the isolated ingredient is no longer balanced by other substances occurring naturally in the plant. In herbal remedies all of the plant may be used, so that the remedy is naturally balanced.

Medical herbalism is very much concerned with the notion of balance; its aim is to restore the body's balance to normal, rather than merely to cure disease. It is particularly successful in treating stress-related diseases, and is at its most effective only if the patient is prepared to co-operate and alter his way of life.

About 200 medical herbalists are registered with the National Institute of Medical Herbalists (NIMH). They will have completed a four-year course (full-or part-time) with theoretical and practical examinations. Members of the General Council and Register of Herbalists qualify by completing a course which is partly by correspondence; there follows an invigilated examination at the Register's headquarters and clinical training with a qualified practitioner. The course can be completed in three to four years, but there is no time limit: candidates may complete it in their own time.

Homoeopathic and herbal remedies

Both homoeopathic and herbal remedies can be bought over the counter in a chemist's or health food shop. However, one of the distinctive features of both homoeopathy and medical herbalism is that the remedies are specially prescribed for the individual patient, and so the professional bodies in both fields recommend consulting a practitioner rather than buying ready-prepared medicines.

Both homoeopathic and herbal remedies are deemed to be 'medicinal products' for the purposes of the Medicines Act 1968, under which it is a criminal offence to supply any drug which is not of the nature or quality the ordinary consumer would expect. Since the Act came into force in 1971, all new medicines have needed a licence to prove their safety, efficiency and quality. Medicines already on the market at that date are gradually being reviewed by a committee of the Department of Health, which is also currently reviewing the safety of herbal medicines; homoeopathic remedies may be tested from 1990.

While self-treatment by ready-prepared herbal nostrums may be effective at curing simple conditions, if symptoms are more serious the patient should consult a registered homoeopath or medical herbalist – or, indeed, a conventional doctor.

CHIROPRACTIC

This manipulative therapy is based on the theory that the correct function of muscles, nerves and joints, especially those of the spine, is essential to good health.

Chiropractors mainly treat mechanical muscle and joint disorders, although many chiropractic patients are seen for conditions such as back pain, neck pain and headaches. Chiropractors also treat sports injuries such as tennis elbow, frozen shoulder, shin splints and so on, and other peripheral muscle and joint disorders.

Treatment is mainly by precise specific joint adjustments to restore flexibility to the region involved, as well as an integrated rehabilitation and exercise programme aimed at maintaining joint mobility and muscle function.

Chiropractors rely not only on the use of their hands for diagnosis; they also use conventional diagnostic techniques, such as x-rays and blood tests.

During your first visit to a chiropractor you can expect him to take a very detailed medical case history, to observe closely how you move, and then to examine you physically; this will probably include an x-ray to check the exact condition of your spine. The length of treatment varies from patient to patient, according to the severity of the problem.

The profession's governing body is the British Chiropractic Association (BCA). It currently has around 280 members, who must adhere to the BCA's code of ethics, and must have graduated from an accredited college, having completed a four-year clinical and pre-clinical training course, leading to a BSc degree in chiropractic; the Diploma of Chiropractic (DC) is granted on completion of a one-year graduate education programme.

McTimoney Chiropractic

This is a branch of the chiropractic profession with its own methodology and philosophical approach. Its main aim is the provision of a safe, effective and comfortable form of whole-body manipulation, particularly suited to the treatment of the young, and of old or frail people. McTimoney chiropractors are the only ones to undertake the chiropractic treatment of animals as well as of people.

The McTimoney Chiropractic School's training course is a four-year one, partly based on home study and partly on practical tuition. The School is supported by the Institute of Pure Chiropractic, which has a register of practitioners, and issues a directory of registered licensed McTimoney chiropractors.

OSTEOPATHY

In Britain, osteopathy is the most popular complementary treatment. It is much more commonly available than chiropractic. It is a system of diagnosis and treatment which lays its main emphasis on the structural and mechanical problems of the body. Osteopaths are more concerned with the mechanics of the body as a whole than are chiropractors. The conduct of this profession is governed by a variety of organisations, some of which are more closely allied to conventional medicine than others. For instance, the membership of the British Osteopathic Association (BOA) consists solely of experienced registered medical practitioners with further specialist training. Members of BOA are eligible to register with the General Council and Register of Osteopaths, which accredits the course on which they have been trained in osteopathy.

The General Council and Register of Osteopaths (GCRO) is the main governing body of the osteopathic profession. It was set up on the advice of the Minister of Health in 1936, to safeguard the public. It lays down standards of osteopathic education and deals with complaints and enquiries from members of the public. It has some 1,200 members who are entitled to call themselves registered osteopaths and to use the letters MRO (Member of the Register of Osteopaths). Three of the schools approved by the GCRO, the British School of Osteopathy in London, the British College of Naturopathy and Osteopathy and the European School of Osteopathy in Maidstone, each offer a four-year full-time diploma course; successful students can use the letters DO (Diploma in Osteopathy) after their names. All these schools provide an osteopathic and clinical medical training which enables graduates to make an accurate diagnosis and to recognise conditions where osteopathic treatment may be inappropriate and the patient should be referred to his doctor.

The initials DO indicating a diploma in osteopathy are sometimes also used by osteopaths who have not had formal training of the sort described; so be sure to check your non-doctor osteopath's credentials.

Another governing body of the osteopathic profession is the College of Osteopaths Practitioners' Association, whose members will have completed a six-year course on open-university lines at the College of Osteopaths, or a four-year full-time course at the Maidstone College of Osteopathy. The Natural Therapeutic and Osteopathic Society and Register (NTOS), mentioned earlier in connection with naturopathy, has a five-year course in Osteopathy taught at the London School of Osteopathy.

The osteopath, on your first consultation, will take a comprehensively detailed medical case history, assess your posture and conduct a physical examination, which will include orthodox orthopaedic and neurological tests. In line with current medical thinking, osteopaths use x-rays only when they are concerned about the possibility of serious injury or underlying problems, such as severe arthritis.

As some of the mechanical problems being treated may have taken years to develop, treatment may have to extend over many weeks; however, recent injuries often respond very quickly to treatment.

Neither chiropractic nor osteopathy is available on the NHS, but some private health insurance policies cover treatment by a registered practitioner provided that the patient has been referred by a GP. Since 1977, the General Medical Council has allowed doctors to refer patients to non-medically qualified practitioners, provided the doctor is satisfied with the practitioner, and remains fully responsible for the patient. Apart from referral by a GP, you may contact a chiropractor or osteopath directly; you can ask one of the organisations mentioned here for a list of members in your locality. (If you choose a practitioner from the Yellow Pages, be careful to check his credentials.)

ACUPUNCTURE
This is one of the most accepted and popular forms of alternative medicine, the therapeutic method of which consists of the insertion of fine needles into specific points on the surface of the body, called 'acupuncture points', thus stimulating the body's healing processes.

There are several theories to explain how acupuncture works, but basically they relate to two different types of acupuncture: the 'traditional', and the scientific, or 'Western'.

Traditional acupuncture is an important element of traditional Chinese medicine, which is holistic in approach, incorporating the use of herbal medicine, exercise and change of diet, and stresses the preventive use of acupuncture. It is based on the hypothesis that health depends on the balance between the positive and negative forces (yin and yang) in the body. If these are balanced, then there is a free flow of energy (chi) through 12 pairs of channels (meridians) which are linked to the body's internal organs. If they are thrown off-balance, the energy flow is impeded and disease may occur. The acupuncture points are located along the pathways formed by the meridians. A trained acupuncturist can locate these points exactly. Diagnosis is made through the general appearance of the body, especially of the tongue, and also through feeling the pulses.

'Western' medical practitioners point out that there is no scientific foundation for the traditional theory of acupuncture. The scientific theory is that acupuncture stimulates the nervous system, and thus eases pain: this theory recognises some but not all of the 1,000 or so acupuncture points of Chinese medicine. Scientific acupuncture is carried out by qualified medical practitioners who have had some training in acupuncture: they use conventional diagnostic methods.

Having diagnosed the problem, by whichever method, the acupuncturist then selects acupuncture points along the appropriate meridians and inserts fine needles at these points. The needles may remain in place for anything from a few seconds to 30 minutes. They may be manipulated, or have a very low electric current passed through them. They are inserted only a few millimetres into the skin and the process is usually painless. Treatments are generally carried out once or twice a week, sometimes more often, if the disease is acute. Any improvement may be immediate, or occur only after four or five treatments.

Most diseases caused by altered physiology are treatable by acupuncture. It has been successfully used for headaches, nervous and digestive problems, menstrual problems and rheumatism; but it probably works only for diseases that are potentially reversible: for example, the bone erosion of advanced arthritis will not respond, although relief of symptoms such as pain and stiffness is possible.

As far as 'scientific' acupuncture is concerned, membership of the British Medical Acupuncture Society (BMAS) is available only to doctors, dentists and veterinary surgeons. Full membership of BMAS is open only to those practitioners whose training and experience satisfy the Society's requirements. Courses in acupuncture are organised by BMAS.

Members of the British Acupuncture Association and Register (BAAR) may be orthodox medical or dental practitioners and other people who have had medical training, not necessarily of the orthodox kind (they may, for instance, be osteopaths or chiropractors); they must have trained at the British College of Acupuncture or at an approved school recognised by the Council of BAAR.

In consulting a 'scientific' acupuncturist, you should be referred by your own doctor.

When dealing with 'traditional' therapists you should

consult only registered acupuncturists, who adhere to strict codes of practice: it is obviously of crucial importance that premises should be kept scrupulously clean and that the needles should be sterilised, to prevent infection.

A lay acupuncturist may have limited access to diagnostic facilities and medical records. He may find it difficult to communicate with your doctor, which would be important where acupuncture had to be integrated with other medical treatments.

There are several associations that govern non-medically qualified acupuncturists: the British Acupuncture Association and Register; the Traditional Acupuncture Society, the International Register of Oriental Medicine (UK) and the Register of Traditional Chinese Medicine. A register of members of the organisations may be obtained from the Council for Acupuncture, which provides a code of practice for the above organisations and ensures that the practitioners have reached a recognised standard of competence.

GETTING THE BEST OUT OF NON-ORTHODOX THERAPIES
There are many practical steps which the user of such therapies can take in order to avoid or minimise problems.

Unless you have been referred to the practitioner by a GP or other medical practitioner, make sure that you check his credentials very carefully. It is a good idea to be guided by personal recommendations, but even then you should check qualifications. You may also choose a practitioner from listings in Yellow Pages, or registers in your local reference library. However, it would be safer to write to one of the professional organisations for names of members in your area (enclose a stamped addressed envelope).

Do not be afraid to ask what particular initials or qualifications mean. If the practitioner calls himself 'doctor', check whether he is medically qualified. If he claims to be a 'registered' practitioner, check with whom he is registered. Be suspicious of claims that the practitioner has a degree in his particular therapy. Currently there are only two recognised degree courses in a complementary therapy. One is in chiropractic at the Anglo-European College of Chiropractic at Bournemouth, which had its first intake of degree students in 1988; the other is at the British School of Osteopathy in London.

Be wary of elaborate advertising. Reputable professional bodies permit only discreet advertisement, informing the public of the opening of a new practice, or the change of address of an existing one. Likewise, be suspicious of exaggerated claims: no reputable professional would claim, for instance, to cure arthritis, although it is permissible to claim to give relief from pain and discomfort.

How much will it cost?

Always check what the fees are when making an appointment to see a practitioner. If you have a choice of practitioners, it may be wise to telephone several to check the fees beforehand, as they may vary considerably. If they seem excessive, check with the professional association.

At your initial consultation, ask how long the treatment may be expected to take, and obtain an approximate estimate for the course of treatment. It may also be worth checking if the treatment you need is covered by any private health insurance scheme you may have (this is unlikely, however, unless you have been referred by your doctor).

Complaints

If, despite these precautions, things do go wrong, the steps you should take are:

○   complain directly to the practitioner concerned
○   if still dissatisfied, write a letter of complaint to the secretary of the appropriate organisation, setting out clearly the grounds of your complaint, in as much detail as possible
○   keep copies of all the letters you send; also keep all the correspondence your receive in connection with your complaint.

As a rule, the professional organisation will charge no fee for investigating the complaint, and will follow a standard procedure. The secretary will usually contact the member concerned, to ask for his explanation. The matter is quite often resolved at this stage, when the background to the practitioner's actions has been explained to the complainant.

Failing that, the organisation will investigate the complaint further. If the matter is sufficiently serious, there will usually be a hearing before a committee, at which both sides to the dispute will be heard, and the member complained of will have to account for his actions. Depending on the investigating committee's findings, the member may be 'acquitted' of charges against him or formally warned or suspended or ultimately expelled from the organisation and struck off the register.

USEFUL ADDRESSES

BRITISH ACUPUNCTURE ASSOCIATION AND REGISTER (BAAR)
The Office of the General Secretary
22 Hockley Road
Rayleigh
Essex SS6 8EB
0268-742534

Membership: voluntary; people with orthodox medical, dental, paramedical and other generally recognised qualifications and with examination qualifications in acupuncture
Style of qualification: MBAcA (Member); FBAcA (Fellow); LicAc (Licentiate in Acupuncture)
Membership list: available in libraries or at the British Acupuncture Association's office, 34 Alderney Street, London SW1V 4EU (01-834 1012)

Fee guidelines: yes
Code of conduct: yes
Complaints procedure: yes
Complaint-handling charge: no
Disciplinary sanctions: fine; expulsion

BRITISH CHIROPRACTIC ASSOCIATION (BCA)
Premier House
10 Greycoat Place
London SW1P 1SB
01-222 8866

Membership: voluntary; restricted to graduates of accredited
   college
Style of qualification: DC (Doctor of Chiropractic) where appro-
   priate
Membership list: free on request from BCA office
Fee guidelines: yes
Code of conduct: yes
Complaints procedure: yes
Complaint-handling charge: no
Disciplinary sanctions: fine; suspension; expulsion

BRITISH HOMOEOPATHIC ASSOCIATION (BHA)
27A Devonshire Street
London W1N 1RJ
01-935 2163

Membership: open to everyone interested in homoeopathy
Style of qualification: (used by qualified medical practitioners
   only) MFHom (Member of the Faculty of Homoeopathy);
   FFHom (Fellow)
Membership list: free on request from the BHA office – names of
   qualified medical practitioners only

BRITISH MEDICAL ACUPUNCTURE SOCIETY (BMAS)
Newton House
Newton Lane
Lower Whitley
Warrington
Cheshire WA4 4JA
092-573 727

Membership: voluntary; restricted to doctors, dentists, veterinary surgeons; full membership conditional on training and experience
Membership list: free on request from BMAS office
Fee guidelines: no
Code of conduct: yes
Complaints procedure: yes
Complaint-handling charge: no
Disciplinary sanctions: expulsion

BRITISH NATUROPATHIC AND OSTEOPATHIC ASSOCIATION (BNOA)
Frazer House
6 Netherhall Gardens
London NW3 5RR
01-435 8728

BRITISH OSTEOPATHIC ASSOCIATION (BOA)
8-10 Boston Place
London NW1 6QH
01-262 5250

Membership: voluntary; restricted to registered medical practitioners who become Members of the London College of Osteopathic Medicine by training course and examination qualification
Style of qualification: MLCOM (Member) or FLCOM (Fellow); MRO also used by those who take up their eligibility to join the Register of Osteopaths

Membership list: free on request from osteopathic clinic at above
        address
Fee guidelines: no
Code of conduct: the rules of the General Medical Council
Complaints procedure: yes
Complaint-handling charge: no
Disciplinary sanctions: expulsion

COLLEGE OF OSTEOPATHS PRACTITIONERS' ASSOCIATION (CO)
110 Thorkhill Road
Thames Ditton
Surrey KT7 0UW
01-398 3308

Membership: Examination qualifications from the College of
        Osteopaths Educational Trust, the Maidstone College of
        Osteopathy or other recognised institutions
Style of qualification: DO (Diploma in Osteopathy); ND (Diploma
        in Naturopathy)
Style of membership: MCD (Member); FCO (Fellow)
Membership list: available
Fee guidelines: no
Code of conduct: yes
Complaints procedure: yes
Complaints handling charge: no
Disciplinary sanctions: warnings; fines; suspension; expulsion

COUNCIL FOR ACUPUNCTURE
Suite One
19A Cavendish Square
London W1M 9AD
01-409 1440

Membership: practitioner-members of the the British Acupunc-
        ture Association and Register; International Register of

Oriental Medicine; Register of Traditional Chinese Medicine; Traditional Acupuncture Society

Code of conduct: code of practice and code of ethics

Complaints procedure: yes

Complaint-handling charge: no

Disciplinary sanctions: expulsion (administered by member bodies)

GENERAL COUNCIL AND REGISTER OF CONSULTANT HERBALISTS LTD

Marlborough House
Swanpool
Falmouth TR11 4HW
0326 317321

Membership: compulsory for practitioners calling themselves registered medical herbalists; examination qualification and training required for this

Style of qualification: DBTh (Diploma in Botano-Therapy); RMH (Registered Medical Herbalist); DHoM (Diploma in Homoeopathic Medicine); Registered Homoeopathic Practitioner

Mem' 'rship list: not available, but names of local practitioners will be supplied on request

Fee guidelines: yes, for new practitioners; based on area in which practice situated

Code of conduct: yes

Complaints procedure: yes

Complaint-handling charge: yes

Disciplinary sanctions: removal from register

GENERAL COUNCIL AND REGISTER OF NATUROPATHS (GCRN)

Frazer House
6 Netherhall Gardens
London NW3 5RR
01-435 8728

Membership: voluntary; requires completion of course at British College of Naturopathy and Osteopathy

Style of qualification: ND (Diploma in Naturopathy); MRN (Member of the Register of Naturopaths)

Membership list: available

Fee guidelines: no

Code of conduct: yes (code of ethics)

Complaints procedure: yes

Complaint-handling charge: no

Disciplinary sanctions: fine; removal from register

GENERAL COUNCIL AND REGISTER OF OSTEOPATHS (GCRO)

56 London Street
Reading
Berkshire
RG1 4SQ
0734-576585

Membership: open only to graduates of five specific inspected and accredited courses

Style of qualification: registered osteopath; MRO

Membership list: annual directory of members; telephone enquiries answered

Code of conduct: yes

Complaints procedure: yes (only about allegations of professional misconduct)

Complaint-handling charge: no

Disciplinary sanctions: censure; fine; expulsion

INCORPORATED SOCIETY OF REGISTERED NATUROPATHS

Kingston Clinic (via the Coach House)
292 Gilmerton Road
Liberton
Edinburgh EH16 5UQ
031-664 3435

Membership: compulsory for practitioners describing them-
selves as registered naturopaths
Style of qualification: registered naturopath
Membership list: name and address of registered practitioner
free on request
Fee guidelines: no
Code of conduct: yes
Complaints procedure: yes
Complaint-handling charge: no
Disciplinary sanctions: expulsion

INTERNATIONAL REGISTER OF ORIENTAL MEDICINE (UK) (IROM)

Green Hedges House
Green Hedges Avenue
East Grinstead
Sussex RH19 1DZ
0342-313106/7

Membership: voluntary; restricted to graduates of International
College of Oriental Medicine
Style of qualification: MIROM (Member); BAc (Bachelor of
Acupuncture)
Membership list: available from International Register office
Fee guidelines: no
Code of conduct: yes
Complaints procedure: yes
Complaints-handling charge: no
Disciplinary sanctions: fine; removal from register

McTIMONEY CHIROPRACTIC

Institute of Pure Chiropractic
PO Box 127
14b Park End Street
Oxford OX1 1HH
0865-246786

Membership: restricted to McTimoney chiropractors; examination qualifications required
Style of qualification: AIPC (Associate of the Institute of Pure Chiropractic); MIPC (Member); FIPC (Fellow)
Membership list: free on request from the Institute
Fee guidelines: yes
Code of conduct: yes
Complaints procedure: yes
Complaint-handling charge: no
Disciplinary sanctions: warning; temporary removal of accreditation; suspension from practising; expulsion

NATIONAL INSTITUTE OF MEDICAL HERBALISTS (NIMH)

38 Holcombe Lane
Bathampton
Bath
Avon BA2 6UL
0225-66835

Membership: voluntary; members must have passed examination of the School of Herbal Medicine
Style of qualification: MNIMH (Member); FNIMH (Fellow)
Membership list: free on request from Institute office
Code of conduct: yes
Complaints procedure: yes
Complaint-handling charge: no
Disciplinary sanctions: censure; expulsion

NATURAL THERAPEUTIC AND OSTEOPATHIC SOCIETY AND REGISTER (NTOS)

'Dynes'
66 High Street
Great Baddow
Chelmsford
Essex CM2 7HH
0245-76677

Membership: voluntary; examination qualifications required, of the London School of Osteopathy, or another recognised institution, or the Society's own
Style of qualification: MNTOS (Member); FNTOS (Fellow)
Membership list: free on charge from NTOS Council, 14 Marford Road, Wheathampstead, Hertfordshire AL4 8AS; may be consulted in libraries
Fee guidelines: yes
Code of conduct: yes
Complaints procedure: yes
Complaint-handling charge: no
Disciplinary sanctions: admonishment; suspension; expulsion

OSTEOPATHIC AND NATUROPATHIC GUILD
Marlborough House
Swanpool
Falmouth TR11 4HW
0326-317321

Membership: compulsory for 'Incorporated Osteopaths' and 'Consulting Naturopaths'.
Style of qualification: DO (Diploma in Osteopathy); ND (Diploma in Naturopathy); MGON (Member); FGON (Fellow)
Membership list: local list free on request (with sae)
Fee guidelines: yes
Code of conduct: yes
Complaints procedure: yes
Complaint-handling charge: yes
Disciplinary sanctions: censure; expulsion

REGISTER OF TRADITIONAL CHINESE MEDICINE
19 Trinity Road
London N2 8JJ
01-883 8431

Membership: voluntary; examination qualifications required
Style of qualification: MRTCM (Member)
Membership list: available from Register Office
Fee guidelines: no
Code of conduct: yes
Complaints procedure: yes
Complaint-handling charge: no
Disciplinary sanctions: fine; expulsion

SOCIETY OF HOMOEOPATHS
2 Artizan Road
Northampton NN1 4HU
0604-21400

Membership: voluntary; examination qualifications from a recognised college of homoeopathy required
Style of qualification: RSHom (Registered with the Society of Homoeopaths)
Membership list: free on request (with sae)
Fee guidelines: no
Code of conduct: yes
Complaints procedure: yes
Complaint-handling charge: no
Disciplinary sanctions: warning; removal from register

TRADITIONAL ACUPUNCTURE SOCIETY
1 The Ridgway
Stratford-upon-Avon
Warwickshire CV37 9JL
0789-298798

Membership: voluntary; requires licentiate certificate of the College of Traditional Chinese Acupuncture
Style of qualification: MTAcS (Member)
Membership list: available from the Society's office
Fee guidelines: no
Code of conduct: code of practice and code of ethics

Complaints procedure: yes
Complaint-handling charge: no
Disciplinary sanctions: warning; fine; expulsion

UK HOMOEOPATHIC MEDICAL ASSOCIATION
Homoeopathic Health Centre
243 The Broadway
Southall
Middlesex UB1 1NF
01-574 4281

Membership: voluntary; orthodox medical and homoeopathic
    qualifications required
Style of qualification: MHMA (UK) Member; FHMA (UK) (Fellow)
Membership list: Register of Qualified Homoeopathic Prac-
    titioners may be consulted in libraries
Fee guidelines: yes
Code of conduct: yes
Complaints procedure: yes
Complaint-handling charge: no
Disciplinary sanctions: warning; removal from register

London telephone numbers

**On 6 May 1990 the 01 telephone
code for London will change to
either 071 or 081, depending on the
local code that follows it. From that
date, people telephoning the 01
code will hear a recorded message
telling them to re-dial using either
071 or 081.**

Veterinary Services

With a number of minor exceptions, the law forbids the practice of veterinary surgery except by registered veterinarians. Veterinary surgery involves the diagnosis of diseases of and injuries to animals, together with advice, treatment and surgical operations based upon such diagnosis.

In order to practise veterinary surgery, it is necessary to become a member of the Royal College of Veterinary Surgeons (RCVS). Membership is open to persons with a university degree in veterinary science, or who have passed relevant examinations in veterinary surgery. The only other people entitled to provide veterinary services are 'veterinary practitioners'. These are persons who are registered under the Veterinary Surgeons Act 1948 or, prior to the passing of the 1966 Veterinary Surgeons Act, held licences as employees of a society providing free treatment for animals, for owners unable to afford a veterinary surgeon. These practitioners are now registered in the Supplementary Veterinary Register. Anybody else who practises veterinary surgery commits a criminal offence. So does any unqualified person who uses the title of veterinary surgeon or veterinary practitioner.

The Council of the Royal College of Veterinary Surgeons has responsibility for the maintenance of the Register of Veterinary Surgeons. The College itself is incorporated by Royal Charter and its rules and regulations are subject to approval by the Privy Council.

Veterinary surgeons may employ staff to act under their supervision in various ancillary capacities, as veterinary nurse, dispenser or kennel attendant, for example. Such persons are not permitted to diagnose any disease, to go out on rounds unaccompanied or to give any medical or surgical treatment to animals except under veterinary supervision. The owner of an animal always has the right to see the vet himself; and animals that have been treated should be returned to the owner only with the consent of and instructions from the vet himself.

A member of the public is free to make his own choice of vet; but a vet can accept or refuse any person as a client, except in the case of providing first aid in an emergency, in which case the vet is under a duty to help the animal.

If an animal has been injured in a road accident, it is best to ask the police to call a vet, in which case they will meet the vet's charges if the owner cannot be traced. Local branches of the Royal Society for the Prevention of Cruelty to Animals (RSPCA) will sometimes meet such expenses, but many lack the funds to do so.

Specialist advice

Under present legislation, vets are not allowed to describe themselves to the public as specialists in any branch of their profession (for instance, 'equine specialist') although this does not prevent a vet from consulting another about a particular problem in which the latter has developed some expertise. If you own an animal of a species not normally dealt with by the vet whom you are consulting, he may legitimately refuse to administer treatment or give advice which he does not feel professionally competent to offer. He does have an obligation to provide first aid, if that is necessary, and to ensure that you are referred to vet who is competent to deal with the case.

If you are not satisfied with your vet's diagnosis or treatment, you are entitled to ask for a second opinion. Tell your vet if you want a second opinion, as he should give you some guidance in this. A vet who is approached for a second opinion should only with the consent of the vet in charge of the case examine the animal.

If you wish to change vets, you should inform the original vet, as it is in the interests of the animal that the successor should be able to ascertain its case history and previous treatment. Provided you have informed the original vet that his services will no longer be required, he has no right to decline to release the case or to try to persuade you to change your decision. The new vet has an ethical obligation to inform the original vet that he has now taken over the case.

If the animal dies, you can request your vet to carry out a post mortem examination, or to ask another vet to do so. However, this may be expensive and the findings may be inconclusive.

Seeing the vet

Provided your animal is not suffering from a contagious disease, you should, if at all possible, bring it to the veterinary surgery. Home visits are time-consuming for the vet as well as expensive for you and the facilities, drugs, equipment and trained help available at the surgery will mean better treatment there for the animal.

However, if the animal is too ill to be moved, contact the vet immediately. Vets are obliged by the RCVS to make 'proper provision at all times for the relief of pain and suffering' of animals: effectively, this obliges the vet to provide a 24-hour service. In large practices there will therefore generally be one vet on duty at all times. Even in smaller practices, the vet must ensure that when he is off-duty clients can obtain help from some other vet, with whom prior arrangements have been made, and who is sufficiently close at hand for a visit to him to be reasonably practical.

How much will it cost?

Veterinary treatment can be expensive (so it may be worth taking out insurance for your pets). There is no set scale of charges, and fees vary with the nature of the treatment and the size and type of animal. The British Veterinary Association

(BVA) publishes a useful leaflet, *You, Your Animals and Your Veterinary Surgeon*, describing the services that a vet should offer and giving guidelines on fees: it explains how they are made up and how much you should expect to pay. Ask your vet for a copy or send a stamped addressed envelope to the BVA.

If you are having your pet vaccinated for the first time, it may be a good idea to telephone several local vets for the cheapest price, as fees vary such a lot; but you should also ask what diseases that covers, how many injections are required for full cover, and the age (the pet's, that is) to start.

COMPLAINTS ABOUT VETS

These may be addressed to the RCVS – but only if the complaint relates to the vet's professional conduct. The courts alone have jurisdiction to adjudicate on complaints of professional negligence. Sometimes both professional misconduct and professional negligence will be involved. Then the Royal College can intervene, unless there is a complete absence of misconduct issues.

The RCVS has a disciplinary committee which exercises its jurisdiction over any veterinary surgeon or practitioner who is alleged to have:

o   committed a criminal offence which in the committee's opinion renders that practitioner unfit to practise veterinary surgery
o   been guilty of disgraceful conduct in any professional respect
o   secured a fraudulent entry in the Register of Veterinary Surgeons.

The sanctions are the suspension or, where appropriate, the deletion of the registration.

Cases are first considered by a preliminary investigation committee, which decides whether there is a prima-facie case to be referred to the disciplinary committee. The disciplinary committee consists of twelve members, at least one of whom is appointed by the Privy Council; at least five members must hear each case. The Privy Council has approved detailed rules relating to the procedure and evidence before the disciplinary committee.

A legal assessor must be present at all proceedings before the disciplinary committee. It is this assessor's duty to inform the committee of any irregularity in the conduct of the proceedings, and to warn of possible mistakes of law. If the committee does not accept such advice, this must be placed on the record.

The person appearing before the disciplinary committee may be legally represented. The proceedings are generally held in public, although the committee has the right to proceed in private. The respondent has the right:

o   to receive sufficient notice of the enquiry
o   to receive details of the case against him
o   to make submissions to the committee
o   to summon witnesses (in relation to the facts, or to give evidence of character)
o   to receive a transcript of the proceedings, upon payment of a fee
o   to learn the reasons for the Committee's decision.

The veterinary surgeon or practitioner whose registration has been suspended or removed may appeal against that decision to the judicial committee of the Privy Council, and the removal or suspension does not have effect until the appeal has been heard.

Typical complaints against a veterinary surgeon or practitioner may be that he has fallen short of the standards of behaviour the profession has set for itself, for instance by failing in courtesy. In such cases it is unlikely that formal action will be taken; but a member of the Council may discuss the matter with the vet in question and give him appropriate advice. It is only if the conduct is sufficiently serious or repeated that it is likely to be referred to the disciplinary committee.

The British Small Animal Veterinary Association is a professional association composed of vets who treat small domestic pets. It does not deal with complaints from the public, as its members are also members of the RCVS.

The British Veterinary Association does not formally deal with complaints from the public (which are the responsibility of the RCVS), but may play an informal role in helping to resolve difficulties between veterinary surgeons and clients.

USEFUL ADDRESSES

BRITISH SMALL ANIMAL VETERINARY ASSOCIATION
5 St George's Terrace
Cheltenham
Gloucestershire GL50 3PT
0242-584354

Membership: voluntary
Membership list: not available
Fee guidelines: no
Code of conduct: RCVS rules
Complaints procedure: no

BRITISH VETERINARY ASSOCIATION (BVA)
7 Mansfield Street
London W1M 0AT
01-636 6541

Membership: voluntary: restricted to veterinary surgeons
Membership list: not available
Fee guidelines: no
Code of conduct: RCVS rules

ROYAL COLLEGE OF VETERINARY SURGEONS (RCVS)
32 Belgrave Square
London SW1X 8QP
01-235 4971

Membership: all veterinary surgeons and veterinary practitioners
Style of qualification: MRCVS (Member); FRCVS (Fellow)
Code of conduct: statutory rules
Complaints procedure: yes
Complaint-handling charge: no
Disciplinary sanctions: warning; reprimand; suspension; removal from register

SOCIETY OF PRACTISING VETERINARY SURGEONS
Green Farm
Shordley
Hope
Wrexham
Clwyd LL12 9RT
0978-761039 or 0934-863217

Membership: voluntary; restricted to people on the Veterinary Register in private practice
Membership list: not available
Fee guidelines: no
Complaints procedure: no

London telephone numbers

On 6 May 1990 the 01 telephone code for London will change to either 071 or 081, depending on the local code that follows it. From that date, people telephoning the 01 code will hear a recorded message telling them to re-dial using either 071 or 081.

401

Funeral and Burial Services

The need for professional services does not end when life ends –
at any rate for the survivors, who may not be in the right frame
of mind for making reasoned consumer decisions. It is therefore
difficult to suggest the best way to find a suitable undertaker; a
personal recommendation from a previously bereaved friend
may be as good a way as any.

FUNERAL DIRECTORS (UNDERTAKERS)

When someone dies, the law puts a duty on the living to dispose
of the body in some hygienic fashion; almost invariably this
means calling on the services of a funeral director (also known
as an undertaker). The official manual of funeral directing
describes a funeral director as 'a man who can enter a house
where death has occurred and take upon himself the whole
responsibility of organising and equipping a funeral. He is a
technical adviser, agent, contractor, master of ceremonies and
custodian of the body of his client'.

In the past, most funeral directors have been small family
firms, but in recent years many have sold out to large
corporations. Most of them are members of the National
Association of Funeral Directors (NAFD). Membership requires
the passing of written and oral examinations, together with an
inspection of the working premises by an agent of the NAFD.
Members may put after their names NAFD (Member of the
National Association of Funeral Directors) or DipFD (Diploma
in Funeral Directing), and many use these letters in their
letterheads, on their premises or in advertising. Members of the

NAFD must display the Association's symbol on their premises.

Every death must be registered at the office of the registrar of births and deaths. If no inquest is required , the registrar will issue a green certificate of disposal, authorising burial or application for cremation.

It is common practice for the funeral director to pay for certificates and disbursements and include the cost in the total expenses of the funeral; in many cases he arranges and pays for everything, except perhaps the catering and flowers.

The NAFD has drawn up a code of practice in consultation with the Director General of Fair Trading. It requires total integrity from the funeral director, so that the client's confidence is respected at all times. It also requires that value should be given for money and that the dignity of the profession should be preserved. A basic funeral must be provided if required; all charges must be itemised, and a written estimate must be given at the time of taking instructions, or as soon as practicable before the day of the funeral. No soliciting of funeral orders is allowed, nor giving any reward for recommendation.

The basic simple funeral must include a coffin, conveyance from a local address, care of the deceased and the use of a rest room, the provision of a hearse and following car, and attention by the funeral director to all necessary arrangements.

Members are required never to exploit a client in the difficult circumstances following a bereavement. All advertising must be in good taste, and clients must be provided with full and fair information about the services offered: this must include explanation of the types of funeral available and their cost, so that no one should be compelled to agree to an elaborate funeral against his inclination.

The costs of a funeral vary considerably according to region. The major part of the expenditure will be the fee for the services provided (based on the type of coffin), together with a charge for disbursements on behalf of the client (over which the funeral director has no control). Occasionally, a service charge is added for making the arrangements. If the actual costs are likely to exceed the original estimate, the client must be asked to authorise the additional expenditure.

If you cannot afford to pay for the funeral until probate has been granted, warn the funeral director that he will have to wait. Many offer a discount for prompt payment.

A Price Commission study suggests that larger firms are generally more expensive than smaller ones. Competition does not appear to rest on price, but on the quality of the service.

Complaining about funeral arrangements

The NAFD's code of practice provides a conciliation and arbitration procedure:

o the client complains to the funeral director
o the client and the funeral director consult local advice services, such as the CAB or the Trading Standards Department
o conciliation by the NAFD: the problem should be referred in writing to the National Secretary of the NAFD
o if a conciliation is not pursued or is unsuccessful, the complainant may go to arbitration under the scheme provided by NAFD, or resort to county court arbitration.

An arbitration fee is charged, but is returned if the complaint succeeds. Both parties must sign an application for arbitration, which is sent to the Chartered Institute of Arbitrators.

Except in unusual circumstances, the arbitration will be based on documents alone. It will be conducted as speedily as possible, by a single arbitrator appointed by the Institute. The advantage of the procedure is that it is independent, yet cheap and quick, but compensation if awarded, may not be as high as it might have been made by a court. However, the complainant may go to court if he is dissatisfied with the arbitrators' decision.

Master Masons

The National Association of Master Masons (NAMM) is another trade association connected with funerals. Its members are monumental or memorial masons. Suppliers of machinery, tools and equipment to the trade may be associate members. To qualify for membership, a firm must be capable of producing finished memorials (without the use of sub-contract labour) and must be willing to conform to a code of ethics and a code of practice. Approximately 450 firms are members; a list can be obtained from the Head Office. Members of NAMM may display the Association's logo on their premises.

Its code of ethics requires members to do everything in their power to uphold and maintain the dignity of the craft; to guarantee that work is of a high standard; to ensure that advertising is of high standard; to maintain prices; to discourage soliciting of orders; and to foster friendly relations with all other members of the craft.

The code of practice requires all memorials supplied to be of natural quarried material. It requires master masons to ensure that exposed faces of memorials are free from scratches; that the memorial is fixed in concrete; that the inscription is legible and clearly defined; that all memorials are set level and fixed in alignment with other memorials in the cemetery; and that memorials and surrounding areas are left in a clean and tidy condition. There are some other technical requirements. Consequently, anyone who employs a firm belonging to the Association has some assurance that the work will be of good quality.

There is no guideline for a scale of fees. The Membership Committee and General Council of the Association may disqualify from membership any firm found guilty of unethical behaviour or uncorrected bad workmanship.

The Association has a complaints procedure as an alternative to court action. On request in writing, it provides an independent inspection and a written report. If this finds against a member he will be required to put things right. A similar inspection and report can be requested in relation to a non-member's work, and would constitute useful evidence in court.

USEFUL ADDRESSES

NATIONAL ASSOCIATION OF FUNERAL DIRECTORS (NAFD)
618 Warwick Road
Solihull B91 1AA
021-711 1343

Membership: by examination
Style of qualification: NAFD; DipFD
Membership list: not available
Fee guidelines: no
Code of conduct: yes
Complaints procedure: yes
Complaint-handling charge: no
Disciplinary sanctions: yes

NATIONAL ASSOCIATION OF MASTER MASONS (NAMM)
Crown Buildings
High Street
Aylesbury
Buckinghamshire HP20 1SL
0296-434750

Membership: monumental (memorial) masons conforming to code of practice; associate membership: suppliers of tools, etc., to the trade
Membership list: free on request
Fee guidelines: no
Code of conduct: yes
Complaints procedure: yes
Complaint-handling charge: no
Disciplinary sanctions: demand that bad work should be put right; expulsion

Abbreviations

ABDO	Association of British Dispensing Opticians
ABI	Association of British Insurers
ABTA	Association of British Travel Agents
ACA	Association of Consultant Architects
ACCA	Chartered Association of Certified Accountants
ACHCEW	Association of Community Health Councils for England and Wales
ACMS	Approved Coal Merchants Scheme
ACT	Advisory Committee on Telecommunications
ADI	Approved Driving Instructor
AECC	Area Electricity Consultative Councils
AFBD	Association of Futures Brokers and Dealers
AMVA	Action for Victims of Medical Accidents
AOP	Association of Optometrists
APR	Annual Percentage Rate
ARCUK	Architects Registration Council of the UK
ASA	Advertising Standards Authority
ASI	Architects and Surveyors Institute
ATOL	Air Travel Organiser's Licence
AUC	Air Transport Users Committee
AVC	Additional voluntary contributions
BAAR	British Acupuncture Association and Register
BAOT	British Association of Occupational Therapists
BAR	British Association of Removers
BCDA	British Chemical Damp Course Association
BCNO	British College of Naturopathy and Osteopathy
BDA	British Dental Association
BDHA	British Dental Hygienists Association
BEC	Building Employers Confederation

BHA	British Homoeopathic Association
BIAT	British Institute of Architectural Technicians
BIIBA	British Insurance and Investment Brokers' Association
BMA	British Medical Association
BMAS	British Medical Acupuncture Society
BNOA	British Naturopathic and Osteopathic Association Ltd
BOA	British Osteopathic Association
BOS	British Orthoptic Society
BR	British Rail
BRA	British Reflexology Association
BSA	British Chiropractic Association
BSI	British Standards Institute
BT	British Telecom
BVA	British Veterinary Association
BWPA	British Wood Preserving Association

CAA	Civil Aviation Authority
CAB(x)	Citizens Advice Bureau(x)
CC	Consumers' Committee
CCS	Consumer Complaints Service
CEGB	Central Electricity Generating Board
CHC	Community Health Council
CIB	Chartered Institute of Bankers
CIFA	Corporation of Insurance and Financial Advisers
CII	Chartered Insurance Institute
CIPFA	Chartered Institute of Public Finance and Accountancy
CNAA	Council for National Academic Awards
CO	College of Osteopaths Practitioners' Association
CORGI	Confederation for the Registration of Gas Installers
COT	College of Occupational Therapists

CPSM	Council for Professions Supplementary to Medicine
CSC	Customer Service Committee
CSP	Chartered Society of Physiotherapy
CTCC	Central Transport Consultative Committee
DC	Doctor of Chiropractic
DHA	District Health Authority
DHSS	Department of Health and Social Security
DIA	Driving Instructors Association
DPB	Dental Practice Board
ECA	Electrical Contractors' Association
ECC	Electricity Consumers' Council
ENACT	English Advisory Committee on Telecommunications
FIMBRA	Financial Intermediaries, Managers and Brokers Regulatory Association
FPC	Family Practitioners Committee
FRU	Free Representation Unit
GCC	Gas Consumers Council
GCCNI	General Consumer Council for Northern Ireland
GCRN	General Council and Register of Naturopaths
GCRO	General Council and Register of Osteopaths
GDC	General Dental Council
GDPA	General Dental Practitioners' Association
GMC	General Medical Council
GOC	General Optical Council
HVCA	Heating and Ventilating Contractors' Association
IAA	Insurance Adjusters Association

IAAS	Incorporated Association of Architects and Surveyors
IB (Scot)	Institute of Bankers in Scotland
IBRC	Insurance Brokers' Registration Council
ICAEW	Institute of Chartered Accountants in England and Wales
ICAS	Institute of Chartered Accountants of Scotland
IIB	Institute of Insurance Brokers
IIC	Institute of Insurance Consultants
IMRO	Investment Management Regulatory Organisation
ISVA	Incorporated Society of Valuers and Auctioneers
LASS	Local Authority Social Services
LAUTRO	Life Assurance and Unit Trust Regulatory Organisation
LCF	Law Centres Federation
LHC	Local Health Council
LIFFE	London International Financial Futures Exchange
LMUA	Lloyds Motor Underwriters Association
LRPC	London Regional Passengers Committee
MSA	Motor Schools Association
MIRAS	Mortgage interest relief at source
NACAB	National Association of Citizens Advice Bureaux
NAEA	National Association of Estate Agents
NAFD	National Association of Funeral Directors
NALIC	National Association of Loft Insulation Contractors
NAMM	National Association of Master Masons
NAPH & MSC	National Association of Plumbing, Heating & Mechanical Services Contractors

NCC	National Consumer Council
NCIA	National Cavity Insulation Association
NFRC	National Federation of Roofing Contractors
NHBC	National House-Building Council
NHS	National Health Service
NICEIC	National Inspection Council for Electrical Installation Contracting
NIMH	National Institute of Medical Herbalists
NPA	National Pharmaceutical Association
NRA	National Rivers Authority
NTOS	Natural Therapeutic and Osteopathic Society
OCPPP	Organisation of Chartered Physiotherapists in Private Practice
OFFER	Office of Electricity Regulation
OFGAS	Office of Gas Supply
OFT	Office of Fair Trading
OFTEL	Office of Telecommunications
OPAS	Occupational Pensions Advisory Service
PA	Patients Association
PES	Public Electricity Supplier
PIAS	Personal Insurance Arbitration Service
POUCS	Post Office Users' Council for Scotland
POUNC	Post Office Users' National Council
PTE	Passenger Transport Executive
PTO	Public Telecommunications Operator
RCVS	Royal College of Veterinary Surgeons
RIAS	Royal Incorporation of Architects in Scotland
RIBA	Royal Institute of British Architects
RICS	Royal Institute of Chartered Surveyors
RMO	Regional Medical Officer
RPB	Recognised Professional Body
RSPCA	Royal Society for the Prevention of Cruelty to Animals

RTPI	Royal Town Planning Institute
SACAB	Scottish Association of Citizens Advice Bureaux
SFAS	Solid Fuel Advisory Service
SIB	Securities and Investments Board
SPC	Society of Pension Consultants
SPVS	Society of Practising Veterinary Surgeons
SRO	Self-Regulating Organisation
TAC	Telecommunications Advisory Committee
TSA	The Securities Association
TUA	Telecommunications Users' Association
TUCC	Transport Users' Consultative Committee
UKCC	United Kingdom Central Council for Nursing, Midwifery and Health Visiting
UTA	Unit Trust Association